DISABILITY, CULTU

Alfredo J. A

MW00583770

Meeting Families Where They Are

Building Equity Through Advocacy with Diverse Schools and Communities

Beth Harry
Lydia Ocasio-Stoutenburg

TEACHERS COLLEGE PRESS

TEACHERS COLLEGE | COLUMBIA UNIVERSITY
NEW YORK AND LONDON

Published by Teachers College Press, 1234 Amsterdam Avenue, New York, NY 10027

Library of Congress Cataloging-in-Publication Data

Names: Harry, Beth, author. | Ocasio-Stoutenburg, Lydia, author.
Title: Meeting families where they are : building equity through advocacy with diverse schools and communities / Beth Harry, Lydia Ocasio-Stoutenburg.
Description: New York : Teachers College Press, [2020] | Series: Disability, culture, and equity series | Includes bibliographical references and index. | Description based on print version record and CIP data provided by publisher; resource not viewed.
Identifiers: LCCN 2020000695 (print) | LCCN 2020000696 (ebook) | ISBN 9780807763858 (hardcover) | ISBN 9780807763841 (paperback) | ISBN 9780807778548 (ebook)
Subjects: LCSH: Special education—Parent participation—United States. | Children with disabilities—Education—United States. | Students with disabilities—United States—Services for. | Parents of children with disabilities—Services for—United States. | Children of minorities—Education—United States. | Minority students—Services for—United States. | Intersectionality (Sociology) | Educational equalization.
Classification: LCC LC4031 (ebook) | LCC LC4031 .H3718 2020 (print) | DDC 371.9—dc23
LC record available at https://lccn.loc.gov/2020000695

ISBN 978-0-8077-6384-1 (paper)
ISBN 978-0-8077-6385-8 (hardcover)
ISBN 978-0-8077-7854-8 (ebook)

Printed on acid-free paper
Manufactured in the United States of America

Contents

Acknowledgments

The idea for this book emerged from one of our most difficult semesters ever. Thirty years apart in age, as mentor and mentee exploring an independent study of parent advocacy, we marveled at the parallel paths that our lives had taken. Between reading, writing, and conversation, and pausing to ask what we could do to support parents like ourselves in their advocacy, *Meeting Families Where They Are* was born. As our idea comes to fruition, our greatest thanks go to the parents who generously shared their time and perspectives regarding their experiences with their children. Their participation contributes a real-world quality to our arguments about the enduring strengths of parents and the challenges of advocating for children who, despite legal mandates for specialized services, often find themselves on the margins of the education system. We hope that this book will offer a renewed vision of the power of parents' love as they collaborate with professionals to reject the prejudices of the past and ensure that all children are valued.

We thank our colleagues and mentors: Maya Kalyanpur, Wendy Cavendish, David Connor, and Father Alfred Cioffi for their inspiring work; Kele Stewart, Bernie Perlmutter, and Angela Galiano of the University of Miami Children and Youth Law Clinic; and all of our communities, school administrators, organizations, and agency partners who valued this work and were happy to share our recruitment flyer with the families they serve. Finally, we thank our colleagues at Teachers College Press: Brian Ellerbeck, whose arms always seem to be open to embrace fresh perspectives on timeless ideas; Karl Nyberg and Scarlett Lindsay for their expert editing: and Alfredo Artiles for his leadership and vision in promoting this Series.

Finally, we thank our families for their inspiration and support in writing this book, especially our husbands: Mel Stoutenberg and Ben Telson, and our children: Devin, Olivia, Bianca, Elijah, and Isaiah Stoutenburg, and Mark and Melanie Teelucksingh.

CHAPTER 1

Constructing Meanings of Human Difference at the Intersections of Identity
Personal and Conceptual Considerations

In this book we are concerned with equity in parental advocacy for children and adults whose age or disabilities make it impossible or improbable for them to advocate for themselves. We begin by asking why advocacy is needed and what it is that parents are trying to accomplish through their advocacy. We note that answers to these questions take different forms over time, yet these answers represent consistent underlying concerns centered on the question of how meanings are constructed to explain human "differences" and what outcomes result from these constructions. We position the concept of "difference" and its construction as a central, though often unstated, bedrock of parents' advocacy.

The work of Martha Minow (1990) provides an overarching framework in our treatment of the issues surrounding the construction of difference. Minow identified three main assumptions that drive these constructions: that having a disability means that a person is intrinsically different from the norm, that the norm is often unstated yet is consistently seen as desirable, and that objective observers' determinations of the meaning of "difference" represent truth, to the exclusion of others' perspectives. With these assumptions in mind, we posit that parents engage in advocacy with two main purposes: first, to influence the construction of disability by asserting their own judgment of their children's differences and their value in the eyes of society; and, second, to create or gain access to opportunities that will enhance their children's development and often, though not always, their approximation to a desired norm.

In investigating the relationship between constructions of difference and parent advocacy, we rely on two interrelated concepts—identity intersectionality (Collins & Bilge, 2016; Crenshaw, 1989) and DisCrit (Annamma, Ferri, & Connor, 2018; Connor, Ferri, & Annamma, 2016). Together, these concepts provide critical lenses for understanding how the

1

intertwining of disability and other stigmatized identity markers such as race, socioeconomic status, education, and gender have resulted in exclusion and oppression. The authors of DisCrit describe their framework as follows:

> [DisCrit] focuses on the ways race and dis/ability have been used in tandem to marginalize particular groups in society. In other words, DisCrit focuses on the interdependent ways that racism and ableism shape notions of normalcy. These mutually constitutive practices are enacted through normalizing practices such as labeling a student "at-risk," for simply being a person of color, thereby reinforcing the unmarked norms of Whiteness, and signaling to many that the student is not capable in body and mind. (p. 19)

In applying intersectionality and DisCrit to the processes that create and affect parents' advocacy, we note that, while all parents are deeply affected by the way disabilities are constructed by society, those with greater social, cultural, and economic capital have a significant part to play in influencing those constructions. We see advocacy, therefore, as a process and a force for change that also has the potential to reinforce existing hierarchies and marginalizations among those for whom they advocate. Thus, those who would assist parents in their advocacy need to understand and respond to these intersections in a process that we refer to as the co-construction of advocacy.

Ultimately, our purpose is to redefine the scope of advocacy by foregrounding a cultural-historical understanding of the changing face of parent advocacy in the United States and a sensitivity to parents' purposes in engaging in advocacy. We also hope to bring understanding to the numerous intersections of identity that differentiate one family's advocacy needs from another. Using the framework of intersectionality as explained by Collins and Bilge (2016), we call for an approach that recognizes advocacy as a fluid and locally responsive process that takes into account the multifaceted identities of families and the complex needs of children designated as having disabilities. With this focus, we aim to stimulate a nuanced understanding that goes beyond assumptions of superficial group identities and reified categories of disability. We hope to contribute to a better understanding of the nature and purposes of parents' advocacy and to change the conception of professionals' advocacy from its original meaning of one who speaks *for* to one who speaks *with*. Toward these ends, we support the key concepts of our work with information from three types of sources: the existing literature on parent advocacy, vignettes from case studies of the lived experiences of parents and caregivers currently engaged in advocacy efforts, and examples of our own advocacy efforts as parents of children with disabilities.

THE AUTHORS' LENSES

We state up front our own positionalities as the authors of this book. Essentially, we represent our ideas through our own multifaceted lenses as women of color who are, or have been, parents of children whose disabilities presented us with a host of unexpected philosophical, social, and practical challenges. Beth's daughter, Melanie, born in Trinidad in 1975, had cerebral palsy and died at age 5 of complications related to her feeding difficulties. Beth's son, Mark, born in 1977, experienced a painful transition at age 18 from a healthy and successful young man to one who would have to meet the challenge of mental illness for the rest of his life. Lydia's son Isaiah, born in 2010, is the last of five siblings and has Down syndrome. We are both fortunate to have been in stable and supportive marriages throughout these experiences. Our lenses are also tinted by different ethnic/national backgrounds, including Lydia's African American and Puerto Rican heritage and Beth's Jamaican heritage and Trinidadian parenting experiences. Our views are also deeply influenced by our professional education and experiences as scholars and teachers in the field of special education. In short, we use the complex intersections of our own lives as a set of lenses through which to view the topic of parent advocacy. Our book is concerned with the strengths and limitations of how such advocacy has been constructed in the past, is evolving in the present, and could more effectively be co-constructed within school and home communities in ways that honor families in all their diversity.

We begin with a simple and true story of Lydia's personal struggle in learning to include her whole self as she advocates on behalf of her son Isaiah. Like his mother, Isaiah is another whole person—a person whose identity might include any number of intersections—rather than a person whose main marker is "disability."

Lydia: Waiting for a Conversation

It was the fall of 2015. I was enrolled in an advocacy training program for parents of children with developmental disabilities. Although having already sought out what I now recognize as "disability studies" through coursework and local trainings, I found myself intrigued as I delved even deeper into disability history in a series of sessions spread over the course of a few months. The topics in each session covered several domains, from the early education of young children to independent adult living, from historical perspectives to contemporary experience, and from policy to practice. After demonstrating a clear need for advocacy, the speaker for one particular session discussed some strategies to be used by advocates in their own communities, raising awareness of the persisting stigmas and negative perceptions that can lead to adverse outcomes. He gave some suggestions for actions that he deemed particularly effective, such as families introducing themselves to law enforcement officers, so that they could become familiar with their child in his or her environments and prevent unnecessary misunderstandings that could potentially lead to arrest. I listened with full attention, waiting for a conversation.

I waited for a conversation because of the recently charged social climate resulting from the shooting deaths of unarmed individuals who are disproportionately Black by law enforcement. I was waiting for the conversation about the intersections in communities where disability and race meet, or where disability and race and poverty meet. I wanted us to have an honest conversation about the increased vulnerability of families at these intersections, for whom a conversation with their local law enforcement did not seem plausible because of power differentials, access, or trust. I wanted to talk about the misunderstandings that may occur among persons of color that result in individuals of color with disabilities being disproportionately vilified and victimized. I wanted to talk about how race held such a master status in society and that failure to address this as a historical and contemporary social condition leaves our families unprepared. I wanted to talk about my son's complex identity as a young Black boy with a noticeable disability. I was waiting for this speaker's advice on how to prepare advocates to talk about these issues for themselves and for others. I looked around the room and, realizing that the only two other Black and Brown parents were absent that day, I knew it was on me. The moment that I uttered the words, "I think we have to consider what this would look like in all communities," I was met with a look of horror followed by an uncomfortable silence. It was as if my words—*all communities*—were code words, carrying a charge that my fellow participants and leaders were not prepared for. I knew it was much more comfortable for them to go back to talking about disability alone. Disability was safe; it was obvious; it was a unified effort. But here I was, presenting another issue on awareness when it had already been decided what we would have awareness about. I was rocking the boat by implying that we should talk about *race* in our social atmosphere. Although the response to my comment was courteous and politically correct, its brevity implied that we were simply not going to go there again.

DISCRIT:
A LENS FOR VIEWING FAMILY AND COMMUNITY INTERSECTIONS

As mentioned at the beginning of this chapter, two central concepts in our analysis are (1) intersectionality as described by Collins and Bilge (2016), and (2) its application to disability by Connor and colleagues (2016) in the form of "DisCrit"—a critical lens for understanding how various identity markers intertwine with disability. It is important to note that the heart of these concepts lies not simply in the fact of multiple features of identity but in the multiple oppressions experienced by individuals whose identities involve several stigmatized markers.

Isaiah: Challenging Oppressions of Race, Disability, and Gender

Coauthor Lydia's previous vignette represents an example of how a conversation purporting to address the needs of children with disabilities treats the perceived disability as the master status of that person's identity, ignoring the importance of other stigmatized identity markers that, in a racist society, signal the potential for harm to the person. Lydia's son Isaiah experiences triple markers—he is Black and male in a society that fears Black males. He is also a Black male with the most stigmatized of disabilities—intellectual limitations that will exclude him from many of the pathways most valued by society.

Our main point about equity, therefore, is that in order to create an equitable field for advocacy, one must take into account family and community identities as parents exercise advocacy, and find ways to co-construct the process with them. To do this, we need to know who the families are. We need to go beyond the templates, categories, and preconceived avenues that may have worked for certain groups of families. Lydia's vignette offers an example of how our current models, ideas, and perceptions of what it means to advocate for children and adults with disabilities are shaped by the assumption that promoting singular voices and strategies can represent and address the needs and concerns of all constituents. Rather, there are many points of intersection with disability at which exclusion may occur, even inadvertently. To mention only a few, these intersections may include the following: emergent bilingual immigrant families of children with disabilities, families who practice nondominant religious faiths, foster families, families who are engaged in nontraditional sexual unions or represent nontraditional sexual identities, and single fathers or single, teenage mothers. In this book we will introduce and reflect on the voices and perspectives of families such as these.

In addition to the inappropriateness of a one-size-fits-all approach, assumptions about what kinds of activities constitute advocacy will also be addressed. Specifically, researchers and community advocacy organizations have tended to pay particular attention to the forms of advocacy that are acknowledged and celebrated by institutions and school contexts, while the everyday functions and expressions of advocacy exercised by families and community contexts are undervalued—although they may have tremendous influence on the quality of life for children with disabilities (Harry, 2008; Hart, Cheatham, & Jimenez-Silva, 2012). Ong-Dean (2009), for example, provided an excellent analysis of how parental advocacy in U.S. school systems came to be defined by the technocratic way in which the Education for All Handicapped Children Act (EHA) and the Individuals with Disabilities Education Act (IDEA) were implemented, and pointed out how this approach has discouraged advocacy among parents with limited cultural/ social capital or material resources. Certainly, our book must address ways in which school-based advocacy can be reconceptualized; but it will go beyond that arena to the challenge of building advocacy in neighborhoods, communities, public media, and adult services.

Applying the Tenets of DisCrit

Applying the lens of intersectionality to issues of disability, we note the socially constructed nature of disability and of racial identity in both past and present contexts and legal systems. Using the framework of DisCrit, we believe that our work reflects all seven tenets outlined by the originators of the concept (Connor et al., 2016). These tenets are as follows:

1. the interdependence of racism and ableism;
2. the multidimensionality of identities;
3. the real-life impacts of the social construction of race and disability;
4. the need to privilege the voices of marginalized populations;
5. the legal and historical aspects of race and disability constructions;
6. the role of Whiteness and ability as a property that acts as a lever to allow change mainly when White interests converge with the interests of the marginalized; and
7. the enactment of activism and resistance in the co-constructed efforts of providers, advocates, and parents.

Of those seven tenets, we particularly use this book as an avenue for foregrounding the voices of parents who, by virtue of race, educational level, social class, or cultural background, have found themselves coming in from the margins as they attempt to advocate for their children. In this effort, we include voices from existing literature as well as from a current qualitative study of parents in a large urban school district who are in the process of advocacy.

Juxtaposed against the question of who speaks for whom and whose voices are heard, we unpack the dynamic and contextually responsive relationship among parent advocacy; cultural, social, and racial capital; and the social construction of disability categories. We describe how, over time, this relationship has taken several forms that are influenced by differing social agendas, changing epistemologies, and the constant exertion of power by those in a position to define and control others. A cultural-historical lens shows four main shifts: from overtly exclusionary constructions based on religious interpretations of disabilities vis-a-vis concepts of "good" and "evil," in which parents could do little more than exist within the paradigm; to pseudo-scientific interpretations of race and disability and the intertwining of the two through false eugenics that resulted in ascribing blame and shame to parents; to "liberatory" agendas in which parents and their supporters used the courts and social movements to remedy the wrongs of past discrimination; to current agendas that espouse equity yet undermine parent power by relying on functionalist interpretations of the law, in which the success of parents' advocacy depends largely on the exercise of cultural and social capital in navigating mechanistic bureaucracies.

To clarify our view of the last two phases, we celebrate the fact that the liberatory project has achieved a type of equity only dreamed of in previous eras. Nevertheless, this dream of equity is seriously undermined by an epistemology that seeks to objectify disability by defining ever more discrete categories of disability and assigning individuals to these categories based on evaluation techniques thought to be scientific. One of the main problems with this paradigm is that several of the disability categories are based on clinical judgment regarding abilities that are intangible and not measurable. In particular, the concept of intelligence, which is at the core of most disability diagnoses, is itself an abstraction that psychology has tried to operationalize in the form of a score on tests of human knowledge and skills. Performance on these tests, however, cannot be divorced from the test-takers' prior opportunities to learn. Thus, as argued by Skiba, Knesting, and Bush (2001), the differential performance of minority students on IQ and achievement tests is a "product of education disadvantage . . . [and] the tragic history of limited cultural and educational opportunity" (p. 70).

Nevertheless, since these categories determine what supports and services children will receive, parents must work within this system to gain the most helpful services and to protect their children from stigmatizing labels and practices that they believe may denigrate their children's value in the eyes of society. After centuries of exclusion, parents' voices came to the table in full force in the form of the EHA/IDEA, and their input is now a requirement of the law. How that input gets enacted, however, is a central concern of this book. It is clear that parent advocacy can have considerable influence, and, despite the field's claim of an objective epistemology, those who have the power to define disabilities respond to the differences in social privilege and power among advocates. These differences reflect schisms in the advocacy landscape that, probably not intentionally, succeed in moving the agenda forward for those with privilege rather than for everyone. These schisms have resulted in a pattern that we refer to as "shifting" and "drifting," as disability categories shift to reflect the pressures of the times and the priorities of professionals and parents, while some students, the ones who can, drift toward the more desirable categories. Later in the book we will address this pattern in detail, with particular reference to how it has played out in the categories of specific learning disability (SLD), intellectual disability (ID), autism spectrum disorder (ASD), and attention deficit hyperactivity disorder (ADHD).

THE CO-CONSTRUCTION OF ADVOCACY

Understanding and supporting parents' advocacy involves attending not only to the complexities of their identities but also to the exclusions and oppressions associated with those identities. This brings us to the third key concept in our book—the co-construction of advocacy—a commitment to work *with* parents rather than *on their behalf*. In doing so, we extend the usual meaning of the term "to advocate," arguing that advocacy may be expressed in many ways. The Merriam-Webster dictionary gives as the source the Latin verb "advocare," meaning "to summon, call to one's aid." The dictionary then offers the current definitions: "one who pleads the cause of another," "defends or maintains a cause or proposal," or "supports or promotes the interest of a cause or group" (merriam-webster.com/dictionary/advocate).

The latter definition is, of course, the term's most common interpretation, and we will focus much of our discussion on this type of advocacy. However, throughout the book we also discuss other, more nuanced or less visible forms of advocacy. We highlight these processes through stories and testimonials that illustrate the contexts and lived experiences of parents who advocate for their children in numerous ways and who include in their representations numerous intersections of their identities. Although special education is perhaps the most frequently referenced context in which parent advocacy has been observed and expressed, we purposefully cast a wider net in order to grasp a fuller range of advocacy experiences across several arenas. We begin with a brief introduction to our own stories of advocacy.

OVERVIEW OF THE BOOK

The book is neither a history book nor a field guide. Although it includes a necessary overview and analysis of advocacy as situated in a sociohistorical context, our predominant purpose is to unearth the less-heard voices of advocates past and present. In this effort, we envision advocacy as wide-ranging, practical, and organic, representing a complicated landscape created by social and familial contexts, inside and outside of educational spaces. Advocacy, in our view, may range from political activism to seeming invisibility. Overall, a framework of equity and restorative social justice will provide the lens through which we seek to understand the past, present, and hopeful future of parent advocacy.

Throughout the book we support the foregoing arguments with examples of, and reflections on, a wide range of research that presents the perspectives of scholars and parent/caregiver advocates from varying social backgrounds. These advocates include more privileged families who paved the way for change, as well as less well-known voices from culturally and linguistically diverse or socioeconomically underprivileged or other marginalized circumstances. Scholars have noted that the voices of the latter group in parent advocacy, historically cast as inexpert in the field of special education, have been muffled (Hess, Molina, & Kozleski, 2006). For example, a powerful ethnographic study by Lea (2006) demonstrated the disdain and disrespect paid by service providers to a group of unmarried teenage mothers who were attempting to advocate for their children with disabilities. The young mothers, meanwhile, simply rejected the advice of the providers and sought their own solutions. We seek to celebrate voices such as these.

In Chapter 2 we lay the groundwork for an understanding of the meaning and purposes of parental advocacy, identifying two main goals—the attempt to bring respect and value to their children and to provide them with opportunities for personal development and social inclusion. Following Minow (1990), we examine how society's construction of difference relies on a model of intrinsic deficit that is assessed by supposedly objective evaluators, and on the assumption that normative development is the hallmark of human value. In Chapter 3 we provide a sociohistorical lens to this discussion by reviewing past and present advocacy efforts in the United States from the perspective of DisCrit, which focuses on society's constructions of difference and the assignation of stigma on the basis of perceived features of individuals or groups. Within that review, we highlight the ways in which slavery, conquest, and the eugenics project intertwined with disability, race, poverty, and gender to create a reified interpretation of "difference" as "deficit." We outline the trajectory of the disempowerment of parents by deficit-laden professional views and an intense rhetoric of exclusion. In Chapter 4 we turn the page to describe the steady countering of that path as parents asserted themselves through individual and then group advocacy for legislation to bring their children into society's mainstream in the second half of the 20th century. Chapter 5 highlights the painful paths that many parents must navigate as they construct their children's "humanness" in the face of this history of oppression and exclusion.

Chapters 6 and 7 outline the liberatory success of decades of advocacy and examine ways in which the double-edged sword of the law liberates yet still constrains parents in their efforts to bring value and opportunity to their children. We note that the legalistic framing of the law, supported by a positivistic epistemology, does not respond equally and equitably to all advocacy efforts (Artiles, 2011; Blanchett, 2010), and we examine the role of racism as well as social and cultural capital in the inequitable successes of advocacy. In Chapter 8, we bring the book to a close with recommendations for more adaptive and equitable models of advocacy through a process of co-construction, by which service providers and supporting advocates work *with* parents rather than *on* their behalf.

QUALITATIVE VIGNETTES AND AUTHORS' REFLECTIONS

This book is very personal to both authors. We speak in our own voices and acknowledge that our analysis is always informed by our own experiences as Black mothers of children with disabilities. We are also academics whose research focuses on the intersections of families, culture, race, and disability. Thus, a special feature of the book is the inclusion of personal perspectives both from us, the authors, and from qualitative interviews with nine caregivers who are currently advocating for improved outcomes for their children. Within the multicultural, multilingual setting of a large urban area, these families responded to a flyer that we posted on the website of a leading advocacy organization and circulated to key personnel at public and private special education programs known to serve diverse racial and socioeconomic populations. The vignettes are condensed versions of specific issues and events that arose in interviews and observations, which we intend to expand into a full-length collection of cases in a subsequent publication. The study included one Caucasian family and seven families claiming identities either as White or Black Hispanic, African American, or varying mixtures of these ethnicities. Socioeconomic status ranged from working class to professional, and primary caregivers included biological parents, grandparents, and a foster parent. Family structures included single parents, married heterosexual couples, and one same-sex married couple. Our goal in this small study was to elevate the voices of parent advocates from diverse circumstances, which would represent at least some of the intersections of identity that might, according to the literature, be likely to experience cultural, racial, or other social biases in advocating for their children.

Throughout the book, we review the contributions of scholars, practitioners, and parents/caregivers to the research, theory, and practice of advocacy. Our intent is to foreground what is known about advocacy among multiply marginalized populations and highlight the potential of these voices as a powerful educator and architect for policy and practice. We propose a new model of what an ideal co-constructed advocacy support program might look like in order to meet the needs, values, concerns, and empowerment for all its constituents.

An important point to note is that although we raise the issues of context, reflexivity, and equity, we do not suggest separate or special types of advocacy, for example, for families of color or for families with limited resources. To do so would be to echo many of the errors of the past by creating further stratifications and exclusions within the advocacy movement.

What we do suggest, however, is that because families of children and adults with disabilities are such a heterogeneous group, those who would support and extend parents' advocacy need to view their work from an equity rather than a deficit perspective—one that honors the diverse experiences, needs, and concerns of all of its constituents. Our book proposes not *training* parents, but *meeting* families where they are, learning their strengths and their needs, while preparing and repositioning them to empower themselves. Instead of speaking *for* our families of disenfranchised backgrounds, we need to speak *with* them. Once more, citing Collins and Bilge (2016), we emphasize an understanding that aspects of identity interact and influence one another in mutually reciprocal ways, so that any feature, such as socioeconomic status, age, or race, might be more or less relevant depending on the context of the advocacy efforts.

Finally, in this book we present the irony of how the very tensions generated by the construction of normalcy as opposed to "difference," which thereby created the need *for* advocacy, may persist and serve to perpetuate marginalization *within* advocacy. It is a call for greater attentiveness to how advocacy is defined and operationalized, with demonstrated sociopolitical power and influence for some constituents, and limited access, representation, and acknowledgment for others. Although designed as a tool to promote equity, advocacy itself may be subject to the very elitism and marginalization it has sought to overcome.

CHAPTER 2

Parent Advocacy and the Challenge of Difference

We hold it as axiomatic that all parents are, or seek to be, advocates for their children. Simply put, parents want their children to be acknowledged and valued by their communities. They also want them to have the best possible opportunities to grow into capable individuals who have a sense of belonging and can build their lives to their own satisfaction. One has to listen to only a few minutes of typical social conversation among parents to hear some claim to the child's positive attributes or accomplishments, whether referring to the child's attainment of early developmental goals, academic or professional successes, or the establishment of a loving relationship with a promising life partner. While some parents may be seen as making extravagant claims about their children's successes, even the most modest will tend to share with close associates the simple joy they are experiencing from seeing their children attain normative life goals.

In all of the above, parents of children with disabilities are no different. The desire to represent and advocate for opportunities for their children is the same, but there are two main ways in which their experience inevitably differs: First, the biggest challenge is in learning to hold onto hope in the face of discouragement from those who would devalue their children and those who claim to have a stronger grasp on "reality" than do the parents. Second, parents must often find ways to reframe what will be "normative" in their expectations and aspirations for their children. Surely, it may be argued that all parents experience such a need to adapt their expectations of their children, but we are focusing here on adaptations to the most basic assumptions about a child's development: the expectations that he/she would be walking and saying initial words soon after their first birthday; that "going to school" would mean learning to master the most highly valued social currency of modern life—literacy; that moving into adulthood would mean establishing his/her own life activities and goals, according to his/her own tastes and desires. Nevertheless, we emphasize that while the rewards of watching and waiting for our children's successes may be long in coming, the tremendous joy experienced at each incremental step confirms our membership in the world of parenthood.

PERSONAL PERSPECTIVES

In the following personal vignettes we ask, When does a parent become an advocate, with whose assistance, and to what ends?

Becoming an Advocate: Lydia's Story

My emergence as an advocate with a public voice came suddenly. Although I had already begun to "fight the good fight" for my son—learning and absorbing everything I could about disability policy, being enrolled in a doctoral program in special education, engaging in community organizations that support various aspects of life for persons with disabilities, having completed a few training and leadership programs at both community and state levels—it was not until April 2016 that I truly found my voice. I was invited by my doctoral program adviser, Dr. Wendy Cavendish, to participate on a panel for the Roosevelt House Public Policy Colloquium entitled *The Intersection of Race and Class in Special Education Policy.* I was in awe listening to the panel presentations by scholars and leaders in the fields related to special education whose seminal works I had read and admired. I was last to present after one of my professors, Dr. Beth Harry, a leading scholar in the field on research with families of children with disabilities, discussed cultural reciprocity. I had not prepared a speech at all because the story I was going to tell had its own design, its own power, its own trajectory. I simply opened my mouth and let the words spill out like paint on a canvas, to illustrate our journey.

Since Isaiah's appearance in our family, his unique presence has transformed our perception of the world, while his heart has had the incredible power of transforming our actions, our affects, our disposition. I did not realize until that point that *I* was—*we* were, as a family—representative of this intersectionality. It was not until I began to sketch and color in the reality of our lives that I felt its magnitude, from the moments I began to trace his presence in my womb until where we were in that present moment. It was beyond my descriptions, my testimonials of injustice and an ongoing struggle rebelliously permeated by hope. What affected me deeply was that somehow, at that moment, at the witness of so many people who knew a whole lot about children with disabilities, I was suddenly placed, positioned at the level of *expert.*

When are we parents ever positioned at the level of expert? Cast into a set of predefined roles as parents of children with disabilities, as members of racial and ethnic minority classes, whose children face the duality of becoming categorically labeled and cast into those same predefined roles—when are we placed at the level of expert? I hold no distinctions or honors. At the moment of that opportunity to be heard, I realized that the door had been opened by people who held some influence in the field of study I had entered. Yet, as Isaiah's mother, I hold a certain dignity that should automatically amplify my voice. That is all it should take for me to be heard. My little boy has dignity as well. That is where we need to begin, when we recognize the dignity of our children and that of our own selves and speak it to the world.

Although parents of children with disabilities certainly are positioned to become natural advocates for their children, it is evident that many parents do not succeed in growing into that role. Even among those who conceptually agree with the need to negotiate for the needs of their children, many do not feel empowered to do so. Lack of empowerment is not simply the absence of such an attribute but the result of historical, institutional, and systemic actions that have intentionally disempowered families. For many parents of children with disabilities, the act of disempowerment may occur even before the child is born, perpetuated by educational, social, political, and economic policies and contexts. Parents belonging to historically marginalized classes, such as racial and ethnic minority groups, or parents whose life experiences are marked by poverty, often also experience similar acts of disempowerment throughout the course of life and across multiple sectors. However, conceiving, giving birth to, raising, loving, and defending the dignity of a child with the duality of having a disability and belonging to a marginalized or stigmatized group very often casts that parent as an adversary to stakeholders who perceive this child's existence as a potential disruption to longstanding norms, systemic practices, and the exercise of power.

Becoming an Advocate: Beth's Story

In 2010, 29 years after the death of my daughter, Melanie, I published a memoir entitled *Melanie, Bird with a Broken Wing: A Mother's Story.* Having started writing that account during the first 6 months of Melanie's life, I had completed it within a year of her death at age 5. The draft sat on my desk for 8 years before I showed it to anyone outside of my closest personal circle. When I was completing my PhD program, I showed the draft to a professor of mine and asked his opinion of it. He congratulated me on the quality of the writing and advised me to do some revisions that would frame the story in terms of my advocacy, relating it to key policy issues of the time in special education. There were two problems with this recommendation: First, for me, it was not a story about advocacy; it was just a story about learning to become a mother to an unexpectedly fragile and intriguing child. Second, the policy issues of that era in the United States were totally different from those in Trinidad/Tobago, where Melanie lived her short life. Certainly, I had worked as an advocate in that community, where, with no services for children with disabilities under the age of 5, I started a school for children with disabilities and took on an increasingly public leadership role in the country's advocacy organizations.

Those, I understood, were acts of advocacy. But my memoir was not about that—or so I thought. I returned the draft to its shelf and moved on with my career as a special educator.

In 2006, after I had published a couple of books with prominent U.S. presses, I worked up the courage to send the memoir to Brookes, with whom I had a good relationship. They turned it down, saying that the press had just published a book with a similar theme the year before, and they didn't think there would be a market for another such book. In 2008, determined that Melanie's story should see the light of day, I self-published the memoir but found that it was impossible to develop the marketing skills needed to for it to gain attention. In 2010, hoping that the published version, complete with photographs, would be more impressive than the original manuscript, I sent it once more to Brookes. They accepted the manuscript for publication within 2 weeks. Since then, the book has done very well, being used mainly in teacher preparation programs for early childhood special educators.

Looking back and realizing the impact the book has had on the many budding and established professionals who send me love letters for Melanie, I see that my story of motherhood was already a story about advocacy. I now see that my own internal struggles with acceptance and understanding were my first steps in advocating for her worth—within myself—which is where it always begins. Every conversation with a medical professional or therapist was an effort to advocate for Melanie's right to be seen as an intelligent and valuable person. Every step I took to establish the school or serve on an education policy committee was an effort to advocate for services for her and others like her. After her death, my decision to make a home for myself as an academic in the field of special education was a final commitment to continue the work of advocacy that she had inspired. This year, I see the publication of my recent study of the school I started in Trinidad/Tobago as the culmination of those beginnings, and today, as I write with my young colleague, Lydia, I see how her advocacy for Isaiah, coming as it does within the context of the well-established legal provisions of the United States, speaks to the very same issue that has inspired my work since Melanie's birth in 1975—an urgent drive to tell the world that our children are valuable and entitled to their communities' loving support.

GOALS AND AVENUES OF ADVOCACY

Implicit in the foregoing vignettes by the coauthors is the centrality of the concept of social capital. Lydia's story of suddenly feeling empowered to speak publicly points to the support that is needed for a parent to move from the day-to-day challenges of advocacy within family, community, and school settings to gaining a voice in a wider public arena. As with Beth's account of her process, it is a story of the availability of social connections and context that can provide the social capital needed to speak to an academic audience or to publish a story that can have broad societal influence.

Historically, power differentials have been the source of a great deal of exclusion within parental advocacy in the United States. We do not assert that this exclusion is necessarily intentional, particularly because we understand that parents are predominantly concerned with paving and tailoring the way for their own children. As we will detail later, in the latter half of the 20th century, prominent families took the lead in developing grassroots movements that would result in policy and systems-level changes, inspired by the very methods employed by civil rights advocates. It was the efforts of these parents that led to the laws that provide services today. However, this brings us to explore the aspects of historical and present overrepresentation and underrepresentation of historically marginalized groups and its effects on who remains empowered. Research has noted a clear irony: Even since the advent of the EHA and IDEA, parent advocates of children with disabilities have continued to be overwhelmingly White and middle class, even though parents of color who have children with disabilities may be in greater need of advocacy in schooling, due to systemic and institutionalized racism that results in disproportionate placement decisions. Advocacy on a public forum, however, becomes available to only a few and hardly represents the daily work of parent advocates in their homes, communities, and school settings.

In Beth's recent book, *Childhood Disability, Advocacy and Inclusion in the Caribbean: A Trinidad/Tobago Case Study* (Harry, 2020), she interprets many parental actions and activities as representing various avenues of advocacy. Specifically, in her research Beth identified three types of advocacy that were evident in the lives of the parents who participated in that study: "everyday advocacy," "breaking barriers advocacy," and "creating a public voice advocacy." Beth described the first type as "taken for granted" daily actions by parents to create opportunities for their child. For example, the mother who, for several years, traveled by three taxis to get her child to and from school every day, or the parent who risked losing relationships with relatives or neighbors to make the point that her daughter, who had an intellectual disability, should not be excluded from social events for the convenience of others. Illustrating "breaking barriers advocacy" was the story of a family who succeeded in getting their academically talented son who had cerebral palsy into a prestigious high school that had never before accepted a student with such a disability. "Creating a public voice advocacy" included examples of parents who initiated and sustained nationwide advocacy organizations for autism or Down syndrome.

It is worth noting that Beth's research did not report a fourth type of advocacy, which will receive most attention in this book: advocacy that uses the law to gain services for children, as in Ong-Dean's (2009) excellent book on that type of advocacy. The reason for the absence was simple:

Up to the time of her writing of that book, Trinidad/Tobago did not have in place any legal mandate for education for children with disabilities nor any legal avenues to seek or secure such services. This simple fact underscores the importance of understanding advocacy in its local and temporal contexts.

Regardless of the level or type of advocacy parents engage in, their efforts center on two main goals: first, parents' intention to draw positive attention to and valuing of their children by asserting their own judgments of their children's abilities, and, second, to access support or opportunities for the children's development and overall well-being. Of course, advocacy for the value of the child and advocacy for the provision of opportunities for the child go hand in hand, since a society is most likely to provide opportunities for those members it values most. Societies that exclude certain children from schooling or from other opportunities that are available to others send the message that the excluded children are not valued or are less valued than others. Throughout the book, we will keep these broad goals in mind.

WHY ADVOCACY FOR THE VALUE OF THE CHILD?

We begin our consideration of the nature of advocacy by asking the simple question, Why is advocacy needed? As we observed in the introduction to this chapter, we note that it seems axiomatic that parents will want to represent their children to the world in a positive light and seek the best possible opportunities for the child's well-being. So, advocacy, in a general sense, may be just a thing that parents do. However, a child with intensive medical or developmental anomalies initiates a chain of much more intensive advocacy. In a situation where a child is born with a condition that seems to threaten his/her health and well-being, whether the likely quality of the child's life or life itself, parents may be expected to respond initially with shock, dismay, or, at the very least, a level of concern that replaces the unequivocal expected joyous welcoming of a newborn. The most obvious source of distress, of course, is the challenge of medical complications that actually threaten a child's life or present the parent with unexpected and extensive care responsibilities. For example, many infants with congenital anomalies have associated health challenges such as the "hole in the heart" problem common among newborns with Down syndrome or intense feeding difficulties experienced by infants with cerebral palsy. Wolfensberger (1983) described parents' initial reaction to such situations as "novelty shock," emphasizing that, regardless of what value was or was not placed on the child's life and condition, most parents would at the very least be unprepared for the practical day-to-day demands of an infant with obvious health or developmental anomalies.

Stigmatizing "Difference"

Beyond these practical concerns, however, lie the intra- and interpersonal aspects of giving birth to a child whose features or developmental trajectory are markedly different from the norm. Depending on the social environment, perceptions of difference may lead to stigmatizing of the child. Ever since sociologist Erving Goffman's (1963) analysis of the origins, nature, and management of stigma, a vast literature on the topic has emerged, cutting across the fields of philosophy, sociology, law, and, most recently, disability studies. This extensive discourse rests on the premise that human societies are regulated by norms that include personal appearance, personal and interpersonal behaviors, health, and developmental patterns. Differences that are seen to violate established norms create confusion and discomfort and lead to the individual being seen as deviant (Stafford & Scott, 1986).

As explained by Goffman (1963), stigma, in its original conception, referred to visible, physical stigmata or bodily features that signaled fear or disgust in the eyes of observers. Goffman's work, however, did not focus solely on disability as a marker. Rather, he described stigma as based on three sources: "Abominations of the body . . . blemishes of individual character . . . and the tribal stigma of race, nation, or religion" (p. 4). Goffman's examples of "character" included characteristics related to homosexuality, addiction, mental disorder, and so on. Based on traditional discrediting of features of difference, Goffman argued, we come to believe that the stigmatized person is "not quite human" and "we construct a stigma-theory, an ideology to explain his inferiority and account for the danger he represents" (p. 5). Moreover, the stigmatizing feature of the individual becomes the "master status" (Hughes, 1945), which comes to dominate all views of the individual and obscure all other attributes. These beliefs are cemented by the application of stigmatizing terminology, which supports further attribution of "a wide range of imperfections on the basis of the original one" (p. 4). Although Goffman often referred to apparently intrinsic features, he also emphasized that the process of stigmatization occurs through social interaction, creating social constructs by which the normal and the stigmatized "are not persons but rather perspectives" (p. 138).

The literature that has built on Goffman's work has emphasized that although distinct targets of stigma are determined by culture and context, the concept itself is seemingly universal but is applied differently across cultures and time periods. For example, homosexuality is known to have been acceptable in Ancient Greece (Pickett, 2018), and through intense self-advocacy in recent times it has succeeded in gaining at least legal standing in most developed societies. Similarly, addictions are increasingly interpreted as biologically based rather than as examples of weak will. Some illnesses, such as mental illness, have historically been stigmatized in all societies, although there are societies in which the mentally ill have been ascribed a positive stigma, being interpreted as seers or supernaturally gifted. Certain illnesses, such as leprosy in previous times and HIV/AIDS, have been the targets of intense stigma, although, in both cases, this has been lessened by the advent of successful medical treatments. Currently, it remains to be seen whether improved treatments for mental illnesses may have similar social outcomes (Corrigan & Bink, 2016).

Critics of Goffman's approach to the topic of stigma, however, decry the absence of a critical view of the political dimensions that promote and institutionalize stigma (e.g., Bhambra, 2014; Tyler, 2018). Tyler, for example, describes Goffman's approach as typical of traditional sociology's "individualistic, ahistorical and politically anaesthetized conceptualization of stigma" as contrasted with "richer historical understandings of the social and political function of stigma as an instrument of social policy . . . " (p. 4). Tyler argues that Goffman's attempts to present an abstract interpretation of the processes of stigmatization and stigma management feign neutrality and ignore the role of power in the creation of social hierarchies. This author makes explicit the connection between the stigma of race and that of disability, both resulting from historical roots of oppression: Citing the self-advocacy of Paul Hunt (1966b), Tyler shows how stigma "as a political economy emerges from the longer penal history of stigma as a cruel system of classification which marks out categories of people in order to impede their freedom and mobility" (p. 13). Further, in direct contrast to Goffman's descriptions of how stigmatized individuals "manage" the "spoiling" of their identities by deftly navigating the social order, Tyler cites Sayad's (2006) explanation of how "the primary form of revolt against stigmatization . . . consists in reclaiming the stigma, which then becomes an emblem of [resistance]" (p. 173).

Self-Advocacy and Re-Claiming the Stigma

The process of re-claiming the stigma was powerfully demonstrated throughout the years of the civil rights movement, with its cry of "Black power!" The replacement of the term "Black" instead of "colored" or "Negro," the promotion of natural African hair in what at the time was referred to as the "Afro," and the claiming of African surnames and clothing styles marked the claiming of pride in all that had been stigmatized. This trend was extended by Black youth's use of the term "nigga" as a term of endearment and belonging and the growth of rap music whose goal was to criticize the racist power structures of the society.

This approach to re-claiming stigma has also been described by disabled self-advocates. While mainstream professionals in disability circles have systematically taught their students to use "people-first language," self-advocates have wrestled with the dilemma of whether to place the disability as the primary or secondary point of identification (Block, Kasnitz,

Nishida, & Pollard, 2016). Simi Linton (2007), for example, described her gradual movement from "people-first" language to the term "disabled woman" as a progression from "denying my disability . . . [to] sailing headlong into it" (p. 120). This approach also drives the popular work of disabled self-advocate Leroy Moore, who harnessed both his disabled and his Black identities to create Krip Hop Nation, described as "an international artistic/activist network focusing on disability justice through music/poetry" (facebook.com/KRIPHOPWORLDWIDE/). Moore (n.d.) explains his motivation in creating this movement as follows:

> Krip Hop Nation is more than music and "bling," it is about advocacy and education and taking back what has been taken from us to oppress us. Language, like other oppressed groups, was taken from people with disabilities and the language was turned on us to oppress us. Before people with disabilities had civil rights, a movement and arts, many had placed labels on us like "crazy," "lame," "cripple" and "retarded," etc. Of course, now with our civil rights and disability studies and culture, we have named ourselves and have used the negative terms to our own benefit to not only shock people but to respect that these words are our history and we must reclaim them. (wordgathering.com/past_issues/issue22/essays/moore2.html)

Paul Hunt (1966a), to our knowledge one of the first published disability self-advocates, addressing the issue of "difference" and stigma, argued that it is natural for people to feel uncomfortable in the presence of visible disabilities that mark extreme difference from the norm. Going directly to the question of the value that is placed on the life of a person with such a disability, Hunt identified five key assumptions that support societal devaluing of the person: that the disabled individual is unfortunate, useless, different, oppressed, and sick. In contrast to these perceptions, Hunt argued, the disabled individual, despite any truth in the foregoing assumptions, inevitably "retains an ineradicable conviction that they are still fully human in all that is ultimately necessary" (p. 147). To appreciate the humanity of all persons, Hunt argued, society needs to adjust its "rigid standards of what is right and proper" regarding the value placed on normative life goals such as work, marriage, and independence, in order to understand that individuals who cannot achieve those goals can also lead useful and satisfying lives. Explaining that he speaks as a person with "severe and often progressive physical disabilities . . . " (p. 145) but with "an alert mind" (p. 148), Hunt says that "an impaired and deformed body is a 'difference' that hits everyone hard at first. Inevitably, it produces an instinctive revulsion, has a disturbing effect" (p. 151). He places the onus on persons with such disabilities to resist the impulse "to hide ourselves in the crowd . . . to bury ourselves in society away from the stares of the curious, and even the special consideration of the kindly, both of which serve to emphasize our difference from the majority" (p. 151). Through such resistance, he says,

> we can witness to the truth that a person's dignity does not rest even in his consciousness . . . his beauty, age, intelligence, or colour . . . to show other people not only that our big difference from them does not lessen our worth, but also that no difference between men, however real, unpleasant and disturbing, does away with their right to be treated as fully human. (p. 152)

But What Is "Difference" and Why Is It Important?

On what basis do we cling so firmly to beliefs about the importance of such differences that we accept that they should become the targets of stigma? What implicit criteria support a society's buying into this process? Artiles (1998), following the work of legal scholar Martha Minow (1990), argued that ethnic disproportionality in special education reflects the conflation of deficit constructions of disabilities with deficit constructions of racial difference in American society. Our framing of the issue of difference is similar to that of Artiles, but with a focus on parents' perspectives of the construction of difference. Minow's analysis of how differences are constructed as deficits proposed five assumptions on which notions of difference are based, as follows: (a) that the difference is a "true" difference—intrinsic to the person, (b) that the norm need not be stated since the "default reference point is so powerful and well established that specifying it is not thought necessary" (p. 56), (c) that the observer describing the "difference" is neutral in his/her perspective, (d) that other perspectives are irrelevant, and (e) that the status quo is "natural, un-coerced, and good" (p. 70). Minow explains that these assumptions are faulty, based not in objective observations but in socially agreed processes that are by no means neutral.

We take the liberty of condensing Minow's (1990) five principles to three: concerns about the intrinsic nature of the "difference," assumptions of the norm as the "default reference point" and part of the natural order of things, and the neutrality and exclusive value of "objective" observers' assessments of the "difference." Applying each of these assumptions to the experience of parents whose children are likely to become stigmatized, we can see how deeply affecting these unacknowledged assumptions can be. We see the first assumption, that physical or developmental differences in infants and young children are intrinsic to the child's self, as leading to the disturbing question of whether this intrinsic difference alters the essential nature of the child as a human being. Second, the developmental norms to which the child is being compared are so deeply embedded in society's consciousness that they represent the natural and desirable condition to which all would aspire. Third, in today's society the official observer is most often a professional in medicine or allied fields such as psychology or speech/language therapy, and the power of the professional gaze is such that other, nonprofessional perspectives are deemed irrelevant. Undoubtedly, the increasing medicalization of childhood development has resulted in an invasive and prescriptive process of evaluation that ensures that all concerned with the infant will be watching closely to confirm that he/she is not presenting any concerning "difference" from established norms.

Given these social processes in the identifying and stigmatizing of difference, parents find themselves in a space that seems to demand advocacy for this child to be recognized and valued. Minow's (1990) assumptions provide a very helpful frame for analyzing the most common avenues of parent advocacy.

Is My Child Intrinsically "Different" and Why Is This a Problem?

The obvious corollary to this question is, "Different from what?" We would say, "different from whatever is normal and valued." As parents we may start by questioning whether there is, in fact, an intrinsic difference embodied by our child. This question is closely tied to whether or not that difference represents a devalued, likely to be stigmatized self. In other words, our concern is tied to the extent to which the difference will cause the child to experience social rejection. Coauthor Beth speaks to this concern directly from her own experience:

Beth's Story

When my daughter, Melanie, was diagnosed with cerebral palsy, a much-loved friend, knowing nothing about cerebral palsy, asked me, "Do you think this means she'll be the kind of person people will shun?" Swallowing my hurt, but trusting my friend's loving intention, I had the momentary presence of mind to reply, "Well, I hope not. But really, people shun all kinds of people!" She replied, "Yes, you know, that's true." But she was right—like her, I too was worried that my daughter would live a life of exclusion and rejection. Consequently, I placed my hope in another "intrinsic" aspect of herself—her intelligence.

For me, I had no hesitation in acknowledging that Melanie's cerebral palsy was indeed "intrinsic." I understood that she had suffered brain damage in utero, related to a hemorrhage I had at about 12 weeks gestation, and the fact that at birth the placenta was noted to be "infarcted," which meant damaged. However, my question was whether that damage would have extended to the portion of her brain that controlled cognition. My question was, simply, would she be "mentally retarded"? I think it's true to say that, throughout her short life of 5½ years, my predominant focus regarding Melanie's development was on evidence of her cognitive abilities. The fact that increasing evidence of her "normal" intelligence was ultimately supported by a CT scan that showed severe damage to the cerebellum but not to the cerebral cortex was a source of huge relief and encouragement for me. This way of thinking was so evident in my memoir of her life that one reader asked me, "Why was it so important to you that she not be 'retarded'?"

When I was asked the question, I didn't know how to answer. Since that time, I've reflected on this a great deal and conclude that there were three issues: First, I like to think that my main concern was for her well-being, which would be tied to her ability to enjoy the world by communicating with others and building her own relationships. Second, I wanted her to be valued by the world, and I knew that intelligence, especially as evidenced by communication abilities, is a characteristic valued in our Western society, perhaps above all else. Third, for myself, I wanted the indisputable joy of seeing her happy and, dare I say, of experiencing the pride that parents generally take in their children's development. I could also say that I would have liked to see her able to become quite independent, but I think that my acknowledgment of her physical limitations came so quickly that I reframed my hopes to focus on the intelligence that would shine through those limitations and endear her to those on whom she would always have to depend.

The question of intelligence strikes deep into the heart of the question of value. Moreover, in Western societies this is tied to the issue of being seen as an independent individual. I believe that both these factors essentially represent the question of what makes a human life worthwhile. We will return to this issue later, citing the work of Kittay (2019), a philosopher whose daughter has multiple disabilities.

Parents in Western and other societies are deeply, if implicitly, aware of the question of what makes a human life worthwhile. As detailed in numerous accounts of the history of disabilities in our nation (Albrecht, Seelman, & Bury, 2003; Caruso, 2015), centuries of negative beliefs about individuals with disabilities created a culture of discrimination that required an intense battle for the civil rights of such individuals. These beliefs were buttressed by religious interpretations that had existed since the Middle Ages and by the steady intertwining of the concept of racial inferiority with that of disability. The next chapter will provide a brief outline of that history.

CHAPTER 3

Constructing Race and Disabilities as Intrinsic Differences

A Cultural-Historical View

The notion of stigma is as old as history. The question arises whether it is a "natural" human tendency to reject or stigmatize individuals whose bodies or developmental characteristics differ significantly from a society's norms. Clearly, interpretations of disabilities represent societal values and beliefs that vary quite widely across the world and change with new legal and epistemological contexts. While we make no claim to being comprehensive in this review, we highlight key concepts and historical transitions that laid the groundwork for centuries of stigmatizing not only of people with disabilities but also of people of color.

"INTRINSIC" ATTRIBUTIONS: FROM THE SUPERNATURAL TO SCIENCE

Prior to the emergence of science, perhaps the clearest trend was that attributions to supernatural causes were common across cultures. According to a history by Caruso (2015), evidence suggests that during prehistoric times some tribes may have cared for persons who were vulnerable, such as those who might have been ill or injured. In contrast, in ancient Greece, infants born with evident disability were left to die, in response to the high value placed on perfectionism. There are multiple references to persons with disabilities in the Bible, and a clear discrepancy is found, for example, between the Old Testament perceptions of "other" and the New Testament teachings of compassion toward all humanity, such as in the parable of the Good Samaritan told by Jesus. Studies of attitudes toward disability in some Asian countries show variable interpretations, including signs of bad "karma" among Indians believing in reincarnation (Groce & Zola, 1993) or, on the contrary, Hmong beliefs that epilepsy and club feet represent spiritual blessings systems (Fadiman, 1997; "Hmong Family Prevents Forced Surgery on Son," 1991).

Caruso (2015) reported that the notion of disability as evil was reified in some versions of the Christian tradition, and in the 1400s, the first institutions in Great Britain were constructed for those who were considered to have some cognitive impairment. About 100 years later, these institutions were exclusively for those deemed "mentally insane" because there was no separation between the constructs of mental illness and disability. By the 1600s, during the Protestant Reformation, religious leaders exerted a great deal of influence on how people perceived disability, the majority of which was often attributed to demonic possession. The following is a description by Wolfensberger (1969) of Protestant reformer Martin Luther's view of a boy with a disability:

> "If I were the Prince, I should take this child to the Moldau river which flows near Dessau and drown him." . . . Luther was firmly of the opinion that change-lings such as this boy are not human, but only a mass of flesh, a *massa carnis*, without a soul, and that "it is the Devil's power to corrupt people who have reason and have soul when he possesses them. The Devil sits inside where their soul should be." (p. 71)

The Advent of Science: Explaining Difference

In Europe, the rise of science and research during the Enlightenment marked a change in the treatment of and sensitivity toward criminals, people with mental illness, and people with disabilities (Cayea, 2006). Among the first documented accounts of an attempt to improve the functioning of a child with disabilities was the report by French researcher and physician Jean Marc Itard of Victor, the famous "Wild Boy of Aveyron," who was discovered in the wilderness in 1800. It was theorized that Victor was abandoned because of his disability, although he could not speak, and his identity could not be confirmed. Itard believed that with some education and formal "training," this child could potentially turn his unintelligible sounds into speech and could be educated in other ways. However, even though Victor had made a great deal of progress toward independence and communication, Itard decided to abruptly cease Victor's education when he reached 17 years of age and shifted his focus toward other cases with more potential for the development of speech. Victor was removed from the home and abandoned to an institutional type of setting, without the continued one-on-one training and care (Cayea, 2006).

In the United States, the ways in which disability could be defined, constructed, and reconstructed in American history have also held strong social, economic, political, and judicial implications. Changing constructions not only affected how persons with disabilities would be perceived by the scientific, medical, educational, political, and lay communities but also determined whether or not services would be rendered, how they would be provided, and where they would be provided. The mid-1700s, for example, represented a time when disability was primarily correlated with illness, and the majority of persons with disabilities resided in American hospitals under this definition. Later in the century, however, as prisons and poorhouses became the main place of residence for persons with disabilities, the definition shifted to become entwined with poverty and criminality. In response, Dorothea Dix and other social reformers of this time period explored the nation's poorhouses and confirmed the disproportionality of people with disabilities residing in them. Dix also publicized the horrific conditions in which adults, children, those with disabilities and without, and persons with mental illness were lumped together with individuals deemed to be criminals, abused, neglected and locked away in cages, in mass incarceration and confinement (Caruso, 2015). Although the exposure of such conditions did generate policy changes that shifted the responsibility for these institutions to the states, such facilities remained unregulated by the federal government.

Science and the Medical Model: Categorizing Difference

The advent of science, while releasing modern society from the hegemony of archaic religious beliefs, nonetheless brought its own version of disability stigmatizing. Prior to the current laws and restrictions protecting individuals from irresponsible practice and research, the medical model served the purpose of both analyzing and generating differences among people, thus creating a system of norms to be used as points of reference for human development and functioning. Gould (1996) has documented the abuses of the scientific method that came to be used as the basis for the emerging "field" of eugenics. Using pseudoscience, in which people with disabilities were subject to experimentation, measurement, and categorization, the medical model served to generate deficit-focused identities. Many of the phrenology, craniology, and other physiological experiments, for example, were conducted to provide empirical support for beliefs in intrinsic racial and gender differences, strategically denoting differences in brain size and morphology. Differences in brain anatomy were hypothesized to be correlated with cognitive, behavioral, and/or emotional normalcy, as well as with a normed point of reference. Norm-referencing in this fashion was a method by which "field experts" could determine who might fit a profile of a criminal in society. Any perceived deficits among children and adults were not attributed to a natural range of human traits and abilities at the population level, as Darwin first theorized, but were considered to be heritable and static flaws. The medical model cast the physician in the role of authority and expert, and the law would take its notes from the medical model for support of legislations crafted to protect the public from the degenerate individuals. This set the stage for the eugenics movement in America, which became inextricably tied to the construction of race and racism.

CONQUEST, SLAVERY, AND COLONIZATION:
THE INTERTWINING OF RACE, DISABILITY, AND "NORMALITY"

Woven into this history was the history of dominated peoples in the United States ever since the invasion by Europeans in the 15th century. As the European colonists encountered people of color on the coasts of Africa and in the Americas and devised the project of slavery, they systematically constructed the role these people would serve, created and defined by political, social, and economic ideologies. It became critical to detail these encounters in terms that would portray the character of the individuals as worthy of disempowerment, conquest, or even mass extinction.

As described by Joel Spring (2016), by the time of Columbus's expeditions to the "new world," European consciousness, forged in the domination of the Roman Empire, was marked by a belief in the superiority of Christianity and Western civilization. To be other than Christian was seen as synonymous with being "pagan," and to be other than European was to be "uncivilized" and "barbarian." The conquest, subjugation, and, where possible, the religious conversion of any "other" cultures was seen as not only the right but also the duty of the conquering Europeans. Within the frame of Christianity, however, were many schisms and intersections, including the belief in the superiority of Protestantism over Catholicism, such that the colonized Irish were seen as the "wild" Irish, not unlike the "wild Indians" of the Americas. In summarizing the scope of the English colonial project, Spring stated: "From Ireland in the 12th century to India in the 19th century, the English were convinced that colonial expansion was just, because it spread Anglo-Saxon culture around the world" (p. 3).

How this expansion became intertwined with conceptions of "race" and "the normal" has been carefully described by Ronald Takaki (1993), who offered a detailed rendering of the progression of English colonialism from the conquest of Ireland, to the Native peoples of the Americas, and then to the creation of the African slave trade. Citing Shakespeare's play *The Tempest*, first performed in London in 1611, Takaki explained how the half-human character, Caliban, represented an exemplar of the English consciousness of the time—the view of the indigenous inhabitants of the colonies in the Americas and the Caribbean as uncivilized savages. Takaki shows how this view gradually came to include perceived "race" as an aspect of the inferiority of such peoples, and how this was further applied to perceptions of the enslaved Africans who eventually came to be identified as an even greater menace than the Irish or the native Indians. Takaki shows how Shakespeare's descriptions of the segregation of Caliban from the rest of the island and his depiction of the "sty" in which he lived actually presaged the oppression and exclusion that would be perpetrated on Indians and Africans in the English colonies. Citing the overwhelming effect of the way the play was staged, Takaki states: "The theatergoers saw Caliban's 'sty' located emblematically at the back of the stage behind Prospero's 'study,' signifying a hierarchy of white over dark and cerebral over carnal" (p. 37).

Caliban was, in fact, already a well-known trope in European social mythology, providing fertile ground for the confluence of Darwinian theory with traditional fabling of the notion of the "monster." In a review of this topic, Gelb (2010) outlined how this traditional concept was fueled by extrapolations of Darwin's theory, by which many believed in both "recapitulation" and its opposite—"degeneration." The former, as described by Gould (1996), was the belief that human nature reflected the process of evolution not only through physical adaptations but also in the gradual evolution of superior moral and intellectual faculties. In this thinking, all who do not appear to fit European norms could be seen as lower down on the scale of evolved humanity and therefore less than human. As explained by Gelb, the opposite trajectory envisioned evolution as also potentially regressive, or "degenerative," producing "beings who were developmentally arrested at a prior, lower stage of evolution: in these the human form served to conceal hereditary vices, marks of an atavistic beast within" (2010, p. 79). The criminal anthropology of Cesare Lombroso compounded this belief system by tying evil and monstrosity to a concept of abnormality.

Through these processes the contrasting of the "cerebral" and the "carnal" became a central theme in the thinking that supported the eugenics movement that swept the United States in the 19th and 20th centuries. This belief provided the key link to interpretations of individuals whose physical characteristics and/or intellectual capabilities were thought to veer too far from the norm of the Christian White male and to represent a less-than-human identity.

A Newly Constructed Identity

The core of racism in the United States was built on these deficit constructions of how the newly dominated peoples differed from the White Christian norm. A utilitarian worldview was central to this ideology, and it became urgent to construct a subhuman identity in order to justify mistreatment— otherwise it would be deemed by the public as inhumane. It was the only means by which treating human beings as subhuman could be accepted globally and as an economic venture. The prohibition of the right to liberty, which set the precedent for the denial of other rights, would go a step further toward casting the enslaved as property. With the accompanying denial of access to various other forms of property and rights, the foundation for perpetual inferiority was set for these generations of slaves and their descendants.

Perpetuated by this newly constructed role of inferiority, of subhumanness, people of color were marketed, sold, negotiated for, invested in, killed, and were killed for. They were the source of a viable labor force that drove the economy of the nation, especially for the southern United States. In the socially constructed identity of African Americans as *property*, their former identity as human beings was thereby extinguished, their names erased, their families broken, their tribes disbanded, and their communities a memory. Trauma and fear would be the tools of oppression, and freedom, a crime punishable by death. The irony of the American value of freedom, embossed in the Constitution, was to be acquired only by some, and those whose human identity and citizenship could be validated.

Among the hierarchy of personhood, or its absence, the Black woman was the most dehumanized (Fenton, 2016). During the centuries of slavery, the reproductive capacity of the Black woman was of particular economic interest for increasing manpower and production through the birth of more slaves. The focus on the procreative capacity of the Black woman meant the degradation of her sexuality (Fenton, 2016). It is important to note that concurrent with this ideology was institutionalized sexism because the female, regardless of ethnicity, was cast into a position of inferiority with the denial of many rights beyond the denial of access to voting privileges. The White female was thereby placed in the subordinate position to the male, another oppression that we will refer to later in our discussion of professionals' casting of mothers versus fathers.

All of the foregoing practices ensured the destruction of the Black family through oppression, violence, and the removal of males and even children for economic exploitation and violent sexual exploitation of the females. It is noteworthy to mention that, while during the time of slavery the focus was on the fecundity and sexuality of the Black woman in favor of procreation because it served to increase property and economic wealth, after the passage of Amendment 13, the shift was toward the reproductive control of the Black woman and the prevention of her procreation (Fenton, 2016).

Post-Emancipation: The Land of the Free

Life after the abolition of slavery did not mean the complete reversal of injustices that so many had hoped for. Even with the passage of the Reconstruction Amendments, which included Amendments 13, 14, and 15, we recall that the economy, politics, social climates, and all systems were still controlled by those who had identified themselves as the dominant race. "Free" as a title did not guarantee quality of life, and in fact many of the former slaves and their descendants suffered greatly after their release from the plantations and in their migration north. On the contradictions of the promises of abolition and its lived experience during postbellum America, W. E. B. Du Bois noted:

> The Nation has not yet found peace from its sins; the freedman has not yet found in freedom his promised land. Whatever of good may have come in

these years of change, the shadow of a deep disappointment rests upon the Negro people, —a disappointment all the more bitter because the unattained ideal was unbounded save by the simple ignorance of a lowly people. (Du Bois, 1903/1994, p. 4)

Conditions for the free Black person were significantly connected to the vestiges of slavery as they related to the freedoms of opportunity, finance, health, education, housing, independence, and survival (Outterson, 2005). Such freedoms have been historically, socially, and economically constructed as properties, with exclusive rights. Harris (1993) described the strategic purpose of dehumanizing African Americans for maintaining and codifying property rights for the elite, adding that "the social relations that produced racial identity as a justification for slavery also had implications for the conceptualization of property" (p. 1781). Citing W.E.B. Du Bois's work, the *Black Reconstruction*, Harris also highlighted the urgency among workingclass Whites to distinguish themselves from Blacks during this era, noting that doing so conferred significant social advantages. Therefore, even after abolition, the establishment of Jim Crow laws maintained "separate but equal" status for people of color, in order to maintain the property and superior status for dominant groups.

Embedded Intersections: Where Race and Ability Meet

As represented by the framework of DisCrit (Connor et al., 2016), and as analyzed in detail by Artiles (2013), we see the history and continuing construction of race and disability in the United States as inextricably bound. Such an analysis reveals complex intersections both within and across presumably discrete categories, and reflects different versions with the changing times. Kimberle Crenshaw's (1989) identification of the importance of identity intersections in the understanding of oppression and marginalization provides an essential lens for this consideration. Crenshaw described intersectionality as a phenomenon that occurs among individuals who are situated in identities that are historically marginalized, and whose experiences within these categories are compounded by overlapping identity markers across multiple domains. Crenshaw and other scholars who have written about intersectionality also criticize single-factor research that approaches any one identity as subordinate to the other, because studying them discretely may place an "additional layer of marginalization" (Fenton, 2016).

The outcomes of identity intersections for people of color during and after the times of slavery could be negotiated in multiple and inconsistent ways. On the one hand, because of their status as a major economic commodity, slaves defined as having a disability could sometimes be protected under the law from the anticipated outcomes of being labeled as "feebleminded" (Carey, 2009). Thus, the question of competence could be manipulated so as to protect the property of slaveholders, that is, their slaves. Derrick Bell (1980) refers to this phenomenon as *interest convergence*, in which practices that may appear to be equitable are widely accepted because they are advantageous to the dominant group. On the other hand, any significant impairments, either physical or psychological, could discount the economic value of such property (Fenton, 2016). Therefore, absolute control of the rights, role, capacity, treatment, and outcomes for persons of color with disabilities belonged to the dominant race.

Given these circumstances, it is not difficult to see how the eugenics movement intertwined with evolutionary theory to support the British project of building colonies based on conquest and enslavement. By the time of emancipation of the slaves, the mythology of the inferior African was embedded in American consciousness and provided an easy link to the concept of abnormality and deficit.

The goal of the eugenics movement was to lead society toward a greater perfectionism, even though this had been refuted by Darwin. Francis Galton, in 1869, just 10 years after Darwin's publication of *On the Origin of Species*, manipulated components of evolutionary theory to argue for selection of certain traits. The eugenics movement also used the studies of the geneticist Gregor Mendel to argue that certain disability-related deficits were not only genetically linked but also dangerously heritable.

Backed up by the pseudoscientific evidence provided by studies in the early 1900s, criminal behavior became attributed to "feeblemindedness" in the individual. The development of the movement was also strongly supported by the Kallikak genealogical studies by Goddard and Green (1913), which labeled and categorized as "feebleminded" multiple generations of persons within the same genetic line (Turnbull, Turnbull, Erwin, Soodak, & Shogren, 2015).

FAMILIES WITH DEVELOPMENTALLY DISABLED CHILDREN IN THE 19th CENTURY

What do we know about families who had children with disabilities during the 19th century? First, we note that available information about the experiences of such families did not include Black or other minoritized families, leaving us with narratives only about White families.

Within that history, as is often the case when reviewing social movements and attitudes at different points in time, we note contrasting narratives existing side by side, with the newer one gradually gaining dominance. In this vein, according to Richards (2004), during the first half of the 19th century individuals with developmental disabilities functioned within their communities, were allowed a place in school depending on the favor of the school principal, and were presented in fictional accounts as stereotypically "benign, if rather maudlin" childlike or angelic figures cared for by loving mothers (p. 68). Richards gives the example of a fictional account published in 1845 in the *Ladies' Repository*, which contrasts the lives of two women, one whose "idiot son" turns out to be a good-natured and well-socialized person, while the other woman's healthy son turns out to be a criminal. In dramatic contrast to this view, Richards describes the simultaneous promulgation by leading reformers and "experts" of the opposite image of the "idiot" as being "generally the offspring of diseased, sinful parents, who, in raising a child so marked by sin, were neglectful, overburdened, and driven to further sin" (p. 70). By the latter third of the century, with the increasing dominance of heredity theories and evolutionary beliefs based on Darwin's work, the word "idiot" had become an official category and was included in the federal census. Family stories began to present the presence of disabled members as a source of shame.

Education of Children with Disabilities in 19th-Century America

Unsurprisingly, the doctrines of this period were mirrored in the conceptualization and practice of education. In the philosophical framework of the 19th century, education was perceived as a property and privilege of middle-class Whites, an idea rooted in philosophers who prioritized intellect as the highest "measure of human worth" (United States President's Committee on Mental Retardation, 1977, p. 3). Philosophers such as Rene Descartes and John Locke "placed such a high premium on intellectual traits" that cognitive ability became equated with success, but only for *some* (United States President's Committee on Mental Retardation, 1977, p. 3). In turn, a compromised intelligence, or lack thereof, would cast populations of people into a trajectory of low worth and, ultimately, failure.

Advocates for the deaf and the blind were the first to challenge the low expectations for people with disabilities during the first half of the 19th century. Edward Miner Gallaudet, for example, founded the first school for the deaf in 1856. Simultaneous with the efforts of Gallaudet was the work of Dr. Samuel Howe of Boston, who, in 1846, was able to secure legislative funding for research from the state of Massachusetts, in order to determine the educability of children with intellectual disabilities. Howe proposed that the study's purpose was "[to] inquire into the conditions of the idiots in this commonwealth, to ascertain their number and whether anything can be done for their relief" (United States President's Committee on Mental Retardation, 1977, p. 3). He conducted a pilot study in the creation of a small private school, which became the first public residential institution, the Massachusetts School for Idiotic Children and Youth.

As mentioned earlier, however, the second half of the 19th century saw the rise of a new paternalistic worldview, presaging the domination by eugenics, and emphasizing the protection *of* these individuals as well as mainstream society *from* those who were different. Because of this approach, the line was blurred between the educational institutions for children with varying abilities and places of containment for children deemed to be mentally ill. Howe lamented the conflation of education with custodial care, and he concluded that although the success of the school he started was not what he had hoped for, which was to "restore" the child with disabilities to "normal function," his data did support the educability and training of children with disabilities in a school setting that could be designed and planned *with* their families (United States President's Committee on Mental Retardation, 1977, p. 4). His later work emphasized that separate schools, even with good intent, were not beneficial to children with disabilities. Following is his comment on a newly constructed school for the blind:

> Society, moved by pity for some special form of suffering, hastens to build up establishments which sometimes increase the very evil which it wished to lessen. . . . Our people have rather a passion for public institutions, and when their attention is attracted to any suffering class, they make haste to organize one for its benefit. (Howe, Ceremonies on Laying the Cornerstone of the N.Y. State Inst. for the Blind, 1866, quoted in United States President's Committee on Mental Retardation, 1977, p. 5)

As one of the primary opponents of exclusion of persons with disabilities from schools and from communities, Howe was among the first to suggest the notion of "idiots' rights," which was refuted by other legislators across the country. Custodial care was in fact the wave of change, and the very residential schools that were emerging when he began his pilot study were growing in other states and transforming into formal institutional settings. In addition, the residents were primarily from local families with little means of support, so upon their release from these institutions the residents had no other supports toward independent living (United States President's Committee on Mental Retardation, 1977, p. 6).

The continuing power of the eugenics beliefs were evident in the fact that Howe, while advocating for the rights of individuals with mental retardation, simultaneously maintained the belief that their existence was the fault of their parents. This view was cloaked in religious beliefs of the day, as expressed in the following statement by Howe:

> It seemed impious to attribute to the creator any such glaring imperfection in his handiwork. It appeared to us certain that the existence of so many idiots in every generation must be the consequence of some violation of the natural laws, —that where there was so much suffering, there must have been sin. (as cited in Richards, 2004, p. 70)

As the march toward education as a "science" continued, by the end of the 19th century, everything from intelligence to behavior was thought to be classifiable and measurable. Most notable and most enduring was the construction of the belief in the bell curve as the measurement tool that would sort the population into categories of intelligence.

The Bell Curve: Origins, Aegis, Power

A third simultaneous current contributed to the confluence of heredity theories toward the end of the 19th century and the diminution of a favorable construction of developmental disabilities. This was the application of the concept of the bell curve to the distribution of intelligence among humans. As outlined by Dudley-Marling and Gurn (2010), the origin of the bell curve concept traces back to a constructed formula that could theoretically express the probability of error in mathematics, which was later applied to the field of astronomy by astronomers Gauss and Laplace. Scientist Adolphe Quetelet, an astronomer, proposed that this model could potentially be applied to the human experience. He looked at the frequency of distribution to describe the "average man," asserting that the average of sampled values for any characteristic would be the referenced norm for that characteristic, with standard deviations establishing the parameters of the normal range. Under the *assumption* that this application was appropriate for explaining human variation, it was readily accepted and presumed to be valid, especially among positivist researchers. The error inherent in this assumption has been pointed out by Peter McLaren (2015) as follows:

> Human behavior, however, is never completely random and is almost always influenced by social factors. The "mean," therefore, is not necessarily a meaningful representation of groups and individual group measures and deviations of the mean do not signify human imperfections. (McLaren, 2015, p. 174)

The epistemological tenor of the time, however, with its focus on heredity and intrinsic deficit, ensured the reification of the concept of the bell curve just years before Darwin's theories on human variation were publicized. Yet in the few years to follow, the theory of the bell curve would have strong alignment with the aims of eugenicists, such as Galton, who applied this ideology to human intelligence. Norm-referencing the White, middle-class, Protestant male would also provide power behind the creation of deviancy, adding that the tails of the distribution curves represented "brilliance at one end and weakness and feeble-mindedness at the other" (Dudley-Marling & Gurn, 2010, p. 12).

THE 20th CENTURY:
THE HEGEMONY OF INTELLIGENCE AS A MEASURABLE CONSTRUCT

By the middle of the 20th century, the interactive effects of race and disability were in full evidence in the field of education. Intelligence testing and the medical model provided a means by which to generate the differences that needed to be evidenced, particularly after the removal of the deeply institutionalized and structural force of oppression that was slavery. The IQ test, for example, would be a pathway for marginalizing children of color by labeling them as disabled. Professor and educational pioneer Louis Terman was a major proponent of the use of the intelligence test to confirm intrinsic deficits. Terman was also a eugenicist. The following excerpt is from his work *The Measurement of Intelligence,* in which he described the educability of children of color:

> And as far as intelligence is concerned, the tests have told the truth. These boys are uneducable beyond the merest rudiments of training. Their dullness seems to be racial, or at least in the family stocks from which they come. . . . Children of this group should be segregated in special classes and be given instruction which is concrete and practical. They cannot master abstractions, but they can often be made efficient workers, able to look out for themselves. (Mendoza, Paguyo, & Gutierrez (2016), p. 73)

The *Plessy v. Ferguson* decision also exemplifies the legalization of discrimination in the education of children, maintaining an institutionalized "separate but equal" position that lasted for half a century. It is no surprise that the Brown decision in 1954 would take decades to be widely implemented and that the vestiges of the Plessy era would form the basis of what would come to be known as the overrepresentation of ethnic minority students in special education disability categories (Dunn, 1968; Mercer, 1973).

Development of intelligence tests, such as those provided by Binet and Simon in 1905, contributed to the ideology that intelligence was static, unchangeable, and could be gauged by administration of a battery of tests. Dr. H. H. Goddard and other scholars thereby constructed the labels of "idiot," "moron," and "imbecile" based on these intelligence tests to determine the measures of a new construct called *mental age* (United States President's Committee on Mental Retardation, 1977, p. 10). Goddard himself believed in the impractical nature of education and the lack of utility to society of individuals with intellectual disabilities:

> No amount of education, it was believed, would alter the constitutionally endowed IQ . . . [and] the menace to society of mentally deficient people, especially of the moron whose feeble intelligence may have been masked by his apparently normal appearance. (Goddard, 1913)

Consider the power behind the intelligence tests, rooted in the same ideology that labeled differences as intrinsic deficits, and how this power can be used to exert control over populations of human beings. Following is a description of the utility of the intelligence test for the advancement of a broader agenda, by Louis Terman (1916), educational pioneer and eugenicist:

> It is safe to predict that in the near future, intelligence tests will bring tens of thousands of these high-grade defectives under the surveillance and protection of society. This will ultimately result in the curtailing of reproduction of feeblemindedness and elimination of an enormous amount of crime, pauperism and industrial inefficiency. It is hardly necessary to emphasize that these high-grade cases, of the type so frequently overlooked, are precisely the ones whose guardianship it is most important for the State to assume. (p. 7)

Terman's words reveal the greater purpose of intelligence testing, an instrument for eugenicists to identify, classify, and therefore eliminate those who were found to be defective.

Controlling the "Menace" of Disability: The Practice of Sterilization

The ways in which these discriminatory practices were implemented were rooted not only in pseudoscientific justifications but also in what we call *pseudoeconomic* and *pseudohumanitarian* efforts. Deceptive, illogical, and constructed rationales that described persons with disabilities and persons of color as financial burdens on systems and their mass extinction as "a greater good" were perpetuated both overtly and covertly through the eugenics movement. Once the 13th Amendment could no longer guarantee the codification of the nonpersonhood of African Americans, and the early educational systems showed some promise for the education of children with disabilities, it became necessary to find biologically, economically, and morally justified means to continue to marginalize the "dually othered" by restricting their access to property, education, and, above all, to *power.*

Thus, the social construction of disabilities in U.S. society throughout the 19th century was built on unfounded theories and practices that increased fear, stigma, maltreatment, isolation, and the removal of rights of people with disabilities. The culture of intelligence testing in the early 20th century gave birth to several categories of individuals based on these outcomes and the subjective decisions of professionals. Among these constructed categories was a classification of "feebleminded" individuals. Persons deemed feebleminded were, as Goddard and Terman contended, "normal" in appearance and "high grade" in assessment. Though arbitrary, these descriptions implied that "feebleminded" individuals could somehow blend within greater society, "passing" for a person without any disabilities, as W. Bullard remarked, those cases in which the defect is least apparent, the so-called border-line cases—those cases which are supposed to stand near or close to the imaginary line which divides the normal from the subnormal or diseased (1908, pp. 240–241).

Remarkably, the feebleminded were classified as the most dangerous threats to the citizens, the "menaces" to society.

One of the primary strategies of the eugenics movement, in order to ensure that its aims gained popularity among the masses, was to generate fear of those who were deemed undesirable. It was common practice to cast people with disabilities into the shadows, locking them away into the invisibility of asylums and institutions. People with disabilities only came into view when they could serve as objects of negative, dehumanizing public curiosity, spectacles in circuses and "freak" shows. Thus, their exclusion from greater society permitted no alternative hypothesis about their inferior status. Rather, the publications and propaganda reinforced the ideology of feeblemindedness as the greatest of danger to the nation's citizens. Consider this excerpt from Walter Fernald:

> The social and economic burdens of uncomplicated feeblemindedness are only too well known. The feebleminded are a parasitic, predatory class, never capable of self-support or of managing their own affairs. The great majority ultimately become public charges in some form. (Fernald, 1912, pp. 90–98)

The power of the word and characterization of *feebleminded* proliferated so rapidly that it soon became a tool by which the dominant social group could assign and remove rights, casting people into the deviant role (Artiles, 2011). It should be noted that anyone could be deemed feebleminded during the early part of 20th century based on observation of one's physical appearance or behaviors. The assignment was not based on professional judgment but could be instituted by any ordinary, middle-class, White citizen.

The Menace of the Feebleminded Female. A primary focus of the eugenicists was how to control the feebleminded female. A concurrent ideology at this time was to associate both intellectual and moral deviance with disability, in particular, toward women. In addition to the aforementioned potential of feebleminded individuals to blend in with society, popularized notions contended that feebleminded females posed an even greater threat to the social order, asserting that they lacked reason and good judgment, were unable to control their sexual urges, and were therefore responsible for the corruption of good men through their "reckless promiscuity" (Stern, 2010, p. 177). Although Dr. Howe was a major proponent of education and rights of people with disabilities and their inclusion in society, he too offered "observations" of females with intellectual disabilities that supported this mythology:

The most lamentable and certain, though less frequent cause of congenital idiocy, is the lasciviousness of some female idiots, whose illegitimate offspring are almost always, like themselves, idiotic and lustful. (United States President's Committee on Mental Retardation, 1977, p. 9)

Making the claim that feebleminded females were loose and dangerous in behavior needed to have some scientific grounding in order to make it credible to the public. Therefore the scientists of the early 20th century busied themselves with professional accounts such as those published by Dr. Howe, associating the behaviors they reported and presumed moral character to be a function of lowered intelligence. This inextricably linked feeblemindedness with criminalization, as described in the following passage from eugenicist Terman in 1916:

Not all criminals are feebleminded, but all feebleminded persons are at least potential criminals. That every feebleminded woman is a potential prostitute would hardly be disputed by anyone. Moral judgment, like business judgment, social judgment, or any other kind of higher thought process, is a function of intelligence. Morality cannot flower and fruit if intelligence remains infantile. (p. 11)

The most threatening feature of feebleminded women was believed to be their increased fertility as compared with non-feebleminded women. With false ideologies of the heritability of traits that were considered to be intellectually and morally deviant, it became the priority, therefore, to bring the sexuality and reproductive functioning of feebleminded women under custodial care, as a means of protection and purification of the population. The reproductive restrictions were promoted as morally, politically and economically sound, as Bullard explains:

They are most expensive to the state because they are the most fruitful source of diseased and mentally-defective children, who are apt to become state charges. One woman of this class, slightly below par intellectually, but not extremely feebleminded, can produce incalculable evil. The plainly feebleminded is more or less obvious and the evil she creates is so plain that it can be and often is guarded against. (1908, p. 242)

Institutionalization of these women was thought to be an enterprise to prevent further pollution of the human race. Segregation based on gender within the institutions was promoted in order to prevent sexual relations between men and women with disabilities. Restrictions, codified in the law, were also placed on the rights of the feebleminded to marry. However, no other legalized act was so profound as the federal- and state-sanctioned sterilization laws:

> The most important point is that feeblemindedness is highly hereditary. . . .
> No feebleminded person should be allowed to marry or become a parent. . . .
> The normal members of a definitely tainted family may transmit defect to their
> own children. Certain families should become extinct. Parenthood is not for all.
> (Fernald, 1912, pp. 90–98)

Following this argument, categorization justified compulsory sterilizations for persons with disabilities. The 1927 Supreme Court decision of
Buck v. Bell legalized involuntary sterilization of individuals with disabilities. Chief Justice Oliver Wendell Holmes wrote, "Three generations of imbeciles are enough" (*Buck v. Bell*, 1927). Castrations were also legalized as
a means of preventing the reproduction among categories of people considered to be undesirable, although this occurred less frequently than the
sterilizations of females (Fenton, 2016). The same was true for people of
color, who had been known only in the condition of enslavement and oppression. As the merging of "feeblemindedness" and racial identity created
an intensified vision of the "menace," the Black female became a particular
target of control.

The Menace of the Black Female. The practice of sterilization marked the
shameful zenith of the eugenics movement, as disproportionate numbers of
women, people with disabilities, and people of color with disabilities, along
with those living in poverty, comprised an overwhelming majority of the
legally sanctioned sterilizations that would occur across nearly 8 decades
(Stern, 2010). However, the Black female with a perceived disability faced a
type of marginalization, maltreatment, and control greater than that experienced by individuals with any one of these identity markers. While historical removal of humanness, of citizenship, and of rights had been persistent
for Black persons with disabilities and for women, the intersectionality of
these groups created an identity perceived by leading eugenicists as needing
to be brought under control. In a multilayered fashion, mythologies about
the sexuality of the Black woman and about feebleminded women, and the
degraded status of women as a whole, made Black women with perceived
disabilities a particular danger and threat to society. They would constitute
a breed of *undesirables* that would taint the human race.

It should be noted, however, that Black women did not comprise the
majority of the category of feebleminded women. An overwhelming majority of feebleminded women were White, poor, immigrant women. As a
result, the United States mandated restrictions on the immigration of "all
idiots, imbeciles, feebleminded persons, epileptics, insane persons . . ."
(Immigration Act of 1907). Where, then, were Black women with disabilities? As noted previously, disability history, while exposing the horrors of
the state of the nation's institutions, tends to overlook the fact that people of
color, subjected to systemic and structural racism, were excluded from such

places. Though sharing the identity of disability with their White counterparts, decades of laws restricted Black women with disabilities from residing in these spaces. Jackson (2001) has noted that although this exclusion may be perceived as somehow protecting people of color from negative experiences, many of these individuals were forced to take up residence in asylums and prisons, whose conditions were even more appalling. Rembis's (2011) analysis of adolescent females in Illinois spanning the period of 1890–1960 found that Black girls were not highly represented in the institutionalized female feebleminded population but were among the 10% of Black individuals incarcerated in state prisons.

Rembis also noted that eugenicists' characterizations of females as deviant were not only expressed by White, middle-class males, but also by White middle-class females in "their perceived ability to speak for the 'less fortunate' working-class women and children, and their status as professionals empowered them to speak in ways that have not been fully articulated or analyzed" (p. 5). Prominent eugenics and birth control proponent Margaret Sanger was a clear example of such highly influential White middle-class women. While approving of fecundity and procreation among White middle-class women, she discouraged reproduction among the poor and women of color with perceived disabilities, in order to eliminate those whom she and other eugenicists would classify as the undesirables of society (Fenton, 2016). The easiest and most effective method for protecting the population was to conduct sterilizations where there were large concentrations of poor, minority women with disabilities, that is, within the nation's institutions. This practice would go unquestioned, under the guise of standard health care, and was routinely performed often without the individuals' knowledge, let alone consent. Forced sterilizations outside of institutional settings also took place, overwhelmingly conducted among immigrant, African American, and Mexican individuals (Carey, 2009).

In summary, the urgency to remove the "threat" of disability from the greater society was perpetuated by professionals, including physicians, researchers, psychologists, politicians, and educators (Berry, 1995). The White middle class was eager to adopt the philosophy of purifying society and establishing a new social order. The professional was placed in the position of authority, and the goal was to push parents toward a decision to institutionalize their child even though many parents were against this decision (Turnbull et al., 2015). Sadly, with less than minimal services for persons with disabilities and their families, institutionalization became the only option for many families, who experienced shame both at the presence of the child and at their own decision to remove the child from the family. Isolated from community environments, families were marginalized. Moreover, the Great Depression of the 1930s and 1940s further undermined families' ability to cope with additional stressors, as well as their ability to meet financial and social needs.

THE 20th CENTURY AND
THE DISEMPOWERMENT OF PARENTS

World War II brought to global attention the horrors that Nazi Germany had perpetrated in the name of eugenics. Though not well publicized at the time, it was later discovered that among the first to be exterminated were individuals with disabilities, who represented the antithesis of the "master race." In the name of "scientific" experimentation, people with disabilities, the poor, and people of color were experimented upon without anesthesia and without ethical principles. When veterans returned home from World War II, many described the horrors and destruction of humanity they had witnessed, and it shocked the world. Veterans themselves were afflicted not only with physical disabilities but also with the lasting effects of trauma.

Another shocking revelation of the extent of disempowerment and exploitation of people of color who were ill or disabled came in the gradual awareness of the multitude of abuses in the United States toward people of color by the medical and research communities. The HeLa cell line, from which we have derived so much of our knowledge about cell function, and which created a cell line for research, amplification, and therapeutic medicine, was taken from a Black woman by the name of Henrietta Lacks in 1951 (Skloot, 2010). She trusted her physicians and the prestigious medical institution for her medical care, but the cells were removed without her consent. Henrietta, a working-class Black woman, died from cancer, without the treatment she sought; her living cells were effectively stolen from her, and from them an entire system of medicine would benefit. In a similar vein, to study the effects of syphilis, a treatable disease, the federal government funded 40 years of experimentation on Black men in Tuskegee, Alabama, who were afflicted with the disease. Under the guise of "research," these men were given a placebo in lieu of the medicine to treat their symptoms. Researchers essentially watched these men suffer and die. In response, Western societies began a slow shift in values as revulsion against these practices led to the foundation for today's standards in ethical research practices. Yet several more decades passed before the horrors of our own institutions for the disabled were exposed.

Throughout the first half of the 20th century, the racism and ableism generated by eugenics beliefs continued to proliferate. One key outcome of this was that professionals continued to advocate for the institutionalization of children with disabilities and the sterilization of poor, minority, and disabled women whose IQ scores or social histories pointed to their unworthiness. Between 1925 and 1950, the population of individuals institutionalized grew to its highest rate. Although one contributor to this increase was thought to be the success of medicine to help populations of individuals with disabilities to survive (United States President's Committee on Mental Retardation, 1977, p. 14), the eugenics vision continued to drive deeply entrenched notions of the "demonic, fearsome defective" (United States President's Committee on Mental Retardation, 1977, p. 15). Many professionals took a paternalistic role toward parents. As Carey (2009) explains, they "supported rights that expanded services for their clients but resisted rights that would limit their professional discretion" (p. 133).

Removal "for the Sake of the Family"

The influence of medical professionals was starkly represented in a 1947 article by Dr. C. Anderson Aldrich in the *American Journal of Mental Deficiency*. Entitled "Preventive Medicine and Mongolism," the article described the practice of prescribing immediate institutionalization of newborns with Down syndrome as a best practice to address the "family tragedy in the birth of a Mongolian idiot" (p. 127). Aldrich described how he would first persuade the father or other influential relatives to agree that the child should be placed in an institution and would then inform the mother that the decision had been made. Aldrich argued that this would relieve the mother of the potential guilt of having to make the decision herself and relieve the family of the burden and shame that the child's presence in the home would inflict on siblings, parents, and even on the marital relationship. It is telling that Aldrich reported that his "method" had "failed" only three times in 14 years; that is, only three families had rejected his recommendation for institutionalization of the infant.

A practical study of how the institutionalization approach worked was presented by John and Nellie Carver (1972), who reported the findings of an interview study with 37 parents of children who had initially lived at home and were placed in a residential institution by the age of 6. Most of these cases occurred during the 1950s. The study was John Carver's doctoral dissertation, and he and his wife had a child with retardation who lived in the institution where the study was conducted. Although the authors spoke sympathetically of the parents' desire to keep the children at home, they were explicitly of the opinion that institutionalization was the best course because of the disabled child "distorting the family focus" and the family becoming "an autocracy capriciously and ineffectually ruled by its weakest members" in a series of "unresolved crises and continued role disruption" (p. 52). The authors' focus on the unacceptability of these children's "differences" was underscored by their description of the apparent folly of parents trying to keep their child at home:

> Sensibly, they had confidence in the doctors, and to a point they accepted the prognosis. But they were going to keep *their* child at home. They were going to set up the home so that they could take care of him. They didn't realize how wide would become the gap between their child's behavior and that of his age-mates who were normal. (p. 45)

From the perspective of increased tolerance for varying lifestyles that has marked the first decades of the 21st century, we would wonder why a widening "gap" among siblings should mean that the child could not be absorbed within the family. Another disturbing aspect of the authors' views was the lack of understanding of the validity of readjustments that parents made to their own perspectives of the child. Rather, Carver and Carver saw parents' reframing perspectives as evidence that they had developed a "soft focus" on the child, and "rarely did they picture him in the harsh lineaments that the reality of this problem seemed to call for" (p. 52). From our perspective today, we ask, But what is the reality? What does reality mean?

Children with less significant disabilities were also deeply affected by the deficit perspective as schools reserved the right to refuse admission to those thought uneducable. The categories based on IQ performance became entrenched, with the term "educable" being assigned to those scoring 50–75 on the IQ test, "trainable" for those scoring 25–49, and "totally dependent" for those scoring 0–24. It was commonly believed among educators that it was not the responsibility of the public school system to inclusively educate the "mentally handicapped," and to do so would cause harm to other children in the setting due to exposure (Smith, 1957).

Professionals' Theories and Family Disempowerment

Following these beginnings in the post–World War II period, professional study of the issues facing families of children with disabilities proliferated, fueled largely by the field of psychology and psychoanalysis. One limiting factor in this process was that the psychoanalytic gaze paid little attention to the contexts and other dynamics of the family while emphasizing the disabling effects of disability diagnosis on the family, particularly on the mother. For example, psychoanalysts Solnit and Stark (1961) described the birth of a "defective child" as a human crisis that initiates a process of mourning on the part of the mother. This theory had a commonsense appeal based on the argument that, during pregnancy, a woman engages in a process of psychological preparation for her ideal child and can only be expected to experience shock when the child presents with complications that appear to defy her dream. However, the approach supported the negativity of the time by using language that today is unacceptable, such as referring to the child as "defective," and it tended to promote a view of the mother as a "patient" who would need psychotherapy for recovery. Still, the authors also described positive ways in which attending professionals could assist the mother to invest in the real child by involving her in planning and caring for the child. A similar and related theory of "chronic sorrow," proposed by Olshansky (1962), represented the idea of mourning in more extreme terms, envisioning a state of permanent sorrow experienced by the mother in particular. Although Olshansky described this sorrow as a normal rather than a neurotic response, the implications of this negative view did little to provide the mother with solutions.

A theory that gained great traction and is still taught today is known as the *disability grief cycle*, accredited to Elizabeth Kübler-Ross (1969), who compared the individual case studies of grieving parents. The cycle consists of concrete stages that include "shock, denial, guilt, anger, shame, depression and finally acceptance" (Turnbull et al., 2015). However, the danger of this theory, as well as similar "stage" theories, is that it reflects a typological thinking, casting the parents and their experiences into generalizable and prescriptive categories. It also assumes a universality of experiences, fixed sequential stages of emotions, and an assumed ability to assess these emotions at any given time. What this theory also failed to address are the multiple layers of structural and societal barriers that placed significant burdens upon the parents of a child with the disability.

Although we believe that these and other theories of parental adjustment to disability hold kernels of truth, their danger lies in the perception that emotional responses render parents dysfunctional, even neurotic. Clinical professionals at this time were committing the same errors that the medical, research, political, and educational professionals had done by generalizing the parental experience and prescribing, rather than customizing, recommendations. The human experience, on the contrary, is very subjective, and each experience is dynamic and unique within its own context. What was particularly dangerous was that these professionals were not only the first lines of contact, communication, and interaction for parents receiving a diagnosis but also the primary deliverers of care and services. Often, for parents in need of support, they were the only sources. Therefore, the professionals had placed themselves in the position of authority, expertise, and power. Under the guise of professional expertise, psychologists and medical personnel persuaded parents to relinquish their children to institutions. They removed the parents' agency and control and therefore positioned themselves to make decisions for the family. Families of children with disabilities were assigned to the fringes of society.

Perhaps the worst of the theories was that of Bruno Bettelheim (1967) regarding the etiology of autism. Bettelheim is best known for his assertion that autism is a disability caused by the parents' negative disposition toward their children and that the child's social withdrawal is a symptom of parent failure. This provided support for institutionalization, as children with autism could be placed under the care of professionals "who allegedly would be more competent and caring" (Turnbull et al., 2015, p. 117). In her study of parents in Trinidad and Tobago, first author Beth recounted a mother's description of the devastation she experienced immediately after receiving her child's diagnosis of autism:

That afternoon I went into the largest bookstore in Miami. I could find only one book on autism and it was called *The Empty Castle*, by Bruno Bettelheim. That book said it was the parent's fault. This child has been neglected. And I thought—When did I do this? I planned, I waited, I adored! When did I unknowingly reject her? Was there something I did unconsciously that caused this child to be like this? I took it as truth since this thing was printed. I think that was the lowest point in my life. (Harry, 2020, p. 219)

We close this chapter with an excerpt from coauthor Lydia's journal.

From Lydia's Journal: Pursuing Hope in Uncommon Places

I recall sharing Isaiah's diagnosis of Down syndrome with my family members and close friends soon after his birth in 2010. I can put their responses into categories. First, there was the grief response. They began to grieve for me, for dreams lost, for the fears of what this might mean for our family, over their understanding of what his disability meant. I had to remind them after a while that he was only a few days old, and his life was just beginning. But for so many people like them, a different life had sort of ended. Second, there was the response of false hope and idealism. False hope ranged anywhere from the suggestion that the professionals had been wrong about the diagnosis to promising to look for some research supporting a possible cure. I listened to them, patiently, knowing what they were grappling with. But my background in biology had understood what the karyotype confirmed, what his genetics had indicated, and that there was no reversal of the number of chromosomes he had been given. Idealism caused them to think of the many actors with Down syndrome they had seen on television or a friend of a friend they knew who was the parent of a child with Down syndrome who made it all the way through college. The third category was somewhat grounded in reality, though at times, too much in reality. Their main question was, What are you going to do, Lydia? This category represented my family members and friends who were nurses, social workers, attorneys, and business leaders. Their practical advice involved making good assessments, ensuring that I maintained my own goals, and not letting his clinical diagnosis shift me too much off of my own self. I remember receiving a checklist for self-care in the mail from one of them who used it in the clinical setting. The checklist still had the title, "For Persons with Mental Retardation or Other Handicaps." I ripped it into small pieces, thinking of my little one, and decided I was going to find hope elsewhere.

The beauty of the digital age is that almost anything you are looking for is readily accessible. However, I did not know how to delimit the information for new parents of children with Down syndrome to only stories of *hope*. Painfully, I read the range of reactions and responses, across contexts, cultures, religions, and global settings. I remember reading that it was not uncommon to hear of newborns with Down syndrome being thrown off of roofs in India. Even within the United States, newborns just hours old were being left without care in a laundry room in the hospital to die. I was shocked that the percentage of elective abortions after confirming diagnosis through prenatal testing was close to 90%. I wept, asking how anyone could do such things. Later, I would learn about the longstanding perceptions within cultures of the "curses" of disability. I had even heard this somewhere within my family, that this was an *evil*. In addition, in our culture of ease and convenience, having a child who may depend on you completely may seem like a death sentence. While I cannot imagine this happening in this day and age, with so much that is known about diversity and the contributions people with disabilities make to communities and families, I know that stigma, despair, and hopelessness still exist. Perfectionism, individualism, and self-exaltation are still staples within our culture.

I realized that hope would have to be actively sought. It would not come in the most convenient and natural of places in this particular case. Hope would run countercurrent in this new life; it would be almost a paradox. I wondered how and why God chose me to care for this little mysterious one. But I knew hope was somewhere in that tiny little fist of his and in the sweet scent of baby breath.

CHAPTER 4

Parent Voices Rising

Challenging Constructions of Difference

Our limited review has so far focused on the first of Minow's (1990) principles of the construction of difference; that is, how human differences have been interpreted as representations of intrinsically different forms of humanity. We have seen how so-called scholars, professionals, and policymakers succeeded in categorizing, excluding, and devaluing those whose differences challenge spoken or unspoken norms of appearance, development, or character. We have noted the power of those voices to persuade the public and to disempower and silence parents of children so labeled.

The year 2020 will mark just 45 years since the passage of the Education for All Handicapped Children Act (EHA), which was reauthorized in 1990 as the Individuals with Disabilities Education Act (IDEA), and just 30 years since the passage of the Americans with Disabilities Act (ADA). These accomplishments were the culmination of years of intense advocacy by parents, community members, legal scholars, and philanthropists, starting in the mid-20th century. The beginnings of this process were marked by the rising voices of parents, at first alone, and then in groups, proclaiming the value of their children and challenging, some subtly, some stridently, those who had presumed to be the judges.

We turn here to the second of Minow's (1990) questions regarding the construction of difference as deviance: Who makes these determinations about difference? Are the observers objective? Do other perspectives matter? We highlight the perspectives of parents in the presentation of this challenge.

ADVOCACY AND THE JUDGES

We introduced this book with the axiom that parents wish to advocate for the value of their children. After centuries of invisibility, parents of the most stigmatized children started to make their voices heard in the period just after the Second World War. Through their published narratives, parents challenged the widespread eugenics-based beliefs regarding normalcy as God-given, proclaiming their love for their "unfinished" children (Abraham, 1958) and calling for compassion toward them as children—even as angels—sent by God to bring a message of wisdom to an uncomprehending world (Evans, 1953).

Implicit in this challenge was a charge to those who would judge their children. Based on our culture's claim of objectivity as a requirement for justice, parents began to ask whether the judge was well-informed, neutral, or fair. The terrible charge of false judgment often came too late, as in the case of Willard Abraham (1980) who, questioning the decisions of decades past, called out to his lost daughter, decrying the guilt and "apparent rejections" caused by lack of understanding, and pleading for a more informed public to "open their arms to babies like you, take you in and make you one of them, instead of the cold rejection which has been the pattern of your lives so far" (p. 82).

In the 21st century, under the aegis of the IDEA, one of the most enlightened laws in the world, parents continue to challenge the evaluations and recommendations made by professionals regarding their children. In the lunchrooms and informal settings of schools, service providers often smirk as they say to each other, "The mother says he can do this at home!" The common professional interpretation of such discrepant views is that parents are "in denial." We beg to differ: We do not claim that parents always know best, but would frame their reaction, rather, as "disagreement."

The difference between "denial" and "disagreement" strikes us often in our research with families who exclaim: "We just want service providers to see our children as we see them." How do parents see their children? How do they want the world to see them? Do their perspectives matter? To address these questions we turn to three bodies of literature: first, the body of parent biographies that have emerged in the United States since the middle of the 20th century; second, the establishment of parent advocacy organizations; and third, the explosion of critical views of the concept of disability, stimulated by the development of the field of disability studies.

It is a powerful testament to the strength of human love that not all parents during the eugenics period gave in to the terrible pressure exerted by the society as a whole and by those who espoused rejection and exclusion of individuals with disabilities. Indeed, we wish we knew who the three families were who, as cited by Dr. Aldrich (1947), had the strength of mind and perhaps the social and financial resources to defy the pronouncements of an eminent doctor! Unfortunately, we cannot identify these heroes and heroines of that time, but we can guess that they may have been among those parents who initiated the change that would sweep the nation during the second half of the 20th century. Indeed, in the midst of the entrenched effects of the eugenics movement, the post–Second World War period saw the birth of parent voice as a public phenomenon. Two simultaneous major trends marked this initiative—the publication of memoirs by well-positioned parents about their children's disabilities and the creation of advocacy groups that moved quickly from local initiatives to national organizations.

PARENTS' PUBLISHED NARRATIVES

The 1950s opened with a spate of parents' accounts of their experience. We consider whether these parents saw themselves as advocates and to what extent the telling of their stories represented attempts to speak on behalf of their children. If advocacy, what was the message being conveyed and what was its purpose? To what extent were these publications driven more by personal need than by intentions of advocacy? That is, it is possible that the drive to tell one's story may serve as a means either of self-vindication or, more simply, as a process of catharsis, which, by focusing intensely on the experience, provides a sense of unburdening for the writer. Parents who are by profession writers or academics, for example, might be likely to use the written form for this purpose.

Regardless of motivation, these accounts are marked by a few clear trends. In all cases, the stories, laden with love and wholehearted reflection, represent the parents' attempts to explain their child to the world by revealing their essential humanity. Some accounts actually describe the kind of hope that Lydia, coauthor of this book, referred to in her journal. Conversely, these accounts are often undergirded by a sense of tragedy and loss, or by the conundrum of whether to challenge or accept the prevailing beliefs of the time, most notably the question of whether these children "belonged" in the family or should be sent to live with "their own kind." Indeed, three clear trends emerge from these narratives: First, as continues to be common in the accounts of parents of children with disabilities, parents expressed deep concerns, often grief, at the fact of their children's disabilities, and described their own struggles toward acceptance. Second, the parents' concerns were deeply exacerbated by unhappiness occasioned by an absence of support and the ethos of social rejection, a rejection consistently underscored by advice from friends and professionals alike that the child "belonged" in an institution to relieve the family of the burden and shame of caring for them within the family. A third trend in these stories is parents' search for meaning in the event of their child's disabilities, a search most often framed in religious terms, such as seeking to understand or to accept "God's plan" for the child and the family.

Overall, the earliest accounts reveal both sides of the acceptance/rejection issue. In some cases, the parents succeed in overcoming society's negativity, either through the power of their religious faith or through the parental love that drove their decisions. In other cases, the issue of social rejection and institutionalization dominates and is accompanied by a strong theme of parents' struggles to overcome a sense of guilt for the decision to institutionalize the child. In some narratives, this theme is so strong that it sometimes seems like the purpose of the story is to provide justification for the decision. However, two of the best-known parent accounts of the time presented loving depictions of the parents' successful resistance to this negative ethos.

Challenging the Norms

At the turn of the 1950s two well-known public figures, author Pearl S. Buck and actress Dale Evans, were the first to call attention to their experiences as mothers of children with mental retardation, as it was termed at the time. Buck, already a popular writer, published *The Child Who Never Grew* (1950/1992), an account of both the intrapersonal and practical challenges she faced in caring for her child who had Down syndrome. In keeping with the norms of the day, Buck ultimately committed her child to institutional care at the age of 11, which she did to ensure that there would be continuity of care after her own death. Despite that decision, Buck decried the rejecting context of the time, exhorting parents to reconcile their sorrow with love for the child:

> There is an alchemy in sorrow. It can be transmuted into wisdom, which, if it does not bring joy, can yet bring happiness. . . . (p. 6)

> Remember this is still your child. Remember, too, that the child has his right to life, whatever that life may be, and he has the right to happiness, which you must find for him. Be proud of your child, accept him as he is and do not heed the words and stares of those who know no better. This child has a meaning for you and for all children. You will find a joy you cannot now suspect in fulfilling his life for and with him. (p. 61)

Evans's memoir, *Angel Unaware* (1953), came on the heels of Buck's, and it echoed the theme of family love and solidarity. Evans's daughter, Robin, had Down syndrome and after living at home with her family died at age 2. Evans framed the story as a tale told by the child, now an angel in heaven, presenting her life as a part of God's plan to bring her parents closer to God and to inspire other families to do the same. In a preface to the 50th anniversary edition published in 2004, Evans quotes her husband Roy's refusal to follow the professionals' advice to institutionalize Robin: "We are taking our baby home. God has a purpose for allowing this, and if we put her away, we will never know it" (p. 10).

The early 1950s also saw the publication of an account by a less well-known parent, Dan Boyd (1951), whose approach was equally positive but differed in that it focused on personal development as distinct from religious commitment. Presenting a uniquely reflective vision of the experience of parenting a child with mental retardation, this father described his own personal development through "three stages"—from total subjectivity marked by self-pity, to a focus on the child rather than himself, and finally to a concern for all children with similar conditions. Interestingly, this perspective paved the way for what came to be known as the "stage theory" of parental responses to disability, which built on Kübler-Ross's (1969) theory of stages of adjustment to dying.

Two stories stand out for their cheerful and positive rendering of the experience of families whose children remained within the family—Carvel Lee's (1961) *Tender Tyrant* and Marie Killilea's (1952) *Karen*. Carvel, the older sister of Jeanie, a girl with mental retardation, told her story with a sly humor that reflected both the highs and the lows of the family's experience. The worst, for this young girl, was a period of social isolation similar to that described by Edith Gramm (1951):

> Jeanie's seventh summer was the worst of our childhood . . . we were helpless to defend ourselves, for these were the locusts of curiosity and gossip. . . . We stood desolate and naked, at the mercy of the elements of humanity. There was no cover for the stark shame of Jeanie's retardedness. (p. 33)

The author, however, described how the "love and laughter" of her family overcame these challenges and concluded that her sister had been sent by God as a lesson, indeed, as a teacher of patience, generosity, compassion, and faith.

Killilea (1952), in her memoir, *Karen*, presented a joyful contrast to other accounts of the same period. Fortunately, the parents were not deterred in their hopes by the potentially devastating pronouncements by physicians— one who advised them to take out an insurance policy to provide for their daughter while she lived in an institution, and another who told them that in China "they take such children up on top of a mountain and leave them" (p. 39). After seeing 23 doctors in 2½ years, and in defiance of the increasing doubts of their friends and family, Karen's parents finally received a professional opinion that matched what they themselves had believed since their child's birth—that their child, who had cerebral palsy, would be able to develop with therapy and was of above average intelligence. Not unexpectedly, Karen's mother's joy at this assessment reveals the tremendous value placed on intelligence.

Acquiescence and Doubt

Citing similar themes of love and social pressure, two other accounts within the decade, Gramm (1951) and Abraham (1958), both published in the *American Journal of Mental Deficiency*, focused on the pain of parents' decision to institutionalize an infant or young child. Willard Abraham (1958), a professor of education, described the painful and continuing ambivalence he felt around the decision to place his infant daughter, Barbara, soon after birth, especially in light of the child's death there 4 months after placement. Two decades later, noting the improvements in the lives of children with

Down syndrome, Abraham (1980) wrote a reflection on the experience, entitled *You Always Lag One Child Behind (Barbara Revisited)*. Seeking to provide support to other parents, he addresses his reflection to Barbara, saying:

> If we are to accomplish something because of you, then it must be only a beginning, a start toward living with children like you and relieving their lives and the lives of their parents of the tensions, misunderstandings, and guilt imposed by a society ignorant, through no fault of its own, of what you were and would have been. (p. 68)

In a similar vein, Edith Gramm's (1951) *Peter the Beautiful: The Story of an Enchanted Child,* described in heartbreaking detail her family's continued efforts to support their much-loved son at home despite the constant undermining by negative social judgments and her own inability to respond to the child's uncontrollable tantrums. The family's first attempt to place him out of home was in a "private institution" at the age of about 4, only to find that, after 12 days, the child had been "beaten black and blue" (p. 273). They took him home but, with no greater success, ultimately committed him to the state institution at the age of 6½. The mother's sense of isolation and alienation from "normal" parenthood, her intense pain at walking away from her child after each visit to the institution, and her sense loss and failure make this account intensely painful reading. She concluded:

> No one street, no single playground marks a neighborhood. Not for us. The world of normal children is a vast yard, fenced and gated. There is no place in the immediate here, nor the far there, where we might go to reclaim our lives and ourselves. . . . Peter is the changeling child I read of long ago. He is enchanted, but the charm is ugly with reality. And love, which can work such magic, was not enough when we lived with him. (p. 274)

Advocacy and Catharsis

Did these family members see themselves as advocates? Clearly, the answer is yes for those who succeeded in keeping their children at home. The accounts of Buck (1951), Evans (1953), Boyd (1951), Killilea (1952), and Lee (1961) were intended to encourage other families and to represent to the world alternative perspectives on the value of children with disabilities. All five authors explicitly stated that their intentions included encouragement to other parents and education of the public generally regarding the disabilities experienced by their children. Evans's (1953) book was at the top of the *New York Times* bestseller list in 1953 (librarything.com/ bookaward/New+York+Times+bestseller), and in her retrospective preface 5 decades later she expressed the belief that her telling of her daughter's story promoted greater acceptance of individuals with Down syndrome. Considering the shame regarding disabilities that had been embedded in the society through the eugenics movement, these parents were not only advocates but pioneers in advocacy.

In asking the same question of accounts by parents who did institutionalize their children in infancy, we come to a somewhat different interpretation of advocacy—one in which parents such as Gramm (1951) and Abraham (1958) sought to advocate for other parents like themselves, rather than for the children. These accounts read like heartfelt efforts to explain themselves to the world, to seek understanding if not forgiveness, and to lend support to other families who might be suffering the same sense of guilt and/or ambivalence regarding their decisions.

Regardless of the decisions made by these families, one thing is clear: the early memoirs demonstrate the tremendous courage of their authors in making public their deepest pain and struggle around an issue that was, for most, a source of shame. Some memoirs, especially those written by parents like Abraham (1958, 1980), who were academics or professional writers, spoke more to a need for personal catharsis and an effort to clarify their own feelings by thoughtful reflection.

From the perspective of the second decade of the 21st century, a couple of searing truths emerge: First, the terrible history of parental loss and children's abandonment would have been greatly diminished had there been the medical, therapeutic, and pedagogical supports that we take for granted today. One wonders, for example, whether the tantrums of "Peter the beautiful" may have been symptomatic of autism or a mental illness, which could have been minimized or modified with medication or therapeutic interventions. Would his family then have been able to keep and care for the child they so loved? In the case of children such as Barbara, who had Down syndrome, we know for a fact that the beliefs of the day were founded on a century of false eugenics propaganda and exacerbated by institutionalization itself, which led to the short life span and minimal development noted among people with this condition.

A second lesson is equally clear: the professional pronouncements about the value of children with disabilities not only impacted parents' sense of self-worth and confidence in their abilities as parents but also came to be literally enacted in ways that deliberately disempowered parents. A 1978 essay by Dorothy Avis recounted some of the ways in which institutions accomplished this disempowerment: the institutions were out of town and "surrounded by fences," parents' visiting hours were limited and visits sometimes supervised, home visits were often discouraged and sometimes denied on the basis of inspection of the homes by a social worker, letters requesting information on residents' progress or status went unacknowledged and unanswered. While some professional attempts at support for families did exist during this period, they tended to be portrayed as "therapies," in which parents were cast as victims or patients (Turnbull & Turnbull, 2015; Wang & Singer, 2016).

After these early beginnings, parents' accounts, too numerous to mention, showed that the eugenics project continued to cast a long shadow over families' responses and decisionmaking for several decades, as parents recounted the misgivings they had to combat as they claimed the right to speak out on behalf of their children. By the 1970s, parents' accounts were beginning to be more hopeful, reflecting a gradually increasing sense of autonomy and greater understanding of the capabilities of children with a wider range of disabilities, such as aphasia (Cameron, 1973) and autism. Notable examples of the latter include Josh Greenfield's *A Child Called Noah* (1972) and two highly acclaimed accounts—Helen Featherstone's *A Difference in the Family* (1981) and Clara Clairborne Park's *The Siege* (1982).

Parents' Reflections on an Era

One very illuminating collection of essays edited by Ann and Rud Turnbull (1978) provided thoughtful reflections by parents who had lived through the institutionalization period. An updated edition (Turnbull & Turnbull, 1985) contained the original essays and follow-up reflections 7 years later. A couple of key themes are dominant in these essays: first, the change from a society that offered no support to these vulnerable children during the 1950s when parent advocacy was just beginning, to the notable improvements in the period just after the passage of Public Law 94-142, the Education for all Handicapped Children Act (1975), when increased availability of day-treatment services allowed many parents to find a middle ground between giving up the care of their children and having their care and training shared by professionals. This view included reflections on the advantages of keeping the child at home through early childhood, with the goal of better preparing them for an ultimate out-of-home placement when parents became too old to continue that care (e.g., Ziskin, 1985).

A second trend was parents' reflections on the institutionalization period and the focus of the 1980s on "normalization" and the move away from institutions to community care. One particularly powerful account was by Elizabeth Boggs (Boggs, 1978, 1985), who had been a leading advocate, helping to create parent support groups and becoming the president of the Association for Retarded Children ("The Arc") in 1958. Boggs's son, David, was born in 1945—in the heart of the institutionalization period. David, who had profound mental retardation, lived with his family until the age of 7, at which time he was placed in a state institution, where he lived, in close association with his parents, until his death in 1971.

In her accounts of the early years and in her reflections 7 years later, Boggs (1978, 1985) argued that the current principle of "normalization," implemented in a one-size-fits-all manner, had become as tyrannical as the previous segregating practices had been. Essentially, she argued that taking to an extreme the assumption that all individuals with intellectual impairments should be trained and encouraged to emulate as nearly as possible the social preferences and behaviors of their nondisabled peers, constituted an oppressive denial of their intrinsic differences. Describing the supportive and accommodating environment of the state school where David lived, his mother saw this situation as "more facilitative and more enhancing" than the community-based residence that could not address his or his peers' "extraordinary need for an adaptive environment structured to their requirements rather than ours" (p. 49). In her reflections 7 years later, Boggs acknowledged with pleasure that the community-based programs David had participated in had helped his development. Her view of the doctrinaire approaches of the inclusion/normalization advocates, however, had changed little. Rather, Boggs gave as an example of the oppressive nature of these approaches her son's love for his favorite toy, a rubber duck that he continually squeezed, which professionals had pronounced as not "age-appropriate" for David. She refers to these principles as "a new set of restrictive rules based on generalized stereotypes about what is good for people, rather than on true respect for individual differences" (pp. 60–61).

The Vehicles of Successful Advocacy:
Racial, Cultural, and Economic Capital

One thing is clear: The parents who had the cultural and social capital, the financial resources, and the education necessary to become public advocates did so with an urgency that wrought profound changes in services and public attitudes. The fact that these social attributes were essential for the performance of such advocacy is evident in the fact that all the accounts we have mentioned so far were written by White parents of considerable educational status. For example, in both Turnbull and Turnbull collections (1978, 1985), the authors of all 15 essays were university graduates, some being journalists, and many holding advanced degrees such as master's or PhDs in psychology, education, special education, science, or law.

The need for social and cultural capital was equally apparent in the only case in the Turnbull collection (1985) that featured an African American family, Curtiss and Willa Knighton and their daughter, Denise. Indeed, this is the only report we found by African American parents during this time period. At the time of their daughter's birth, Curtiss was serving as a lieutenant in the army in Korea. Upon his return, he worked in a military hospital as a psychiatric social worker, which gave the family access to medical evaluations that revealed Denise's aphasia and profound hearing loss. These parents responded with incredulity to an initial recommendation that they plan for future institutionalization of their daughter and "simply ignored this recommendation" (Knighton & Knighton, 1985, p. 273). Through numerous moves required by the military, including a stint in Germany, the family sought out and accessed every possible service for their daughter. After Curtiss retired from the military, the family moved to Washington, DC, where they engaged in fervent advocacy for better services from the board of education and became active in the DC ARC. Despite many setbacks, their ability to access services through the military and through a range of social contacts resulted in revelations of Denise's artistic talents and opportunities to learn sign language at Gallaudet College. Advocacy by her parents resulted in Denise gaining employment as a teacher's aide with the DC ARC. This upbeat and inspiring story ended with Denise's marriage at the age of 31. The parents concluded:

> As parents of a young handicapped child, we were often troubled by the professional system and the medical model that operated within the military system. At times, the system has hurt us badly, but we were not destroyed then and we are not now. We resolved that we would invariably fight back. We fared better with the military medical system because we worked from within it and possessed some professional knowledge. However, knowing the difficulties we had, we readily understood how parents working from outside a system can be absolutely devastated by it. (Knighton & Knighton, 1985, p. 273)

Neither racial nor socioeconomic diversity were explicitly stated in the published advocacy narratives. In the case of the Knighton family (1985), professional status and social connections intertwined with their ability to "work within the military system" despite several setbacks. Moreover, it is noticeable that the Knightons, the only African American family included in the Turnbull and Turnbull (1985) collection, did not mention race in their account. Here we see the power of crucial identity intersections such as socioeconomic status and education in trumping race in the development of a public voice, and, possibly, a downplaying of the role of race.

The absence of ethnic minority voices in this literature is in no way surprising. The racism of the post–World War II period, marked by Jim Crow laws in the South, is perhaps most shocking in the fact that soldiers returning from risking their lives for the cause of freedom returned home to an inhospitable environment that literally denied them the same rights that their White army peers took for granted. The GI Bill, which through its new mortgage program provided White GIs the opportunity to buy into the new concept of suburbia, excluded Black families, and urban "renewal" projects resulted in the creation of Black and Hispanic ghettos (Rothstein, 2017). In this context, it is clear that a group advocating for a marginalized population, such as persons with disabilities, would have to gain solid ground itself before permitting the inclusion of other marginalized groups. This exclusion was evident, for example, within the deaf culture: Ironically, the institutions and organizations that served the needs of the deaf followed discriminatory laws that excluded people from membership and rights, even when they held the deaf identity. For example, Gallaudet University, formerly Gallaudet College, had a long history of exclusion of Black deaf students. It was not until the passage of *Brown v. Board of Education* in 1954 that the college admitted its first African American male deaf student, Andrew J. Foster, that same year. Similarly, Ida Wynette Gray, the first deaf African American woman to graduate from Gallaudet College in 1957, was also admitted post–*Brown v. Board of Education*. Furthermore, membership in the National Association for the Deaf (NAD), which former president of the National Black Deaf Association Benro Ogunyipe described as the "premier national advocacy organization for the rights of deaf people," excluded women and African Americans from voting and membership, respectively. Their privileges were not assigned until the Voting Act of 1964 and the Civil Rights Act of 1965 were passed (Ogunyipe, 2016).

In addition to exclusion of non-White families through the explicit de jure and de facto racism of the period, the postwar parent advocacy movement in the United States reflected a complicated portrait of competing societal beliefs and goals regarding individuals with disabilities. Despite widespread horror at the revelations of Nazi atrocities, a newly optimistic vision of the American dream, as expressed in the rise of middle-class suburban family life, struggled to counter the entrenched beliefs of a century of eugenic pseudoscience. In the context of increasing national prosperity and government policies supporting affordable housing for White GIs returning from the war, the national ideology quickly absorbed idealized images of White suburban family life that inherently rejected the inclusion of perceived abnormality or "deviance." As professionals in the rising fields of psychology and child development promoted child-rearing philosophies that should create perfect families, the perception was that a good family would be destroyed by the presence of a child who would not "fit in." As a result, residential institutions for placement of such children thrived. As noted by Castles (2004), approximately half of all parents, and a greater proportion in the case of Down syndrome, had been instructed by their doctors to immediately institutionalize their child, and the rate of new admissions of children under age 6 doubled between 1945 and 1955.

THE EMERGENCE OF ADVOCACY ORGANIZATIONS

The wave of change brought about by the advocacy of parents such as those cited previously occurred alongside the birth of local and national parent advocacy organizations at the end of the 1940s. These early efforts gained fuel from the civil rights movement of the 1950s and 1960s. As we will detail in a later chapter, these simultaneous movements came to full fruition in the enactment of the EHA in 1975 and its subsequent reauthorizations in the form of the Individuals with Disabilities Education Act in 1990. As described by Turnbull and colleagues (2015), the decades succeeding the EHA have seen parents go through a series of role changes in their interactions with professionals, as follows: parents as the cause of the child's disability; families as recipients of professionals' decisions; families as organization members; and families as service developers, as teachers, as political advocates, as educational decisionmakers, and as partners with professionals.

Parents Reaching Out

Simultaneous with the increase in institutions, mothers of children with mental retardation who resisted or could not afford institutionalization were beginning to reach out publicly for support. As described by Castles (2004), the earliest of these efforts was a 1946 advertisement in a New Jersey newspaper in which a mother pleaded for others to "band together and do something for our children!" (p. 351). This was followed by a similar plea in a New York newspaper in 1949. The time was right for these efforts because another feature of the period was the rise of civic and community service organizations such as Kiwanis, Rotary Clubs, and, in schools, Parent Teacher Associations. Thus, the appeals by parents of children with disabilities brought hope to many who found themselves excluded from mainstream parent organizations because of the perceived shame of their children's conditions. The very act of joining a parent group took tremendous courage on the part of mothers, who had to struggle against pressure from their families and peers and against their own internalized doubts that they were doing something wrong (Castles, 2004).

Castles offers a disturbing account of the power of the hegemony of "normalcy" and the stigma by which mental retardation was seen as a marker of "genetically based social deviance" that might reveal the "bad stock" of the entire family or, as quoted earlier by Richards (2004), the "sins" of the parents. She quotes the words of one mother:

> I silently shuddered as I thought that we were joining the ranks of freaks in the eyes of our community. What we found was, for me, an amazing sight. There was a group of nice, average, Americans talking in that animated manner which characterizes any meeting of a P.T.A., service club, or church gathering. (Castles, 2004, p. 354)

Of course, it goes without saying that the "nice, average Americans" in that group would not have included non-White families.

The Arc. These early efforts constituted the beginnings of organizations such as the Association for the Help of Retarded Children (AHRC) and the New Jersey Parents Group for Retarded Children (Jones, 2004).

In 1950 these and similar groups from 14 states joined together to establish the National Association of Parents and Friends of Mentally Retarded Children, which, in 1952, became the National Association for Retarded Children (NARC), now known as The Arc of the United States. According to the organization's website (thearc.org), by 1974 NARC had grown to include well over 225,000 members affiliated with more than 1,750 state and local member units.

The goals of these organizations were both to improve public awareness of children with mental retardation and to provide or promote much-needed services. In keeping with the beliefs of the time regarding the likely negative impact of such a child on the family unit, advocacy organizations were not necessarily against institutionalization. As noted by Jones (2004), for example, parent groups in New Jersey advocated for increased public and private support for the state institutions. The difference between the practices of these groups and those recommended by medical personnel such as Dr. Aldrich (1947), cited previously, was that they advocated for continuing family relationships with the institutionalized child through regular visits and outings, rather than placing the children and "forgetting" them.

While it is beyond the range of this book to delve deeply into the work of national advocacy organizations, we offer just a brief view of the origins and apparent focus on diversity in a few leading organizations. While the current website of The Arc reveals an explicit press for diverse leadership and membership, the change over time is revealed by Robert Segal's 1970 study of four Associations for Retarded Children, including the NARC. The author explains that the original membership of these organizations represented a predominance of middle- to upper-middle-class families and an "almost exclusively White" membership. Segal reports:

> The membership of the four associations was almost exclusively White, despite the fact that in two of the cities, Boston and Providence, there was a rather large Negro population; and in the other two cities, Hartford and San Diego, there was a fair proportion of Negroes. (p. 49)

Segal was advised by participants in the study that this situation was the result of several related factors, including "a subtle form of racial discrimination," "little, if any concerted effort . . . to recruit Negroes," and a "membership fee" that served as a deterrent. In one case, the informant simply stated that the "board had been anti-Negro," so that when attempts were made by Black families to attend events "the Negroes were made to feel that they would not be welcome" (p. 50). Segal concluded that the success of the NARC was largely due to the socioeconomic characteristics and available social contacts of the membership.

By contrast, the website currently details a dramatically different vision of the organization. Some 5 decades since the survey cited above, its goal is now listed as "to be the leader in diversity in the disability community" (thearc.org). Strategies toward this goal include increasing outreach and accessibility of programs to minority populations, as well as reducing male and White representation on the board of directors and in management and staff. Interestingly, the 2017 report noted greater success on this goal for the former group than for the latter, with a decrease of male representation on the board from 52% to 46% and an increase of minority representation from 13% to 29%; for national staff representation and senior management, male representation did decrease, but so did minority representation.

United Cerebral Palsy. The pattern of leadership outlined in the 1974 ARC survey was typical of most advocacy organizations initiated during the postwar period. United Cerebral Palsy (UCP), for example, was initiated in 1948 by an advertisement in the *New York Herald Tribune* by the president of United Paramount Theaters and ABC television, Leonard Goldenson, and his wife, together with a New York businessman by the name of Jack Hausman. Both families had children with cerebral palsy and used their own resources and influence while also recruiting other parents who shared similar experiences. Currently, and in contrast to The Arc, UCP's website (ucp.org) does not mention racial or socioeconomic diversity, and while the CEO appears to be Hispanic, the surnames of the board of trustees' members appear to be predominantly English, with one African American member. The website does state that the organization serves a diverse range of disabilities, including individuals with Down syndrome, autism spectrum disorder, physical disabilities, and traumatic brain injury.

The National Center for Learning Disabilities. The National Center for Learning Disabilities (NCLD) was founded in 1977 as the Foundation for Children with Learning Disabilities and, in 1989, changed its name to NCLD. This organization was founded at a time when the concept of learning disability (LD) had enjoyed increased attention as a bona fide disability with an etiology in "minimal brain damage/brain dysfunction" (Kirk & Becker, 1963). Concerns about the racial and cultural issues involved in the creation of this category were raised initially by Sleeter (1986), who observed that the category was supported by White, middle-class parents whose children stood to benefit from a category that would be less stigmatizing than mental retardation and would likely be populated by fewer minority students. The latter point was further analyzed by Collins and Camblin (1983), who noted that two features in the official definition of LD ensured the exclusion of Black students: the clause that excluded social disadvantage as a source of the disability and the requirement for a 15-point discrepancy between IQ score and measurements of academic achievement. The underrepresentation of minorities in this category, or, one might say, the overrepresentation of White students, was in fact the case during 2 or more decades after the establishment of the LD category, and it was not until the turn of the 21st century that Black and Hispanic overrepresentation was noted. Although the racial profile of this category has changed significantly over the years, it is notable that the website for the NCLD (ncld.org) does not mention targeting diversity, and the board of directors appears to have one African American and no Spanish surnames among 19 members.

The National Autism Association. The National Autism Association, founded in 2002 by a parent, shows a similar profile to that of the NCLD. Currently, the website information on the organization's senior membership indicates an apparently totally White leadership in its board and honorary members (nationalautismassociation.org).

Culturally and Ethnically Oriented Organizations

The latter decades of the 20th century began to evidence the rise of parent advocacy organizations representing specific racial or cultural/linguistic groups with disabilities, both nationally and in specific localities. It is easy to understand why parents with social and economic power would be the initiators of advocacy organizations, given their resources of time, finances, and social networks. As explained by numerous scholars of critical race theory (Delgado & Stefancic, 2017), these advantages intersect with and are furthered by racial privilege that is endemic in the social structure of the United States. Breaking the structural barriers of this system can be so difficult that parents of minority groups would inevitably turn to creating their own organizations.

Two such organizations are the National African American Autism Community Network (NAAACN), and the National Association for the Education of African American Children with Learning Disabilities (NAEAACLD, guidestar.org/profile/31-1621724). The website for the NAAACN describes it as "a nationwide coalition of organizations who support and educate African American communities affected by autism" (National African American Autism Community Network [NAAACN], n.d.). Citing a 2018 statement by the Centers for Disease Control and Prevention, the website explicitly calls attention to "the disparities between diagnoses, access to early intervention and special education services in underserved communities. " Its goal is to serve as:

> a link between the African American community and mainstream developmental disability, behavioral health and governmental institutions, all of which often fail to address issues specific to African Americans impacted by autism. We want to help build and strengthen African American parents and caregivers so they can effectively support and advocate not only for their children, but for their community. Autism Speaks provides technical assistance, capacity

development, and other resources to NAAACN. Together, our organizations firmly believe that the most effective advocacy for any community, especially one that is underserved and historically marginalized, must come from individuals within that community who have walked the same path. (NAAACN, n.d.)

Parent Technical Assistance Centers

The success of the parent movement can best be seen in the impact it has had on federal policy. Under the 2004 reauthorization of the Individuals with Disabilities Education Act (IDEA), the Office of Special Education Programs at the U.S. Department of Education provides grants, through a competitive process, to centers whose purpose is to provide technical support to parents of children with disabilities. There are nearly one hundred Parent Training and Information Centers (PTIs) and Community Parent Resource Centers (CPRCs) in the United States and its territories (ed.gov/about/offices/list/osers/osep/index.html).

The broad reach of the centers is exemplified in the website of the Center for Parent Information and Resources (CPIR), which provides resources for national and regional centers around the country, and reports 900,500 contacts with parents, students with disabilities, and professionals (parentcenterhub.org/2017-data-collection-results).

This website describes its work as serving

parent training and information centers, operated by local parent organizations, that help ensure underserved parents of children with disabilities, including low-income parents, parents of children who are English learners, and parents with disabilities.

A particularly well-known center is Minnesota's Parent Advocacy Coalition for Educational Rights (PACER) center, which was initiated in 1977 with a project called Parents Helping Parents. According to its website, the center continues to be staffed primarily by parents of children with disabilities throughout the state. A look at the array of programs reveals a strong focus on trainings for professionals and parents in cross-cultural communication and service provision (pacer.org/about).

Sinergia, based in New York, NY, and founded in 1977, is explicit in mentioning the mission for "providing multicultural, lifespan services for people with disabilities" with a focus on language, housing, cultural, and economic barriers. Dedicated to the support of families who may be experiencing discrimination or other vulnerabilities, the name *Sinergia*, which in Spanish means "synergy," makes reference to "two forces combined" and "refers to what families and individuals can achieve when they work with advocates who support their goals and respect their cultures" (sinergiany.org/about/about).

EXPOSING THE INSTITUTIONS

The powerful grassroots movements initiated by parents in the 1950s found their momentum in the 1960s with the support of prominent figures in politics and industry and, most effectively, President Kennedy. The president took what was then a novel approach toward disability advocacy by creating a collaborative panel of experts with diverse backgrounds and perspectives similar to the interdisciplinary and collaborative methods we use today across multiple sectors (Wolf-Branigin, 2007). The influence of the Kennedy family, with its own history of supporting a family member with an intellectual disability, also had an impact on the actions and initiatives of volunteer organizations. In addition, physical development became a priority for funding and program development, providing the impetus for the founding of the Special Olympics, whose first international games were held in the summer of 1968 in Chicago (United States President's Committee on Mental Retardation, 1977, pp. 78–79).

According to the President's Committee on Mental Retardation (1977), although knowledge about persons with disabilities was increasing along with the demand for better treatment and standards of care, the population of institutions still continued to rise and, in 1969, reached its peak at 190,000 residents. In response to the question of why this practice continued to grow in spite of the tremendous strides in understanding intellectual disability, the President's Committee described this paradox as a "cultural ideological lag and the persistence of an established and vested institutional mechanism" (p. 15). Wang and Singer (2016) point out that although the peak number of residents in institutions represented only 5% of people with mental retardation in the United States, the institutions, with their stigmatizing power, were the main source of the public's understanding of this disability. It would take something significant to provide both the pressure and force to level these structures, which were not only physical but ideological in nature.

Dismantling the "Snake-Pit" of Institutionalization

The challenge to the institutions was raised in 1965 by Senator Robert Kennedy, who charged that the conditions in New York's Willowbrook State School amounted to a "snake-pit" (Disability Justice, 2017). Willowbrook warehoused some 6,200 people instead of the 4,000 for which it was built. Despite Senator Kennedy's public plea, the institution was subjected to severe budget cuts in 1969, leaving residents to be cared for on a ratio of 1 caregiver to 50 residents. Kennedy's charges, however, opened the doors to a flood of initiatives by parents, journalists, academics, and litigators.

On the academic front were leading scholars such as Wolf Wolfensberger and Burton Blatt of Syracuse University. Blatt's (1966) pictorial exposé,

Christmas in Purgatory, uncovered the deplorable conditions found in five institutions in different states. In a paper written for President Kennedy's Committee on Mental Retardation, Blatt (1969) described the "degradation and despair" that he encountered in these institutions, where children were chained, restrained, and crying out for help (p. 39). In reflecting on the motivations of those in charge of the institutions, Blatt proposed that the neglect, abuse, and isolation of the residents did not mean that the attendants were cruel or necessarily evil, but that they "have come to believe, for various reasons, that those in their charge are not really human" (p. 46). Reinforcing Blatt's work, Wolfensberger's promotion of the principle of normalization fueled the scholarly arguments toward the dismantling of institutions nationwide. As outlined by Carey (2009), Wolfensberger argued that the removal of the child from his or her home was unjust and that the delivery of services could be integrated into the community, separate from places of residence, so the services should be customized to meet the specific needs of persons with developmental disabilities.

Within a few years, the challenge to the institutions moved to the courts, where the landmark case *Wyatt v. Stickney* (1971) decried the inhumane conditions at hospitals and institutions in Alabama. Addressing the conditions in the Bryce and Searcy hospitals for persons with mental illness and the Partlow State School for those with developmental disabilities, the court's ruling established that all persons who had been involuntarily committed to state institutions had a constitutional right to treatment that could prepare them for return to living in the community (Disability Justice, 2019a).

During the same period, most forcibly in the public eye were journalists' televised exposés, such as Bill Baldini regarding Pennsylvania's Pennhurst Institution and Geraldo Rivera regarding New York's Willowbrook State School (Disability Justice, 2019b), which presented unforgettable images of neglect and abuse of the residents at these facilities. Rivera's access to Willowbrook was facilitated by a doctor who had recently been fired from the facility and by 21-year-old Willowbrook resident Bernard Carabello, a man with cerebral palsy who had lived in the institution since the age of 3. Interviews with Bernard reveal a man of obvious intelligence who explained that his mother, who spoke no English at the time of his birth, found herself with no support to care for her son and, on the advice of a doctor, had placed him at Willowbrook. Rivera's exposé provided the impetus for a class-action suit against the State of New York that was settled in 1975 with a consent decree which, despite several counter challenges from the state, succeeded in setting the precedents for national reforms focusing on the provision of supports for community-based living.

Murray Schneps (2014), an attorney whose daughter, Lara, had been placed at Willowbrook in 1969, published a memoir some 4 decades after the Willowbrook case. Schneps (2014) explained the overwhelming sense of hopelessness he and his wife felt on realizing that Lara would need constant care and that there were no day programs available to help her and no options for who would care for her after their death. When Willowbrook claimed to be offering residence with therapy programs for the youngest children, and advised parents that the waiting lists were so long that the longer they waited to admit the child the less likelihood there would be for her admission, these parents felt they had no choice. However, Schneps soon found that there was no therapy provided and that a "palpable atmosphere of intimidation" by the institution's administration worked to silence parents, who, in Schneps's words, "were afraid to anger their children's caretakers. They were afraid to make matters worse" (p. 41).

After realizing the dire circumstances that existed at Willowbrook, the Schneps family took their daughter back home to live with them, and Murray Schneps became one of the leading advocates for the closing of Willowbrook and the establishment of small group homes. In 1972, Schneps presented the following statement as part of the Willowbrook class action suit initiated by the New York Civil Liberties Union:

> Shortly after she became 14 months of age, on July 31, 1969, my wife and I painfully, sorrowfully, guiltily and under absolute compulsion, "voluntarily" delivered our daughter Lara to Building 14 at the Willowbrook State School. The feelings of helplessness, hopelessness, bitterness, emptiness, timidity, fear, pain, guilt and compulsion of this absolutely involuntary act, shall never be forgotten by me for as long as I live. (p. 102)

Although parent advocacy was an essential part of this battle, Schneps noted how difficult this was for parents: "Most of the parents were fearful and were easily cowed by the State or any authority. They were beaten down by the continued suffering of their handicapped children and did not have the tools, the power, or the internal toughness to do more than comply" (p. 134).

Parallel Discrimination:
Institutions for Blacks with Disabilities or Mental Illness

The segregated nature of U.S. society throughout this period was, of course, reflected in the nation's institutions. While it seems likely that many Black or other minority group families may not have been able to afford placement in the institutions, or may have chosen to keep their children at home, institutions or "asylums" for "Negro" citizens with disabilities or mental illness also proliferated (Hughes, 1992). Moreover, institutions that had originally accepted both Black and White residents, but had housed them separately, became increasingly segregated as the numbers of Black applicants grew. For example, the Partlow State School in Alabama, which became the target of the *Wyatt v. Stickney* litigation in 1971, was built in 1919 as the Alabama Home for Mental Defectives. It was renamed Partlow in 1923 and in 1946 added a separate building for "Black feeble minded" children (asylumprojects .org/index.php/Partlow_State_School). The *Wyatt v. Stickney* case (1971) came about at the time that the State of Alabama, under Governor George Wallace, was vigorously resisting school desegregation orders resulting from *Brown v. Board of Education* (1954). Consequently, the desegregation issue was also central to the motivation for litigation against these institutions, as both Bryce and Partlow were "predominantly White, with black patients and residents assigned to separate quarters to the rear" (Yackle, 1989, p. 23), while Searcy was all Black.

The continuing construction of Black people as "other" and "less than human" was evident in the way psychiatrists at the turn of the 20th century interpreted mental illness in this population. Hughes (1992), in a review of attitudes toward mental illness in Alabama between 1861 and 1910, noted that an increase in Black patients was interpreted by White psychiatrists as a sign of overexcitement in response to the gaining of freedom, and it is clear that institutionalization became a vehicle for further segregation. For example, Stuckey (2017) placed the building of the Crownsville Hospital for the Negro Insane in Maryland in the context of a strong resistance to what Whites perceived as a "Black invasion" of the city of Baltimore. Moreover, Stuckey's review of the institution's records revealed that patients' diagnoses included alcoholism, dementia, epilepsy, manic depression, and imbecility.

While the conditions in institutions serving White residents were abominable, it is not surprising that levels of inequity were surpassed in institutions for Black residents, including higher death rates, lower rates of "recovery" as compared to permanent patients, lower expenditures on personnel and supplies (Stuckey, 2017), and malnutrition (Hughes, 1992). Placing this institution in the context of racism and eugenics, Stuckey (2017) stated: "That eugenic ideologies functioned as infrastructure for Jim Crow is no accident; the rhetoric of 'racial hygiene' added medicalized reinforcement for the removal of people with more melanin from society" (p. 2). Stuckey continued:

> Unlike Provident Hospital [for Whites], Crownsville was not founded as a result of advocacy within Black communities; rather, it can be argued that Crownsville operated as the receiving station for a forced exodus and a "ghetto-clearing." The opening of Crownsville Hospital was fueled by Baltimore's preeminent brand of Jim Crow segregation as well as by progressive and often misguided reform aimed to assist the "insane." (p. 4)

Supported by unfounded theories of racial difference, psychiatrists believed that the more animal-like nature of Blacks predisposed them more to mania than to depression, which was more commonly diagnosed among Whites (Hughes, 1992; Summers, 2010). Other stereotypes of dysfunctional

Black characteristics included "laziness," which was identified as a medical diagnosis under the category "dysaethesia aethiopica" (Stuckey, 2017); "drapetomania," a mental condition that caused slaves to want to escape; and, on the contrary, a condition indicating that Blacks in the immediate postemancipation period had been "made mad by freedom" because they were constitutionally "unfit for the competition and pace of life made necessary by emancipation" (Hughes, 1992, p. 456).

With regard to family advocacy and support, while all institutions encouraged minimal contact with families, Hughes's study of Southern asylums indicated that there was much less contact with family members, which he suggested might have reflected the intense poverty experienced in Black families and the lack of resources to support dependent family members.

Toward Empowerment

Throughout the 1980s and 1990s, deinstitutionalization would continue. In response to the reauthorization and amendment in 1994 of Title VII of the Rehabilitation Act of 1973, centers for independent living emerged across the country, offering services for people with disabilities and their families in a nonresidential setting. Wolfensberger (1983) continued to be a prominent scholar in the normalization process and renamed the principle *social role valorization*, emphasizing that the goal was to create and acknowledge valued social roles for individuals with intellectual impairments. This reenvisioning of the normalization principle was important in its call not just to "normalize" but to value individuals with intellectual disabilities by placing them in roles that are valued by the society.

From our critical perspective, however, we see the concept of social role valorization as once more playing into the narrative of the norm, by insisting that individuals will be more valued if they are contributing to the productivity of society. As Kalyanpur and Harry (2012) argued, this argument is based on the assumption that the value of a human life lies in its potential for economic productivity—a reflection of the contract theory of human value. Nevertheless, the principle of normalization formed the basis for the currently much-touted concept of *inclusion*, which today represents a much sought-after, though by no means universal, goal of education (Harry, 2020; Richardson & Powell, 2011).

In concluding this review of the period, we celebrate the relentless work of parent advocates and reformers who in the second half of the 20th century transformed the lives of individuals with disabilities and their families.

CHAPTER 5

The Social Construction
of Humanness

In reviewing the history of the treatment of Americans with intellectual and other significant disabilities, we have found the most hurtful, yet the most explanatory, statement in this history to be Burton Blatt's interpretation that the caregivers at the worst of the nation's institutions "did not believe their charges were human" (1969, p. 46). Yet the thought of sorting human bodies in terms of their essential humanity was not confined to those with disabilities. Indeed, this perception echoed the entrenched racism inculcated by slavery—a perception that was proclaimed from the hilltops of Europe to the trenches of America's Jim Crow practices. German philosopher Immanuel Kant, for example, stated:

> The Negroes of Africa have by nature no feeling that rises above the trifling. . . . So fundamental is the difference between these two races of man, and it appears to be as great in regard to mental capacities as in color. (as cited in Ronald, 1993, p. 109)

So, who is Human? In this chapter we turn to our interviews with parents to illustrate many of our points about the devaluing of people with disabilities. First, however, we begin with an excerpt from coauthor Lydia's journal, which indicates that the history described in the foregoing chapters is not so far away.

From Lydia's Journal: Promises Not Delivered

It is tempting to archive the errors of the past, when less was known about human difference, when sense-making relied on theories that were based on deficits and generated differences. With technology and advancements in medicine, education, psychology, sociology, and almost every field, it would be almost unheard of to think that professionals have not also improved in the ways in which they deliver the diagnosis of a child with a disability to parents and discuss his or her prognosis with them. Today's world is filled with the promises of informed decisionmaking, collaboration, value systems, and cultural competence. Yet my own experience illustrates the failure of these promises in their real-life, clinical application.

In 2010, when I received the news of increased risk for "fetal abnormality" during prenatal testing, I asked for the numbers. The probability of having a child with some disability had increased because of my age (34) and because of some detected alpha-feto protein levels. Ultrasound confirmed that the most likely disability was trisomy 21. At about 20 weeks' gestation, I learned that my risk for having a child with Down syndrome was 1:14. At this point, the only way to definitively confirm would be to have an amniocentesis or chorionic villi sampling (CVS). Because I was a high risk for preterm delivery, I knew these tests would put me at further risk. But my greater reasoning for refusal of these tests was because I simply did not need to know.

When the genetic counselors informed my obstetrician that I did not want to proceed with further testing, the climate changed during the prenatal visits. Instead of the warmth of "how are you feeling?" he was short with me, hostile, and proceeded to lecture me every time about the risks to my own health of having a child with a disability. He insisted that he wanted me to make an informed decision, and even though I reassured him that I had, he would always describe me in his physician's notes as, "34 y.o. African American woman refuses amnio . . . " before writing down his clinical notes for the visit.

The most shocking event occurred during my postnatal 6-week checkup. I went alone, which was one thing I regret because it left me vulnerable at a very critical point in my life. In response to my disagreement with his reproductive recommendations, the obstetrician said very plainly, "NEVER get pregnant again. I'm serious, don't come back here pregnant. Don't you see what happened last time [pointing to the carrier where Isaiah was sleeping]? Don't you see how selfish you are for making this choice? Don't you see what a burden you have put on society, on the medical system? Don't you see how selfish you are to your family, to your other kids? This child may never walk; he may never talk. He may need multiple surgeries that someone has to pay for. He may never work; he may never learn. He will be dependent upon you forever. Forget your marriage, it is over! These things never work out after this. And forget you, you can forget yourself, whatever dreams you had, being attractive again. You are giving your life over to him. That was your choice."

It hurt me to my soul that this could be said in 2010. I wondered if he would have had the same conversation with another woman in my same situation whose skin was not my shade of brown. Although I did not know much about professionals' attitudes toward disability, I knew he had violated a trusted relationship; he had abused his position of authority to cast me into a submissive role and remove my power. He bared his teeth because of my defense of my child from the womb, and because of that I did not regret my decision to keep my child, raise him, and love him. There I was, an educated Black and Hispanic woman with a newborn with a disability, and there was nothing he could do about it but to try and disempower me.

Implicit in Lydia's journal entry is the legacy of the eugenics movement of the 19th and 20th centuries, with its entrenched negativity toward and fear of people with disabilities and people of color—indeed, any persons perceived as "different" from mainstream norms.

DEFINING THE VALUE OF A LIFE

In the latter part of the 20th century, with increasing availability of medical interventions, decisions about whose life is worthwhile became a centerpiece of medical ethics. As practitioners struggled with this notion, the idea that essential features of "humanity" could be defined was perhaps best demonstrated in the criteria proposed by Fletcher (1972), a medical doctor who included the following in his list of characteristics of personhood: minimal intelligence" as measured by the Stanford-Binet test, with a score of IQ 40 indicating an individual who is "questionably a person" and a score below IQ 20 indicating "not a person"; evidence of characteristics such as "self-control," "self-awareness," "a sense of futurity," "the capability to relate to others," "curiosity," and, as a precursor to all of these, "neo-cortical function" (p. 1). With regard to neo-cortical function, Fletcher stated, "In the absence of the synthesizing function of the cerebral cortex, the person is non-existent. Such individuals are objects but not subjects" (p. 3). Fletcher subsequently reduced these 15 indicators to 4: neocortical function (the sine qua non), self-consciousness, relational ability, and happiness (Fletcher, 1974).

Fletcher's perspective was essentially the same as that of the 16th-century Protestant reformer Martin Luther, whom we cited earlier as recommending the drowning of a boy with a disability because of his being solely "a mass of flesh . . . without a soul" and inhabited by the devil. Fletcher's view in 1974 differed from Luther's only in that he had replaced the religious overlay with a coat of scientific whitewash.

Numerous scholars in medicine and in education countered Fletcher's approach. For example, Frohock (1986), a pediatrician, illustrating his arguments with detailed, poignant accounts of infants in a neonatal care unit, demonstrated the tremendous complexities and dilemmas facing those who cared for the infants, as well as those who advocated for them. Relating the thinking of his time to centuries of Western thought, Frohock identified "the life of the mind"—rational thought and capacity for reflection—as that which "marks us off from other animals" (p. 97). However, he argued, where does one draw the line as to how much and what quality of thought would be required, and what would we say of infants, who have not yet developed, and may not even develop, rational thought? Frohock's case examples highlighted the dilemmas of decisionmaking regarding medical treatments, pointing to some cases in which recommendations that a child would not benefit from treatment were contradicted by the child's subsequent development, as opposed to other cases in which decisions about treatment were overly aggressive, resulting in impossible expectations for the child's development. In summarizing the approach taken at the time in the neonatal clinic, Frohock pointed to the power of advocacy on behalf of the at-risk infant or child: "The current procedure in the nursery has one built-in safeguard that inclines decisions toward, rather than away from, aggressive therapy. If *any* interested party—parent or physician—want the child treated, the child is treated" (p. 121).

A succinct review by Clinkenbeard (1989) of the ethical debate of the time noted that although there were variations in the foci of different scholars, consciousness and capacity to reason were common to all proposals. Clinkenbeard concluded that while the debate was interesting and possibly helpful for both moral discourse and clinical decisions, "In a social context marked by the labelling and rejection of the mentally handicapped, the use of such criteria is morally dangerous" (p. 91).

The debate around humanness and disability took a sociological turn when Robert Bogdan and Doug Biklen (1977) introduced the term *handicapism* (later known as *ableism)* to represent the "set of assumptions and practices that promote the differential and unequal treatment of people because of apparent or assumed physical, mental, or behavioral differences" (p. 14). Bogdan and Taylor (1989), working toward what they called "a sociology of acceptance," investigated the processes by which caregivers interpreted the identities of those in their care. They proposed that "the definition of a person may be found in the relationship between the definer and the defined, not determined . . . by personal characteristics of the abstract meanings attached to the group of which the person is a part" (p. 136). Based on a study of the views of more than 100 persons who provided care to severely disabled people, these scholars identified four processes that caregivers relied on to construct their understanding of the identities of the disabled individuals: (a) attributing thinking to the other; (b) seeing individuality in the other, for example, as seen in specific aspects of personality, likes and dislikes, feelings and motives; (c) viewing the other as reciprocating; and (d) defining a social place for the other, such that the person's membership in the group is evident in his/her inclusion in the life of the group. Case studies of individuals with cognitive disabilities have lent empirical support to the positive attributions of such caregivers. Particularly revealing was a study by Goode (1983) of the poorly understood cognitive and communicative abilities of "Bobby," a young man with Down syndrome.

These views were further developed by the growing influence of feminist scholars such as Martha Nussbaum (2002) and Eva Kittay (2019). While the range of these philosophical arguments is too extensive for our consideration here, we note that they tend to fall into camps of contractual or utilitarian approaches, in which justice is seen, on the one hand, as a social contract among individuals who can participate reciprocally for a mutual benefit, and, on the other hand, as a "capabilities" approach, which identifies key human characteristics that allow an individual to live a "truly human life" (Nussbaum, 2002). While Nussbaum began her theory with a list of 10 capabilities (including affiliation, senses, and practical reason), her later work (Nussbaum, 2009) directly addressed applications of this approach to individuals with disabilities. Here, building on the work of Eva Kittay (2019), Nussbaum adjusted her theory to include Kittay's theory of "care," connecting them by arguing that "good care supports the capacity of the cared-for" (p. 159) to develop or enjoy the capabilities specified by Nussbaum's theory.

We found the essence of the debate over the valuing of persons with disabilities to be alive and well in our interviews with parents. For example, in the following vignette, Patty's angst exemplifies Kittay's description of a parent's "worst ache" (Kittay, 2019, p. 31)

Patty: "Nobody does it like you."

Patty self-describes as a Black Hispanic adoptive grandmother. She has been working for several years as a NICU nurse. Patty's adult daughter has two children, one of whom, Richard, Patty has adopted. Patty is caring for both children. Richard is a bright 7-year-old boy enrolled in a self-contained classroom at a public school nearby. He has been diagnosed with Williams syndrome and assigned the label of Intellectual Disability (ID).

> But I, uh, you do get concerned because you know—and I figure [sigh] you don't really know. You really don't know how it's gonna end. You know or—if you're not there is your next—nobody does it like you, you know? But um . . . you know—I pray a lot over him. I think that like . . . like a mother's prayer? It's the best thing you—anybody could do for a child. And so, I just hope God is gracious and whoever comes around him, he finds good people that'll love him. And . . . just to find all of the programs that are available. And have a plan B.

THE MEANING OF DISABILITY

Social rather than medical interpretations of disability became dominant through the 1990s, and by the end of the decade, the field of disability studies, initiated by the work of self-advocate Michael Oliver (Oliver, 1990; Oliver & Barnes, 1998), had stimulated a robust discourse on the construction of disability. Centering on the importance of seeing the abilities rather than the disabilities of individuals, these scholars raised the question of whether a disability should be seen primarily as a condition intrinsic to the individual or as the outcome of society's lack of response to the needs of individuals with varying physical, sensory, or cognitive capabilities. Proposing the social view, Oliver and Barnes argued that disability should be interpreted not as a tragedy but as a result of oppression. As explained by disability studies scholar Nirmala Erevelles (2011), "disability is the embodied experience of social oppression constituted via the inhospitable social, cultural, and economic structures in mainstream society" (p. 181).

The conversation was initially interpreted as a dichotomous approach to espousing a "medical model" as opposed to a "social model" of disability (Oliver & Barnes, 1998). However, since its beginnings, and with much controversial discussion, the field of disability studies has shifted its view to be more inclusive of both the medical and the social explanations. The World Health Organization (WHO), in its *World Report on Disability* (2011), presented the view that treating these interpretations as dichotomous was fallacious. Rather, the WHO described disability as a "dynamic interaction between health conditions and contextual factors" (p. 4). Citing the International Classification of Functioning, Disability, and Health (ICF), the WHO report proposed a "bio-psycho-social model" as a "workable compromise between medical and social models" (p. 4).

As argued by Erevelles (2011) and Oliver (2013), however, the central issue is not so much a matter of which definition is to be honored. Rather, we must be concerned about the "material" consequences of our beliefs. To make this point, Erevelles pointed specifically to the role of capitalist social and economic structures that, through the process of labeling required for eligibility of services and financial support, simultaneously assign persons with disabilities to the "regulatory and controlling benevolence of the welfare state" (2011, p. 182). The latter was in fact Oliver's (2013) original concern, which he reiterated in a reflective article 30 years later. Here he argued that, despite the considerable attention garnered by the disability studies movement, people with disabilities were particularly vulnerable to dips in the global economy, as in 2008, when, as financial resources diminished, the bureaucracy surrounding the concept of disability intensified. In his words:

> Just as we had predicted, emphasizing impairment and difference was a strategy that was impotent in protecting disabled people, our benefits and services. . . . Hence cuts in our benefits are being justified on the grounds that the intention is to give more to those who are severely impaired. . . . Our differences are being used to slash our services as our needs are now being assessed as being moderate, substantial or critical, and many local authorities are now only providing services to those whose needs are critical. (p. 1026)

The irony inherent in this argument highlights the meaning of what Minow (1990) referred to as "the dilemma of difference": the dilemma of whether creating special structures for people perceived as "different" helps or hinders them. On the one hand, the obvious remedy to exclusion would seem to be explicit recognition and provision of services for that group; on the other hand, the designation of "special" status can increase stigma and result in controlling rather than supportive social measures. Moreover, in Oliver's argument, such categorization can also create divisions among people who experience disability status.

Patty: The Underprivileged Disability

Patty, the grandmother/adoptive mother of 7-year-old Richard, who is diagnosed with Williams syndrome, described her initial frustration in discovering that so many practitioners in both the health care system and in the school were just as unaware about her child's disability as the individuals in the community were. A second wave of frustration, however, came from the impact of her child being assigned the Intellectual Disability (ID) label. Patty spoke about her multiple attempts to volunteer at the school, just to find out what strategies the teachers used in the classroom to support students with ID, so that she could replicate them at home. In addition, as Patty began to navigate the school system and the agencies that support families with disabilities, she encountered several roadblocks. One such roadblock followed the discussion about the results of her child's psychoeducational evaluation. Patty was told that her child's IQ level was fixed and that he may permanently stay at the developmental level of a 4-year-old. Patty was unaware of the perception that intelligence is static, despite interventions and targeted support. Patty, wanting to see if her child had possibly improved in his scores, asked if he could be reevaluated. She was told that the testing would not be repeated unless they wanted to change his services. Because of the nature of her child's ID label and the lack of understanding of what that means, Patty expressed how this label implies that parents should simply accept what they are given rather than challenge what they receive, let alone request supports. She further described how making requests may have a negative impact on empowerment as a parent advocate:

> So whatever you get? You know you can't speak out because it's almost like you're an underprivileged because it's intellectual disability. So I was asking around, I don't know, I think it was in the school, I asked, "Do you have information, a program to teach me? About intellectual disability? So that I can know how to deal with him? Like what does intellectual disability mean?"

THE PAINFUL CONTOURS OF PARENT ADVOCACY

Regardless of the social versus medical focus of the experience of disability, the question of the value of an individual life creates for parents, persons with disabilities, and advocates what Ashley Taylor (2013) referred to as a "deep discomfort" because the very fact of continuing to address this question serves to support rather than rule out the possibility of making decisions about who should be excluded.

What lies at the heart of this issue? Does the debate matter? And if so, why? From the perspective of parents, we believe that it matters deeply, if only because, as members of a community, we are affected by how others see us. We are affected by how we think others see our children. Further, what do beliefs about the value of our children's lives mean for their rights as individuals? What does it mean for our advocacy? How much should we ask for? How little should we accept? What rights ought all children be entitled to?

Carlson and Kittay (2010) highlighted the core of the issue with this question:

> Are those with cognitive disabilities due the same respect and justice due to those who have no significant cognitive impairments? Are the grounds of our moral obligation different when a human being may lack certain cognitive faculties that are often understood as the basis for moral personhood? Are those with significant cognitive impairment moral persons? . . . Are the people with cognitive disabilities, especially those labeled as "mentally retarded," distinct, morally speaking, from nonhuman animals? (pp. 1–2)

Parental Autonomy and Life-or-Death Decisions

At one end of the spectrum of parents' advocacy are the hard decisions that have to be made in cases in which medical interventions may actually prolong suffering, as in the sad story of *The Long Dying of Baby Andrew*, told by the parents of an infant born with brittle bone disease at 24 weeks gestation (Stinson & Stinson, 1979). In that case the parents' advocacy was for relief for their infant—for his right to die, rather than to be kept alive.

At the other end are decisions regarding the right to live, which sometimes means gaining consent for interventions that will save a life. It also means determining whether parents automatically have the right to make life-or-death decisions for their children. In the United States, several such cases have ultimately been determined by the courts. For example, the issue of who could make such a decision was at the center of the case of Phillip Becker, who had been placed by his parents in an institution at a young age (Herr, 1986). Phillip had a heart condition related to Down syndrome, and when his parents refused to give consent for the surgery, a family who had formed a bond with the young man turned to the courts and ultimately gained the right to give the needed consent. The case turned on "the power of absentee parents to deny their child not only life-prolonging medical treatment, but also any chance to live an emotionally satisfying life" (Herr, 1986, p. 1). The author of this report went on to state:

> This litigation involving Phillip Becker has forced society to consider the value of a retarded child's life and the possibilities for such a child's future. It documented Phillip's abilities as a mildly retarded 15-year-old to learn, to grow, and to give and receive affection. It also revealed problems of low parental expectations and conflicts of interests that can arise from the birth of an infant with Down's syndrome. Ironically, Phillip's natural parents would invest great emotional energy and legal expense in waging a bitter custody fight over a child they never invited to their home until litigation had begun. (p. 1)

Another case reflecting caveats to parental autonomy was the case of Baby Jane Doe in 1984 (Fuller, 2013), in which the parents of a child with spina bifida approved only conservative treatment rather than the surgery. The courts found contradictory conclusions regarding the parents' right to refuse surgery and, based on Section 504 of the Rehabilitation Act, the federal government brought suit against the hospital, that the baby was being discriminated against based on her handicap. Numerous legal complications in this case centered on the question of who had the right to make decisions for the child's health and whether a hospital would be guilty of neglect or abuse by refusing appropriate treatment. The government lost the case and the parents' privacy rights prevailed, but the baby died before an emergency petition could be filed (Herr, 1986).

Since that time, the rules regarding withholding of treatment have become more stringent, requiring that

> If a case involves parents or their doctors choosing to withhold treatment, the review boards are obligated to report the case to child services as an instance of medical neglect. Under the rules, withholding treatment is only permissible if the newborn is irreversibly comatose, if treatment would only prolong its death, or if treatment would be inhumane. Furthermore, the law also holds that a physician's decision for neonatal care cannot be based on quality of life, or other abstract concepts. (Resnik, 2011)

Parental Autonomy and Quality of Life Decisions

Perhaps the most challenging situations are those in which the central question is who determines what constitutes a child's quality of life. This issue can be intensely disturbing when it raises the possibility of interventions that actually alter the individual's physical being, such that the parents, wanting their child to live, also want to control the actual nature of the child and his/her body. In the case of Ashley X (Gunther & Diekema, 2006), doctors agreed to parents' request that a 6-year-old girl undergo hormone treatments to restrict her growth, as well as a hysterectomy, removal of her breast buds, and an appendectomy. These treatments were seen as preventive measures to facilitate her physical care as well as to protect her from the discomforts of menstruation and the likelihood of sexual abuse. The case immediately provoked an intense debate regarding the ethics of such intervention (e.g., Brosco & Feudtner, 2006; Kittay, 2011; Turnbull, Wehmeyer, Turnbull, & Stowe, 2006). While even the most intense critics agreed with the parents that Ashley's small size and childlike body would make her care much easier for caregivers, many questioned whether this was mainly in her interest or in the interest of her parents/caregivers. Essentially, critics cited numerous objections centering on ethical principles.

An article by a team of parent advocates/scholars (Turnbull, Wehmeyer, Turnbull, & Stowe, 2006) proposed counterarguments based on principles of an individual's bodily integrity and on the principle of justice:

> Growth attenuation results in a fundamental alteration of a person's very self. When imposed by parents and physicians on those who are unable to consent because they are minors or lack mental capacity to do so, grave constitutional issues arise. . . .
>   Given that they [the parents] will benefit from the intervention and have sought it for that reason (and for their child's sake). . . . The conflicts of interest and power imbalance require an independent advocate for the child and the child only. (p. 349)

The Institute of Clinical Bioethics (2013) concluded that the "Ashley treatment" violated three principles of ethics—respect for persons, beneficence, and justice—and set in motion a potentially slippery slope that recalled the nation's history of sterilization based on the eugenics movement. In fact, the Washington Protection and Advocacy System found that the hospital had violated the child's rights by doing the hysterectomy without a court order.

On the most practical level, disability advocates have pointed to the social failures that allow the entire burden of Ashley's care to fall on her family, and they have called for family support policies with medical intervention only as a last resort (Brosco & Feudtner, 2006; Epstein & Rosenbaum, 2019; Turnbull et al., 2006). Epstein and Rosenbaum cite case studies of parent advocates who argue for the importance of having a community of support that can engage in "supported decision-making," and they propose a "human rights model of disability . . . full rights and dignity of all people to be free from stigma and from being viewed through a medical-only lens" (p. 135). These authors praise the California Lanterman Act, with its mandate for community-based living and support, which they explain "resulted from many years of parental activism and lobbying" (p. 220). They also cite the UN Convention on the Rights of Persons with Disabilities (CRPD)

(United Nations, 2006), which, under its Article 12, argues that people with disabilities enjoy legal capacity—capacity for rights and capacity to act—on an equal basis with others in all aspects of life.

In addition to ethical dilemmas, there is the concern that one cannot know exactly what a person, even with the most profound disability, understands or feels. Eva Kittay (2011), speaking of what her own daughter who has multiple disabilities may or may not know, explicitly includes in her critique the decisions to remove Ashley's sexual organs:

> As the childishness in her face fades, Sesha's body has taken the form of a woman. I don't know if Sesha can rejoice in her breasts, if she notices them at all, if she would miss them, or if she compares herself to other girls. What I do know is only that I don't know. Nothing about Sesha—with all her profound incapacities—tells me that Sesha is incapable of these feelings. I can say that I, as her mother, delight in her womanliness. It is very much a part of Sesha, as she is now. . . . To have the mind of a baby and the capacities of a baby are not the same thing, for the disabled person may well have an understanding and a set of emotional responses that far exceed her capacity to act. (pp. 621–622)

Perceptions of Quality of Life at the Intersection of Race and Disability

Parents who must navigate the intersections of race and disability may have little control over the interpretation that others have about their children. Some of the implicit biases about race are so historically and socially entrenched that it becomes a part of clinical and school decisionmaking. In a highly cited publication, researcher Peggy McIntosh (1989) describes unpacking her privilege as a White woman in the United States. Among the most profound items on her list of privileges is number 11, which states, "I could arrange to protect our children, most of the time, from people who do not like them" (p. 47). One could conceive of parents' ability to protect one's children as a basic right, something that any parent would feel free to advocate for, yet it may also be a privilege to some families. For instance, can the parents of children of color or parents of children with more stigmatizing disability labels make identical arrangements to protect their children, while situated within systems where racism and ableism continue to operate?

Children of color are often subjected to criminalization across various settings, including schools. Nowicki (2018) reported on data from 2013 to 2014 to the Governmental Accountability Office (GAO), indicating disproportionate rates of discipline for boys, Black boys and students with disabilities. According to the report, Black boys and girls were subjected to disciplinary actions at rates 3.5 times and 5 times greater than their White counterparts, respectively. The reported described six forms of discipline, including out-of-school suspensions, in-school suspensions, referrals to law enforcement, expulsions, corporal punishments, and in-school arrests. Particularly disturbing were the trends reported on Black girls, noting that these children "were suspended from school at higher rates than boys of multiple racial groups and every other racial group of girls" (p. 14). Other studies have shed light on the devalued ways in which Black children are perceived. A 2014 study conducted among 137 law enforcement officers reported dehumanizing perceptions of Black boys, perceiving them as 4.53 years older than their actual age, less innocent, and more responsible for their actions at a younger age (Goff et al., 2014). Researchers in this study concluded that Black children are "less likely to be afforded the full essence of childhood and its definitional protections" (p. 539). Comparably, a national survey at the Georgetown Law Center on Poverty and Equality comprised of 325 participants who were predominantly White (74%) and female (62%) reported their perceptions of Black girls as being less innocent and in less need of protections compared to their non-Black female counterparts (Epstein, Blake & Gonzalez, 2017).

The source of this troubling pattern is the deeply rooted fear of Black children, who will one day become Black adults. We draw a comparison here between the denial of adulthood to a child with a disability, as in the Ashley case, and the denial of a childhood identity to a Black child. In the former case, Ashley's parents were the agents of denial, while the combined subversive forces of racism and ableism may often be the source of Black children's loss of their childhood identity. We present here this vignette of Marie, a Haitian mother of a 7-year-old son who carries multiple labels—learning disability, speech and language impairment, and giftedness. Her comments reveal how medical professionals instilled fear in her of her own son, based on their narrow focus on typical norms of childhood growth. Given what is known about embedded fears of Black men, we interpret the doctor's perspective as being influenced by implicit bias.

Marie: "The neighborhood could be cruel to them."

Marie is a Black Haitian single mother of two children, who works as a flight technician. Her eldest son, Stephen, is enrolled in a K–5 center. Although he was initially assigned the label of LD/SLI, he has since been identified as gifted.

Marie explains her concerns about how fast her son is growing. She recalls how at the age of 5 he was already towering over the other children in his kindergarten class. His size and stature have gotten the attention of the pediatricians, who are evaluating him as if he were an older child. These professionals also noted how the public would also perceive him as being older. They presented the possibility of administering a hormone in order to slow down his growth. Although Marie was adamantly against her child taking medications, the doctors' concerns caused her to be worried about what this could mean for her ability to manage him in the future. She described her reaction to what they presented to her:

> And I was thinking, okay, now I'm a petite woman. He's 7. They're already saying they evaluate him as a 10-year-old. He's big. And I say like, when he gets older, would that "mind thing" [become a problem] . . . 'cause right now he loves me, he loves being around me.

Marie was relieved when the doctors decided not to give him the hormone treatments. She described her fear for him in the community, in spite of people's potential fears of him,

> I'm not saying it's a good neighborhood, but the neighborhood could be cruel to them, depending on um, the household. 'Cause when we get them out and we have like a certain way to do things with them and then when they get out there exposing themselves to the things that they've never been exposed to, like I would say crime and bullying, I'm afraid that they're gonna kind of—I'm not saying afraid but like I'm—I'm new to this.

Prenatal Decisions About the Value of a Life

At the most extreme end of the debate around the value of life is the question not simply of how to treat the presence of a disability but whether to *prevent* the birth of a child with a disability. For several decades, courts in the United States have been challenged by "wrongful birth" suits, in which parents have sued medical practitioners either for failure to provide available prenatal testing that could have identified the presence of an illness or disability in the fetus, or failure to advise the parents of the possibility of such an occurrence. These cases rely on the logic that knowledge of the condition in the fetus allows the mother the opportunity to decide whether to continue or to terminate the pregnancy (Andrews & Hibbert, 2000).

Even more challenging are "wrongful life" cases, which are brought on behalf of the child rather than the parents, in which the individual with the disability (or his/her advocate) brings a suit on the basis that the person should not have been allowed to be born. The latter cases continue to be largely disallowed by U.S. courts because of the "problem of having to define the child's very existence as an injury" (Schuster, 2016, p. 2367).

At the heart of this entire debate lies the question posed at the beginning of this section, whether "difference" is to be valued or rejected: Turnbull et al. (2006) argued that the answer lies in the former approach: "Only by confronting the unwelcoming culture and celebrating the difference that culture deems unacceptable has progress been made for people with disabilities and their families. Less able is not less worthy" (p. 11).

Desiring the Norm

The dilemmas around the value of life can be heartbreaking. While it is true that parents' motives are often marked by concern for the safety and welfare of the child, we also believe that they are undergirded by the question of how to value what is not normative. Martha Minow (1990), in her analysis of conceptualizations of "difference," argues that the rejection of perceived differences reflects two factors: First, she explains that the norm is so embedded in our consciousness that we are sometimes not even aware of its dominance. Second, Minow challenges us to ask whether the norm is necessarily better or more desirable.

Philosopher Ashley Taylor (2013) specifies some of the norms that are so deep as to appear intrinsic: "Norms of intelligence, competency, independence, and appearance govern how individuals with intellectual disabilities are recognized, not simply as disabled, but as human or non-human." It may seem hard to believe that our perceptions of "humanity" can be so deeply affected by such norms, until we consider how we assign value to various individuals. For example, research by Glaser and Strauss (1967) showed how nurses caring for dying patients saw them in terms of "high or low social loss" depending on their knowledge of characteristics such as the patient's age, marital or occupational status, social class, or race/ethnicity. The value of the life of a young mother with two children, for example, would be considered as "high social loss," based on the perception of the person as useful and therefore valuable. Moreover, the researchers found that the nurses' treatment of these patients was also affected by the perceptions of their social value.

The power of such ideas has far-reaching effects on how we respond to news of the death of a person perceived as having "low" social value. Citing the work of feminist philosopher Judith Butler, Taylor (2013) says:

> "Livable lives" are lives that are included (recognized within) these norms. Non-livable lives are those that are excluded, foreclosed, rendered invisible. Where lives are unrecognized, individuals become exposed to physical violence precisely because that physical violence is not at present recognized as harm. Their pain, their loss, is un-grievable.

The notion of the "un-grieveable" life resonates deeply with the first author, Beth, in her experience around the death of her daughter Melanie at age 5. A conversation with a well-meaning person, who knew of Melanie only as a child with serious disability, revealed his lack of comprehension that he was talking with a mother whose child had just died:

Beth's Story: The "Ungrieveable" Death of Her Daughter

Some weeks after Melanie's death, I had an encounter with our local pharmacist, a kindly older gentleman who knew my family only as customers and who had never met Melanie or talked with me about her before this time. He said to me, "I'm sorry to hear about the baby. I know she had some disabilities, eh?" I said, "Yes, she had cerebral palsy." He replied, "Yes, so I imagine it must be something of a relief." Too hurt to answer, I left the pharmacy as quickly as I could. Later, upon reflecting on the conversation, I knew that I should have said, "It's true that my life is easier without her. But it's also much emptier."

The Appeal of the Norm

Why is it so hard for people to value nonnormative ways of being? Why do we so fervently wish for those we love to conform? Some of the parents in our study touched on this question, tying it to adaptations they made toward reframing their vision of their children.

We begin with a vignette from Carlos and Betty, during the very delicate prenatal period. Their testimony of these early experiences takes us through their personal process, from the recognition of the "appeal of the norm," to the tensions with medical professionals, to the loving acceptance of their child as he is.

Carlos: "No one wants it for yourself, right?"

Carlos and Betty are Hispanic parents of two young children. Carlos is working part-time as an adjunct instructor at a university while his wife Betty works as an assistant at a law firm. They have one typically developing child who is 7 years of age and a son, Alex, who is 2 years old and has Down syndrome. Alex is attending a birth through age 2 program offered through a university system, which has a program that includes children with and without disabilities. Currently, he is being served under the label of developmental delay (DD).

Carlos described the challenging process of accepting his child's diagnosis. During the prenatal testing period, he went through a series of tests in his mind, first questioning the validity of the tests themselves, then holding out hope that they could possibly be that family who could beat the odds and have a child without Down syndrome. He emphasized not having any embedded biases or perceiving people with stigma, having been around people with disabilities in his community and having a family member with Down syndrome. However, he described how difficult it was to internalize and accept the diagnosis himself. Even though he is on the receiving end of his child's diagnosis, Carlos frames this event as becoming a part of the disability community rather than the disability experience becoming a part of his own life.

> But like—no one wants it for yourself, right? Like that's not something that you want. So. That was—that was—the hard part was just . . . Now, it's not me and them. Now I'm a part of them, so it becomes us. And so it was like making that transition.

Carlos noted how his wife, Betty, had a more personal experience because of the increased number of encounters she had with medical professionals. In these encounters, Betty described often feeling pressured both over the phone and during the in-office visits to continue invasive prenatal testing, in order to confirm the diagnosis for Down syndrome. Because there was a limited amount of time to terminate the pregnancy, as Betty reached the 20-week gestational mark, the pressure intensified. Even beyond this period, the clinicians suggested that the family consider alternative options, such as adoption. Betty and Carlos rejected their persistent assumptions that they would not want to keep or care for their child. Despite numerous objections, Betty had to really put her foot down by telling the clinicians, "He's our son; of course we are having him."

Similar to Carlos and Betty, Linda recalls her own mix of emotions initially, accepting multiple diagnoses. However, she describes the freedom that comes with acceptance:

Linda: "That was not a very good experience for me."

Linda is a Hispanic mother who lives with her husband and three children. She and her husband are both public school teachers at an elementary school and high school, respectively. The youngest two children attend the school where Linda works, while their eldest child, Anthony, or "Tony," attends a private school some distance away. Tony was diagnosed with Down syndrome shortly after birth and received a secondary diagnosis of ASD at age 6. He is now 12.

Linda describes how concerned her providers were about Tony's small size, that he was perhaps not thriving in the womb. No one had suspected Down syndrome, in the time before more advanced prenatal testing. However, Linda expresses how the negative impact of the practitioners' questions outweighed her own shock:

> That was not a very good experience for me. If I have to say something, like support. I felt . . . I mean the doctor knew I didn't do the test to detect that. And you know, he and the doctors, I think could have been more sensitive you know, like in the delivery. And instead I just kept hearing the question

of, "Did you do the screening? Why didn't you do the screening?" At that
point, what was the point of the question, you know? It should be more
about reassuring the mom, reassuring the dad. . . . They made me feel like
ashamed, you know? Like if I did something wrong.

Linda expresses how the practitioners' questions combined with her prior
experiences of children with Down syndrome had a tremendous effect on her
emotional state:

I went into a depression, to be honest. Because I don't think my husband
knew about Down syndrome. And I did. . . . We had to do a semester of
teaching children with special needs. And we had to do hours at a school.
I just saw, you know the difficulty they had with learning . . . with self-care.
I was more aware of the diagnosis and the challenges. . . . I don't think
my husband understood it. . . . My husband's philosophy is "It's how God
wants him to be."

Eva Kittay (2019), a professor of philosophy who has a daughter with
multiple disabilities, offered a keen analysis of what she refers to as "desir-
ing the normal" (p. 25). Kittay explained that although the social revolution
of the 1960s broadened her horizons of acceptable norms, when she was
faced with the birth of her own child who defied all developmental norms,
"the desire for normalcy once again held me in its thrall. The desire for
normalcy was at the heart of the pain and despair that so tore our hearts in
those early days" (p. 26).

Why? Kittay stated the heart of the question when she asked, "How
will this child grow into an adult that others can love and cherish? Will she
be viewed as a valuable and valued member of society, included as a full
citizen, not merely a pitiful charity case?" (p. 27). Kittay noted the inevita-
ble limitations that can face parents of a child with severe multiple disabilities as they strive to accomplish three key goals of parenthood—promoting
safety, growth, and socialization for acceptance. She concluded that these
goals can be so daunting that the parent may ultimately be faced with a
larger challenge that requires "socializing of the community to accept the
child even more than it requires socializing the child" (p. 30). Above all,
and greater than the "selfish" motives of what may become of the parents'
lives, is the "worst ache"—the fear that the child will not experience the
intrinsically valued experiences of "friendship, meaningful dignified work,
membership in a community, love, and family" and may, instead, experience
"frustration and sadness—rejection and exclusion" (p. 31).

Kittay reported the continuing ambivalence that haunted her even as
she reframed her understanding of her child's life—that there can be a difference between "a good life" and "a normal life" as the family establishes
new norms by which their child's successes and joys can be celebrated. Yet,

when faced with dissonance between these family-based norms and those of the public, the parent is once more challenged to hold firm to his or her definitions of the child's value:

> The desire that refuses to go away is then, first, a desire to have one's own worth and that of one's children confirmed. Our sense of self-worth depends in large measure on the willingness of others to recognize our worth and that which we value. We require the affirmation of a community that what we are and what we value are, in fact, valuable. . . . For social creatures such as humans, the desire for acceptance into a community is hard to abandon. (p. 33)

We believe that every parent of a child with a disability will recognize Kittay's description of a feeling reported by Helen Featherstone, when a prospective babysitter fled at the sight of her son. Kittay explained that, at that moment,

> Her [Featherstone's] sense of normalcy fell apart—if only for a moment—when she viewed her child through the stranger's gaze. . . . What falls apart is the vision of your child as the individual he or she is and not just someone with the impairment he or she has. . . . What is imperiled is the connection you have with this singular person, and you must steel yourself not to allow these intrusions to stand between you and the love you have for your child. (p. 46)

Kittay concluded that we need to commit to developing "more capacious" norms, by which we allow for wider parameters of normalcy—norms that allow for both conformity and individualism. In our research with families, some parents, like Carlos and Linda in the following vignettes, addressed the issue of learning to set norms aside in order to know and love the real individual who has become a member of their family.

Carlos: "Accepting who he is and how he is"

Carlos describes how a part of his acceptance was not only understanding what his child can and cannot do but also shifting his overall perspective as a parent. While there may be differences in the expectations of parenting versus the reality of parenting for any family, the fragility of his son's life changed his views dramatically.

The circumstances surrounding their child's birth shook the family perhaps even more than the diagnosis of Down syndrome. Alex was born with the inability to expel blood from his lungs and was then diagnosed with failure to thrive. Carlos and Betty's concerns were about his health as they questioned, "Is he gonna make it?" The fear for Alex's life, Carlos adds, overshadowed any concerns they had about his disability and functioning. They focused their energies instead on his survival.

Carlos says that these circumstances, however scary and traumatic, were integral to their transformation as parents, in valuing Alex's life and his differences. As Alex began to grow, Carlos recognized the change in himself as a father:

> In the meantime, there's—just learning how to take care of him, how to deal with him. Learning how to put aside my expectations of who he should be and what he should be doing. Oh, "he's not doing this, he's not doing that." So, putting all that stuff aside. And just . . . learning. How to accept who he is and how he is, for what he is. Rather than . . . continually placing these expectations upon him that . . . he won't meet.

Linda: "Free to love them"

Although Linda had suspicions about her child's delays that were dismissed by medical professionals, she still describes the utter shock of receiving a second diagnosis of ASD by noting, "that was like a second blow, to be honest."

However, in spite of the challenges, she does note many positives that come from the therapies he is able to receive. In addition, despite the sometimes-difficult road, Linda's words also express an appreciation and acceptance of who her child is:

> I just realize as I've gotten older and I see my kids growing up, that you just have to let them be who they are. And you just have to accept them with and without their limitations. And once we realize that this is who they are and we don't try to make them do more than they are capable of, or more than they want to do, more than they enjoy doing, then we really are just free to love them and we just accept them. Everybody's happier.

Wider Parameters of Normalcy Within Culturally Based Definitions of Disability

The issue of parameters of normalcy has been addressed from several angles, with parent advocates offering widely varying perspectives on the meanings of disability. One aspect, usually relevant to milder disabilities, is differential definitions based on different cultural traditions (Harry, 1992) and families' socioeconomic status or level of acculturation to U.S. practices (Gutierrez & Sameroff, 1990; Harry, Allen, & McLaughlin, 1995; Ninio, 1988).

Harry's (1992) study of Puerto Rican families' disagreement with the school district's assessments of their children revealed that the parents held much wider parameters of normalcy than did school personnel. Family members argued against a notion of "mental retardation" as applied to children who were walking, talking, and demonstrating appropriate social behavior. The latter characteristic was particularly important, being expressed in the Spanish tradition as "bien educado/a," as not meaning well "educated" in an academic sense, but well brought-up, well behaved. One grandmother, for example, was incredulous that her 7-year-old granddaughter, who "speaks clearly in Spanish and English" and was "bien educada," could be labeled as "mentally retarded." For school district assessors, the child's level of language development in her native language was estimated as being about 3 years behind normative development. For the grandmother, this level was a bit slow but certainly not at the level of "retardation." The grandmother went on to offer her definition of *handicapped* as someone "who can't walk or talk or can't help themselves." A similar study by Harry, Allen, and McLaughlin (1995) of African American parents found the same kind of distinction, with a father defining "mental retardation" as a condition of great dependence, by which a person would require a lot of attention, rather than in terms of school-based assessment.

Another aspect of differential definitions of normalcy and disability by parent advocates is found in cross-cultural literature on families' attributions of the causes of disabilities. For example, spiritual attributions have been documented among the Hmong families who challenge medical treatments for epilepsy and define the condition as a sign that "the spirit catches you and you fall down" (Fadiman, 1997) and define a child's club foot as a divine tribute to the travails of an ancestor whose feet had been wounded in battle (*Omaha World Herald*, 1991). The latter case embodied a dramatic illustration of parent advocacy by which the family, living in California, refused to allow surgery on the child's foot. When a California court ruled that the surgery should proceed, the family pursued the case all the way to the U.S. Supreme Court, which returned the case to the local court, where the family's wishes were eventually supported and the order for surgery withdrawn.

In our broader understanding of the meaning of parent advocacy, we note also that several studies have identified differential attitudes and coping mechanisms linked to cultural traditions of extended family, collectivism, and spiritual/religious beliefs. For example, Rogers-Dulan and Blacher (1995) proposed a framework for understanding the coping strategies of African American families, in which they described African American cultural characteristics including religious connectedness, culture/ethnic traditions, and more extended or augmented family structures. Similarly, a study by Vasquez (1973) found greater resilience and acceptance of the child's disability among Mexican American and African American mothers as compared with European American mothers, while Mary (1990) noted a focus on motherhood as requiring self-sacrifice among Hispanic mothers. Meyers, Borthwick, and Eymen (1985) found that ethnic minority families were more likely than White families to keep their children at home than to place them in an institution. A study by Hanline and Daley (1992) noted specific strengths among African American and Hispanic families. In comparing these families' coping strategies with those of Caucasian families of children with and without disabilities, the researchers noted a greater reliance on informal family networks for support, with Hispanic families placing particular emphasis on family pride and African American families displaying a less detrimental view of having a child with a disability than the other groups. By contrast, although the Caucasian families in the study had a wide network of supports and utilized various coping strategies, they displayed lower levels of family pride and family accord, which tended to be negatively impacted by the disability diagnosis.

In the following vignette, parents in our study describe the challenges of being alone in a world with a new and unwelcome diagnosis. Like some of the other parents we have introduced already, this couple has had exposure to people with disabilities. Yet because of their baby's rare condition, it was hard for the birth mother to feel as if anyone else could relate to what she was feeling, let alone support her.

Sonia and Zoe: "Normalizing" the Disability

Sonia and Zoe are a biracial, same-sex married couple and the mothers of two young children. They both work at a county program that supports adults with disabilities. Their eldest daughter, Giselle, who is 3 years of age, has Down syndrome and was born with a genetic condition that has attenuated her eye development and function. She is enrolled in a specialized school that supports children with visual impairments. She is being served under the label of Other Health Impaired (OHI). Her younger sister attends this school and serves as an example of typical development for age-peers with disabilities in an inclusive classroom. Sonia had experienced some depression after she realized the extent of her baby's visual impairment. However, once the baby was enrolled in a program for blind children and their families, Sonia's spirits lifted as she came to know other mothers whose children had visual impairments. More importantly, the teachers' modeling of positive attitudes toward the children presented a contrast to the medical practitioners' focus on the novel genetic diagnosis they had identified in this baby. Sonia's wife, Zoe, describes Sonia's emergence from depression:

> They were normalizing it—you know? Like, "She's gonna be okay. We see kids like this every day." Once Sonia got to going to those classes, and the playgroups twice a week? I think she started to come back. Sonia started to come back. . . . She needed that, you know, more than Giselle did. And I think it made all the difference in the world.

On Being a Whole Person

We bring this chapter to a close with quotes from two fathers, Michael Bérubé (Bérubé, 1998) and Rud Turnbull (2011, 2014). Both attest to the joy of experiencing their child whole, for who he was, rather than as a child with a disability.

Bérubé, reflecting on the "cognitive dissonance" he experiences in trying to imagine the view of others who may see his child through the lens of disability, says:

> Almost as a form of emotional exercise, I have tried, on occasion, to step back and see him as others might see him, as an instance of a category, one item on the long list of human subgroups. This is a child with Down syndrome, I say to myself. . . . It never works: Jamie remains Jamie to me. (pp. xi–xii)

In the first of two quotations from Turnbull, we note the scholar's voice, arguing for a more holistic approach to decisionmaking regarding the meaning of the quality of life. Turnbull (2014) states:

> There are risks in measuring only the quantifiable, in measuring only the domains now identified. . . . It may be that an antidote to a potential perversion of the science of quality of life . . . is to acknowledge that . . . quality of life does not obtain without our careful attention to the source and nature of personhood; without our engagement with issues around the social construction of dignity; without our actionable concern for self and others; and without our careful attention to the routes that compassion, trust, and dignity can lead us to follow. (p. 410)

In Turnbull's (2011) memoir of his son, Jay, who passed away at the age of 41, the author speaks as a father, concluding with a series of reflections shared with Jay's sisters, Amy and Kate. Among these reflections we see the following, an excerpt from a poem that presents a resounding answer to the question of the value of a life:

Being Whole

Amy affirms, "Jay was a whole person."
Kate elaborates, "To be whole is to have all parts of life,
The imperfections coupled with the perfections,
with acceptance of that wholeness by one's self and by others." (p. 207)

CHAPTER 6

Advocacy Toward the EHA

Converging Interests and Intersections

The second half of the 20th century marked a sweeping process of change that represented intense and continuing intersections of race/ethnicity, language, and disability. While the growing voices of White, middle-class parents of children with disabilities had dominated the landscape of disability advocacy through published personal narratives and the creation of advocacy organizations in the 1950s and 1960s, the civil rights movement on behalf of nonwhite citizens was sweeping the nation. As the society's entrenched racial inequities were forced into the public eye by the school desegregation order of *Brown v. Board of Education of Topeka* in 1954 and Rosa Parks's challenge in 1955 to racial segregation in public settings, education became the battleground for equity. Identity markers of race and disability, which had been essentially conflated through the eugenics movement, would now experience a new style of categorization that was conceptually more benign yet functionally perpetuated racial divisions. With these changes, the landscape of parent advocacy would shift into a new gear, using the law as its main vehicle.

PARENT ADVOCACY: THE LAW AS THE VEHICLE

The fundamental argument of the Brown decision became the building block of all civil rights arguments of the period—that "separate educational services are inherently unequal" (*Brown v. Board of Education*, 1955). Following this principle, the stage was set for explicit and focused political action on behalf of citizens with disabilities. Indeed, the early 1970s saw a spate of lawsuits related to the right to an appropriate education, all of which were initiated by parents and produced landmark decisions affecting the practice of special education.

Breaking the Barriers to Schooling: PARC and Mills

The first two of these cases did not represent race, although racial differences were evident in both. In 1971, parents of 14 children with developmental disabilities, represented by the Pennsylvania Association for Retarded Citizens (PARC), achieved a seminal decision in their case challenging the state's right to exclude children deemed "uneducable and untrainable" from public schools. Based on due process and equal protection rights under the 14th Amendment to the Constitution, the PARC case concluded with a settlement guaranteeing admission of all children to schools, regardless of their disabilities. Following swiftly on the heels of PARC was *Mills v. Board of Education* (1972) in Washington, DC, on behalf of seven Black children who had been denied admission to the public schools on the basis of alleged disabilities. These decisions in favor of the plaintiffs proved a powerful precedent for parent advocates, and 27 federal court cases followed quickly across the states (Disability Justice, 2019c).

Most relevant to our interest in identity intersections is the fact that the Mills case did not use either race or disability in its arguments. Rather, the case was framed as a class-action suit representing the entire class of children of school age in the District of Columbia who had been denied access to public schooling. While 12-year-old Peter Mills and six other children represented by their parents were Black and were all alleged to have some kind of disabling condition, the suit was brought on behalf of all residents of the District of Columbia who were eligible for a public education but had been denied, regardless of disability or race. Moreover, the plaintiffs were described as being "poor and without financial means to obtain private instruction" (*Mills v. Board of Education of District of Columbia*, 1972). The documents reported that the parents of most of these children had sought public school placement but had been denied, after which they filed the lawsuit on September 24, 1971. We can only assume that the broad-based class action approach was thought to be more effective than a claim on the basis of race or disability might have been.

As critical race theorists Delgado and Sefancic (2017) have observed, however, race is always in the air, as we can see by the way racial affiliations were or were not reported in the PARC and Mills cases: In the PARC case it is notable that the court documents included the names of the plaintiffs but did not mention their race. By contrast, in the case of Mills, the court documents specifically stated that, although the children were "Negroes," the case was representing all children who had been excluded from public schooling in the District of Columbia. Comparing these documents, we can only assume that the absence of a racial descriptor in the PARC case suggests that the court felt no need to specify race because the children represented the society's normative point of reference.

Litigating Race, Language, and Disability

Race, cultural affiliations, and language did become the centerpiece of three other lawsuits brought by parents of children with disabilities that occurred during the same period. The first was the suit known as *Diana v. State Board of Education, Arizona* (1970), which challenged the use of English-language IQ testing for the placement of Spanish-speaking children into programs for mental retardation. Although the case was settled out of court, it had a long-lasting impact on the principle of nonbiased assessment that subsequently became authorized in the Education for All Handicapped Children Act of 1975. *Diana* was followed by the *Larry P. v. Riles* lawsuit, which was initiated by parents of six African American children in 1971 and was not finally settled until 1977, with further amendments affirmed in 1986. The court in the Northern District of California upheld the parents' challenge that the IQ tests being used to place children in classes for "educable mentally retarded" were biased against African American children. A similar challenge, though not directly related to special education, was *Lau v. Nichols* (1974), in which the U.S. Supreme Court ruled that the San Francisco school system's failure to provide English language or other appropriate instruction to students of Chinese ancestry denied them "a meaningful opportunity to participate in the public education program" and was in violation of the Civil Rights Act's ban on discrimination based on race, color, or national origin in any program receiving federal financial assistance (*Lau v. Nichols*, 1974).

In 1973, the disability rights movement made perhaps its most significant leap forward. Indeed, the most noticed political protest on behalf of persons with disabilities occurred in relation to what had been the least noticed legal mandate for disability rights—Section 504 of the Rehabilitation Act. Passed with minimal fanfare in 1973, Section 504 has been described by Ong-Dean (2009) as "nothing more than a paragraph appended to a bill funding vocational rehabilitation for people with disabilities" (p. 15). However, in 1977, as activists realized that the Department of Health, Education, and Welfare (HEW) was taking years to establish regulations for the law's implementation, parents, self-advocates with a range of disabilities, and supporters staged protests at the head office of HEW in Washington, DC, in regional HEW offices in major cities, and in the HEW office in San Francisco, the latter "sit-in" lasting for several weeks (Shoot, 2017). With its sweeping affirmation of the right of "handicapped individuals" to receive services under any federally funded program, this law set the stage for advocates' pursuit of laws that would specifically entitle all children with disabilities to a place in schools.

The convergence of disability and racial rights movements within the paradigm of civil rights gave power to the pursuit of equity. By 1973, there were laws in 45 states mandating education for children with disabilities and, building on these successes, advocates continued their pressure for federal legislation. These efforts culminated in the passage of the Education for All Handicapped Children Act of 1975, to be later reauthorized as the Individuals with Disabilities Education Act of 1990. The battle for recognition had been won and its permanence marked by assurance of an entitled place in the education system for every child.

Paradoxically, however, this convergence contributed to a new version of segregation, as scholars and activists soon began to note the disproportionately high rates of African American and Chicano students in special education programs (Dunn, 1968; Mercer, 1973). Harry and Klingner (2014), in a study of the contributors to racial disproportionality in special education, envisioned the convergence of racism and handicapism (Bogdan & Biklen, 1977) as a "collision" fueled by the history of the role of eugenics in the mental testing movement:

> Thus, sometime in the early 1970s, the special education movement and the desegregation movement officially collided. Those whom the society had rejected, and had excluded from its public schools, would meet in the special education system. The concept of deficit, by then an ingrained part of the educational belief system, would become the chief metaphor to encompass difference. (Harry & Klingner, p.15)

THE CONSTRUCTION OF DISABILITY UNDER THE LAW

Earlier, we referred to four broad phases of the construction of disability and parent advocacy. We described the first two of these as representing a pathway from extreme oppression and exclusion that was based at first on superstition and later on pseudo-scientific eugenics. We viewed the third phase as a progression toward advocacy and leadership driven by parents and social reformers who possessed the cultural and social capital needed to make their voices heard. We turn now to the fourth phase, the liberatory project of rights enshrined under the law, which includes a philosophy based on equity, although it is one that we see as being undermined by mechanistic and bureaucratic implementation.

By using the term "liberatory" we mean that parents' advocacy has had the powerful effect of liberating not only children from physical and educational exclusion but also liberating parents from centuries of exclusion and shame. Nevertheless, the trajectory of parent advocacy has been more liberating for parents who are able to use the law to their advantage and even to contribute to its definition. This is not to say that it is parents' advocacy alone that has produced the policies and practices under the law, but rather a confluence of advocacy, professional and research conceptualizations, and the bureaucratic interests of schools themselves.

The first issue we must consider with regard to the law is the framing of disability itself. In order to be eligible for services, students had to qualify for specific types of disabilities. There were clear misunderstandings and inequities in the traditional conflating of many disabilities, such as cerebral palsy, sensory impairments, and even mental illness, with intellectual disabilities. In addition, eugenics-based designations such as "mongol," "cretin," and "imbecile" needed to be cast off to reflect less stigmatizing and, hopefully, more scientifically based nomenclature. Perhaps most important, the definition of *mental retardation* had undergone a revision in 1969 by the American Association on Mental Deficiency (now the AAMR), by which the desired criterion for the diagnosis was changed from an IQ score of 85 to 70, which included a much wider spectrum of cognitive abilities within the "normal" range. Here, we see a prime example of the meaning of the concept of disability as a social construction: with the stroke of its pen, the AAMR was able to redefine the official parameters of the most reviled of disabilities.

Thus, the framers of the EHA began with a list of 11 disabilities, which sought to distinguish between behavioral, sensory, physical, and cognitive disabilities, and between levels of disability within the cognitive category. However, the conundrum of the horrific stigmatizing of mental retardation (MR) remained and soon came to be identified not only with past abuses but also with the conflation of race and disability. Some years prior to the EHA, researchers Dunn (1968) and Mercer (1973) had already alerted the field to the misuse of the MR category for continued segregation of Black and Hispanic students and, only 7 years after the passage of the EHA, the National Academy of Sciences (Heller, Holtzman, & Messick, 1982) was commissioned to study the issue of minority overrepresentation in the MR category. A parallel current during the run-up to the law was the development of the concept of specific learning disability, which created a clear distinction between global intellectual impairment and learning difficulties in specific areas, such as reading, mathematics, and even communication. In this era of the creation of new knowledge about disabilities, decisions about their construction responded both to scientific study and social pressures. These processes began in the 1960s and continue to this day.

Shifting Categories and Drifting Students

In addressing the liberatory phase of the parent advocacy movement we celebrate its tremendous success in bringing parents' voices to the center of the disabilities agenda. However, power imbalances within the movement itself has generated two major processes, which, following Ong-Dean (2009), we refer to as *shifting* and, we would add, *drifting*. At the forefront is the pattern of shifting within disability categories—a process that has created an informal but powerful hierarchy of categories among disabilities. This hierarchy functions to lessen the stigma of certain disabilities, usually in a way that tends to benefit children from higher-status ethnic or socioeconomic groups. Ong-Dean attributes this shift partly to the advocacy of "privileged" parents whose cultural and social capital allows them to be heard, and also to the changing response of school districts as new or "emerging" disabilities become established and resources to address them become more available.

Specific learning disability. The most obvious example of the shifting/drifting pattern is the relationship between the categories of specific learning disability (SLD) and what was previously referred to as mental retardation (MR). The concept of a learning disability that was specific to certain domains was built on the work of Strauss and Lehtinen (1947) and culminated in the creation of the SLD category by Kirk in 1963 (Kirk & Becker, 1963). This model presumed an etiology initially referred to as a "minimal brain dysfunction." Unempirical though it was, this concept took root in the field and created a condition tied to a sophisticated understanding that a person could have normal intelligence yet have brain anomalies that affected academic learning. This construction of a learning disability resulting from intrinsic deficit has continued to have considerable sway, supported more recently by empirical work that demonstrates correlations between differential patterns of brain activity and an individual's reading ability (Shaywitz & Shaywitz, 2004, 2009). As is always the case with correlational studies, however, there is no proof of the direction of the effect; that is, the research does not demonstrate whether existing patterns of brain activity affected the reading skills or whether learned reading habits affected the brain activity. Moreover, Shaywitz and Shaywitz's finding (2009) that "intensive evidence-based reading intervention brings about significant changes in brain organization so that brain activation patterns resemble those of typical readers" (p. 5) raises the question of whether poor reading may be a result of learned reading habits rather than a deficit in brain functioning. Poor reading habits may well be developed as a result of poor or inadequate instruction, as is often the situation in schools serving poor children of color (Harry & Klingner, 2014). Thus, the intrinsic deficit assumption of SLD continues to be moot.

Regardless of the logic of the SLD category, for parents, this was a far more acceptable diagnosis than the concept of global intellectual delay, and those with the greatest privilege were able to build on this concept (Ong-Dean, 2009). Moreover, there were two aspects of the definition of SLD that effectively limited its applicability to many students of color. First, the requirement for a discrepancy between IQ score and academic achievement effectively limited the likelihood of students of color attaining the discrepancy, since they have tended to score lower than Whites on IQ tests. Another crucially important feature of the original definition was the "exclusionary clause," which ruled out social/environmental disadvantage as a potential contributor to the disability. Once more, this meant that students of color were less likely to qualify for this more desirable label. Ong-Dean reports that the period from 1976 to 2002 was marked by an increase in SLD diagnoses from "about 1.9 percent of the public school population to about 5.5 percent," while the percentage of students classified as MR "declined from about 2.7 percent to 1.0 percent" (p. 65). Most notably, the SLD category was populated primarily by White and middle-class students. Ong-Dean argues that the reversal of this trend occurred gradually as the SLD category became institutionalized and supported by increased funding, causing school systems to begin to apply it more broadly. To this we would add that another reason for the shift was that the IQ/achievement discrepancy criterion was replaced within the first decade of the 21st century by the use of response to intervention (RTI) assessment procedures, thus eliminating one of the predominant factors of the definition that had tended to exclude students of color.

Ong-Dean (2009) described the history of SLD in terms of two contrasting trajectories as students of color gradually "drifted" into the SLD category: a "high road" to SLD by which high-status parents earned much-needed accommodations for students struggling with academic learning, and a "low road" that school systems created in response to their own need to move low-performing students out of the mainstream and also to reduce the placement of children into the controversial category of mental retardation, which had been marked by overrepresentation of children of color ever since the inception of the EHA in 1975 (Donovan & Cross, 2002; Heller, Holtzman, & Messick, 1982).

The politics of the racially driven organization of special education was also applied within the SLD category itself, in terms of the kinds of services that different groups of students would receive. For example, the complexity of the historical SLD landscape has been dramatically illustrated by a study of service delivery decisionmaking in one school district that was resisting racial integration in the early 1970s (Saatcioglu & Skrtic, 2019). This study analyzed how the school district deliberately reconfigured the resources and status of three types of SLD placements—regular classroom, pull-out, and self-contained—so as to ensure that Black students with SLD would be served in different service-delivery settings than their White counterparts. Specifically, the high level of resources and status initially accorded to regular classroom placements where White students predominated were transferred to self-contained classrooms, literally reversing the placement model and ensuring that this setting would become the setting of choice for White students.

The foregoing study shows how impossible it can be to assume that a disability label will work in a particular way for any group of students. These findings provide a vivid illustration of Artiles's (2013) discussion of the importance of an intersectional lens in understanding how race and disability intertwine. Cautioning against essentializing any discrete category or identity marker, Artiles argues for a contrapuntal analysis—an examination of the relationships among apparently contradictory information—in order to understand how complex identity markers intersect, even within so-called disability categories.

The autism spectrum and attention deficit hyperactivity disorder (ADHD). A further feature of the shifting and drifting trend was, and continues to be, a preference for conditions that are highly associated with clinical diagnoses, as is currently evident with autism and ADD/ADHD. Once more, we cite Ong-Dean's (2009) cautious analysis of the dramatic increase in ASD diagnoses, by which he explores reasons that include environmental causes, a change in definition of the category, and the role of affluent parents in accessing this diagnosis and effective treatments for the condition. Definitional changes within this category have been intense, moving from a conceptualization of autism as a form of infantile schizophrenia, to a psychoanalytic, parent-blaming approach (Bettelheim, 1967), to the more recent interpretation as an impairment in communication. One of the greatest improvements related to this category has been the dramatic transition of parents from the role of "victim" and "patient" to perhaps the most powerful parent lobby ever seen.

The shifting/drifting process in categories, however, has reflected clear patterns of parental power by which children of influential groups move toward the "elite" categories and away from the categories by which the school system, not the medical system, determines eligibility, such as intellectual disability (ID) and emotional behavioral disorder (EBD). Further, research has continually reported racial disparities in the category of autism (Liptak et al., 2008; Morrier & Hess, 2012), and has recently identified this as the only category in which White children are currently overrepresented in some states (Travers & Krezmien, 2018).

The category of ADHD also comes under scrutiny, as research by Zirkel and Weathers (2015) reported that, nationally, White children were twice as likely as Blacks and Hispanics to receive services under a Section 504 plan. Since ADHD does not qualify a student for services under IDEA, Section 504 offers an option for specialized services. Further, Zirkel and Huang's (2018) update of the national average for the prevalence of students receiving 504 plans revealed that rates increased from 1.02% in 2009–2010 to 2.29% for the 2015–2016 year. Zirkel and Weathers's (2015) discussion of likely contributors to this pattern include the litigious approach of parents of high income and their use of the category to gain accommodations for their children on SAT and ACT exams.

The implications for racial privilege here are evident, as students with a diagnosis of attention deficit hyperactivity disorder (ADHD), while not eligible for services under IDEA, frequently receive services under the Section

504 protections. As pointed out by Erevelles (2017), students with an ADHD label are more likely to be placed in inclusive settings than are students designated as having emotional behavioral disorder (EBD), a category known to be assigned disproportionately to Black students, and to result in disproportionately high rates of exclusionary placement. Thus, Erevelles asks, "Where are all the Black students with 504 plans?" (2017, p. 122).

It is clear that categories of ASD and ADHD now carry less social stigma and have greater priority in funding and services, thanks largely to a powerful parental lobby. Meanwhile, the school-based, nonmedical categories of ID and EBD show overrepresentation by students of color while simultaneously carrying greater social stigma and greater exclusionary school placements (Losen & Orfield, 2002). The drift away from these categories, therefore, can be perceived in a remarkably similar way to the "white flight" phenomenon, which described the intentional movement of overwhelming numbers of White students away from U.S. public schools by their parents during the desegregation movement.

At the present time, however, based on our research with parents in a large, urban school district, it appears that the pattern of ethnic representation in the ASD category may be undergoing yet another shift, in which the ethnic distribution of the category is changing. Our interviews with parents suggested that this school district may be experiencing exactly what Ong-Dean described:

> As a particular disability diagnosis ages, however, we might expect a shift in its social profile. As the diagnosis becomes institutionalized, it becomes easier for schools to recognize, more school professionals are equipped to identify and accommodate the disability, and federal or state funding for it expands. Thus, schools' resistance to recognizing it will lower, making it easier for less privileged parents to persuade the school there is a disability. (p. 66)

THE LABEL AS A NEGOTIATING TOOL

In our interviews with parents, the ASD label provided a fascinating set of examples of the range of possible advocacy styles and interpretations of the disability. Two parents, Ana and Myra, had children who had been designated as having ASD. Three others, Rhonda, Marie, and Patty, had the experience of the label being "dangled" but never applied to their children, for differing reasons. Much of the confusion around this label reflects its perceived desirability as a tool for negotiating increased services and both parents' and practitioners' ambivalence toward its appropriateness. Our vignettes under this section represent the wide array of mothers' differing experiences with this process.

Patty: "An elite diagnosis"

For years, Patty noticed that the neurologist would write down that her son
had autism. As a nurse, Patty scoured the documentation thoroughly; however,
as a new parent of a child with a disability, she was not sure whether there
was something she might have missed. One day she asked the neurologist if
he actually had ASD:

> "Did you ever test—"
> "No, but—do you want him tested?"
> I go, "No, but you keep writing down he's got, um, the autism spectrum.
> Makes it look like he's got autism."
> Then he goes, "Well that's the only way that the insurance is gonna pay."

With the subsequent testing that she requested, it was determined
that her child in fact did not have autism. However, in this encounter,
she recognizes the power of both (a) the neurologist and (b) ASD as the
gatekeepers of services. Patty describes the latter as a coveted label, adding,
"It's an elite diagnosis . . . you know this is like . . . 'If you want to get into the in
crowd? Get some autism.'"

As a positive, Patty found that the neurologist was generally responsive to
parents' recommendations. Because of this leverage with getting coverage for
services, she notes how the label was an important tool for parents to have,
although she questioned if it was appropriate for all children.

> So, if the neurologist recommends it, then the insurance approves it.
> So the neurologist is important. I don't think my son needs one . . . but
> it's not bad to have . . . but if you ask him, "Can you please give him
> behavioral?" "Oh, you want behavioral, sure here." . . . So it's good in that
> um, he's giving you . . . like a leeway. He's thinking: This is a parent, she
> knows, she deals with this kid. She says he needs something . . . and he
> agrees. But at the same time, it's like, "Are we making progress with what
> you're giving me?"

Ana: "Whatever helps her to get ahead"

Ana self-describes as a White Hispanic mother of two children. She works
in the communications department at a large university hospital network.
She is married and is the sole income provider for her household. She is the
mother of two children ages 6 and 3, who have both been diagnosed with
ASD.

   While her son was diagnosed through the referring agency, she sought out the diagnosis for her daughter, paying for a 2-day comprehensive evaluation. She is admittedly much more concerned about her son than her daughter because of his greater social and communication challenges.

   Ana notes how the prevalence of ASD in the population has been increasing yet adds that she doesn't recall ever seeing any children with ASD when she was growing up. She questions whether every child diagnosed may actually have ASD; however, she places emphasis on the importance of this label for receiving supports:

> Maybe we're getting better at diagnosing it, um . . . it is not, you did not hear about this when I was growing up. I'm 44 and I can tell you I've never met a kid with autism when I went to school. I don't know if we're just doing a better job of catching it. I don't know if we're overdiagnosing. Again, going back to my daughter, she has a little bit of quirks, so I'm not saying she's where she needs to be. I don't know that she is autistic but I take the diagnosis and it worked because of the resources that come with it for her. Whatever helps her get ahead, you know.

Contrary to what our parents had heard about the power of the label, as well as the insistence of some of the professionals and community members, some of them rejected the label. While they were clear about the label being essential to receiving services, two Black mothers, Rhonda and Marie, described how they, in fact, rejected the label for their children, understanding the social implications of the label and what it meant for their child and their family.

Rhonda: "I don't want the label."

Rhonda is a single, African American mother of two children. She works in the field of law enforcement and corrections. Her eldest daughter is enrolled at a local college and is commuting. Rhonda's youngest daughter, Amira, has visual impairments and has been diagnosed with ID. She is a 17-year-old senior in a self-contained public school classroom.

   Rhonda's experience over the years with Amira was inundated with both confusion and hesitation to assign her a label. Like many of the parents in this study, she noticed some differences in her child from a very young age. Some practitioners suggested that Amira's profile may be consistent with features of ASD. However, she was never assigned that label. Consistent with other parent accounts of the elitism of the ASD category, Rhonda recognized the value of the label to provide services but was confused by practitioners' ambivalence on the diagnosis:

Because the big name was always autism. Autism. When they start
tapping into the spectrum or whatever, they started saying, "Well, she's on
the spectrum." But nobody's willing to give her that diagnosis.

However, other parents in the community encouraged her to advocate for
the ASD label, recognizing its power in obtaining additional services. Several
parents on her daughters' cheerleading team offered her their perspective,
perhaps not recognizing how difficult it was for Rhonda to actually obtain that
label:

And then I have parents that tell me, they say, "If you want to get services,
let them give her the label. Give her that label, give her the label!"

Amira was ultimately placed in an EBD classroom and assigned the label of
ID, leaving Rhonda dissatisfied with the whole process of labeling. She explains
how the EBD label was given as a result of the school's available classroom
placement rather than a result of evaluation or even the appropriateness of the
placement of children with disabilities who are in the classroom:

She wasn't in normal classes, but they—they kept putting her in, what
they called—I want to say . . . EBD and . . . recommended ABA [Applied
Behavior Analysis] therapy . . . but I feel like at that time, that's not where
she belonged. Because nobody tested her, so how did you come—how did
you come to this?

Rhonda's preferences, however, are for the labels to be removed
altogether. She contends that this is not a rejection of her understanding
of her child's learning differences, but rather the consequences of what the
labeling means for her child, and her frustration with the professionals' lack of
understanding,

. . . to understand that she does have developmental delays. She's getting
speech, but I don't want it separate. I don't want her separated from
whatever, I don't want the label.

Marie: "They are kids, that's what they do."

Similar to Rhonda, Marie's providers suggested that her son may have ASD.
Because of his dual label of learning disability and speech impairment as
well as the new gifted label, some of the practitioners suggested that he may
fall under the category of autism. She describes her visit to the pediatrician,
who then issued the referral to see a neurologist for an evaluation and
diagnosis.

You know it's because they couldn't just look at him and say, "He has this." They kind of—based on . . . the questions they were asking, the answers I would give them, "Oh he might. But if he has it, he has it mild. But I'm not a specialist to know what's going on." And that's why they referred me to see [the neurologist].

However, using her own experiential knowledge and intuitiveness, she opted not to go to the neurologist. In our interview, she recalls witnessing another parent she knew whose child was exhibiting some challenging behaviors. She describes the child's excessive crying and difficulties separating from his mother. Subsequently, this child was referred to a neurologist, where he received the diagnosis of ASD and was medicated. She didn't know for sure if this would happen to her own child, but she did not want to take the chance,

I have no idea. Because . . . I have a friend that has a child like this. She went and they put him on meds. . . . I should have gone [to the neurologist]. But I would not accept anyone to give my kid meds. Because he's not like crazy or running around. 'Cause they are kids . . . that's what they do, they learn. [My friend's son] was like high . . . autism. So they had to put him on meds. But I said okay, if I go to the neurologist, would they give my son either a high one [dose], to make him hyper . . . because he's not talking. But whenever he's mad he uses his body and he's a big boy.

What is very powerful here is the association that Marie made between her child's frustrations with communication and the potential interpretations of others. Her description seems to suggest her own recognition of autism and why her friend's son perhaps needed some type of intervention, although she made a clear distinction between his challenges and those of her own son. She also raises the implications about her son's physical size and that fact that he "uses his body" as something that made him potentially vulnerable to the ways in which practitioners could evaluate and treat him.

Our final vignette related to ASD exemplifies the pattern of the "high-profile" parent described by Rehm, Fisher, Fuentes-Afflick, and Chesla (2013).

Myra: "I would say, 'Just look at the rule book!'"

Myra, the only mother in our study who identified as White, non-Hispanic, is both the grandmother and mother of children who have been diagnosed with ASD. She is currently residing outside of the United States but travels back and forth to serve as an educational and health care advocate for her grandson, who is now attending college.

Myra describes the many battles she had with the school district several decades prior, when her son was in public school. At the other end of the advocacy spectrum from mothers like Rhonda or Marie, Myra wanted the label of ASD for her son and engaged in advocacy trainings and self-education to learn what she felt was needed to be effective.

> I wanted him to get services, and the principal told me, "Do you really want to label him?" I said, "If I don't give him a label he's never going to get help." And that was a novel idea, and she said, "You think he's going to be like this when he's an adult?" I said, "Do you think he's *not* going to be like this when he's an adult? You want to take a chance?" Because he was explosive, and if it wasn't for the public school system and all that they did to help him when I was at work (because I was widowed, and I had two children, working hard and still had to be available for my children), if it wasn't for them my son wouldn't be where he is today.

At one point, Myra took the process to the level of a hearing in order to get what she felt was needed.

> I wanted him to go to a special class for LD gifted . . . so we had a meeting and I came with my books as my honor and my weaponry. . . . It was at the local school level. I had gone to the district and accumulated all sorts of advocates who were from the school board, not the board itself, but from the district. The special ed, um . . . director from the district came, and he was infuriated and walked out of the room, telling everybody you're not doing a thing for this kid and left. He was so frustrated. . . . In the beginning they went around the room and everybody gave their, you know . . . it was like a canned kind of thing, you know? Already prepared, like I was just going to sign and leave. Um . . . and when it got to me, they just left me out, and I stood there for a second, and I said, "Mmm, are you leaving somebody out here?" And everybody looked around and said, "I don't think so . . . " and I said, "Well, what happens with the parent? I thought I was part of the team." And they hadn't a clue because none of them had read the rule book, but I read it in detail and every time I would tell them something I would say, "Just look at the rule book!"
> Well, after the meeting was over I finally got the respect of the region director. I was a little shocked, but very pleased, and I bumped it over to the district level because they didn't want to pay for the services. . . . That was a huge room! And, I kid you not, there were 15 people there in a huge circle! It was like going to a political negotiation table. In the end he got everything. Everything! He got adapted P.E., speech therapy. He got um . . . um . . . occupational therapy sensory integration . . .

THE LABEL AS EXCLUSION OR CONFUSION

The following testimonials are perhaps some of the most painful that we have encountered. Though we have interviewed these families ourselves, listening to the audio and reading the transcriptions have sent us back into the place of sorrow that we, as mothers of children with disabilities, visit from time to time. Contrary to what others may assume this sorrow to be, it has little to do with the diagnosis or what the children can and cannot do—we have accepted these things long ago! It has more to do with the injustice of the world, as we see practitioners, perhaps not even realizing how much power they have, hurting the mothers the most. To see others suffering as we have, simply hurts.

Patty: "Is the baby's name William?"

As outlined earlier, Patty was caring for her grandson, Richard, who has Williams syndrome. Patty describes how her daughter, Justina, who is Richard's biological mother, received her son's diagnosis of Williams syndrome. He had remained in the NICU for almost a month, diagnosed with failure to thrive. During that time the providers were unsure of his diagnosis but reassured the mother that his condition was not due to a lack of nutrition from the placenta or "her fault," as she might have believed. However, it was not until post-discharge that they were able to come up with a diagnosis. As Patty explains, the delivery of the diagnosis was very distressing to Justina, who was already medically fragile and coping with a mental illness:

> And after they discharged him, then my daughter, Justina, went for an appointment. Um, the doctor says to her, "Oh, so is the baby's name William?" And she's like, "What—William? No. His name is Richard." Then the doctor tells her the baby has Williams syndrome. Justina says, "What is that?" He goes, "Ah, don't worry about it! I guess we'll both look it up!" And takes her to . . . a laptop. She said she was devastated. She called me crying. She goes, "Oh my God, you don't know what just happened to me."

Following the diagnosis, the provider delivered a grim prognosis for Richard, leading Justina to believe the worst possible scenario—that her child would die. It was this very exchange, the confusion and lack of support, that sent Justina into a cycle of depression. When Patty took over full responsibility for Richard, Justina was grateful, saying: "Mom, I don't think I could have handled a special-needs baby."

Sonia: "In the dark"

Sonia describes her baby's diagnosis with Down syndrome as coming weeks after her delivery. The primary focus among the doctors at the hospital was on the child's rare medical condition, a condition in which her eye development had stopped. Described as a translocation, this is a rare type of Down syndrome that has effects on the eyes, skin, and kidneys. Sonia explains that because the baby's eyes were very small and had no vision, the geneticist and other specialists were so preoccupied by this rare condition that they seemed to forget that they had both a mother and a baby to deal with. As Zoe describes,

> He [the geneticist] was very scientific and just . . . black and white. I think he wanted it to be something, you know, for him to have discovered this new genetic disorder.

Because she did not have the typical facial features of a baby with Down syndrome, Giselle was not diagnosed at birth. In addition, she was feeding well in the NICU, and despite the doctor's insistence, there was no need for the baby to remain in the hospital. It was Sonia who suggested that the baby may have Down syndrome, while the doctors insisted that she did not:

> That was the first thing I said. When the doctor came, I said "She has Down syndrome." And he said, "No, she has something very rare." And if they would have told me she had Down syndrome, I would have felt so much better, right? Just because I understand it and I know it. . . . It's not the rarest thing, you know. And I would have been, Okay, it's not so crazy. But they had us going—oh, it was horrible.

Going home, however, was a difficult experience for these mothers, not knowing how to interpret the diagnosis. Because the baby was born around the holidays, the medical offices were closed, so the couple spent weeks without being able to communicate or reach out to anyone for support. Sonia describes her overall confusion and lack of support:

> Down syndrome was 2 weeks later. We were already home. I had been home for a while with this blind baby, thinking all these crazy things, you know. What she has—I had no idea.

CHAPTER 7

Parent Advocacy Under the Umbrella of the EHA/IDEA

With the establishment of the EHA, parents' role as representatives of their children became official. This is not the only law to mandate parent involvement in children's schooling, as this was the case in the establishment of Head Start in 1965 and, later, in the No Child Left Behind Act (NCLB) and the Every Student Succeeds Act (ESSA). This pattern represents a powerful shift in the conceptualization of the role of parents in children's schooling, from the responsibility simply to support the school's efforts, to taking responsibilities that include both supportive and leadership activities within the school. Best known for delineating these roles is the work of Epstein (1995), whose list included communicating with school personnel, volunteering at the school, supporting home learning, and participating in decisions about children's learning. Under special education law the vision is more expansive, with parental consent required for evaluation and placement of a child in a special education program and for the initiation and ongoing review of the child's Individualized Education Program (IEP). The prescriptions for due process in the case of disagreements between parents and the school underline that it is the intention of the law to hold school personnel accountable for delivering an individualized program appropriate to the child's needs. However, a seminal ethnographic study by Mehan, Hartwick, and Meihls (1986) demonstrated that, within a decade of the law, the decisionmaking process in IEP meetings had already taken on a routine nature, by which parents' agreement most often represented a ratification of decisions already made by professional teams.

As we know, however, the law is always a two-edged sword, ensuring and protecting, while also constraining and limiting. With regard to education as a whole, Fennimore (2017) used the lens of critical race theory to analyze the impact of the legal framing of parent advocacy on nondominant or minoritized groups. Referring to Epstein's conceptualization as "seemingly non-controversial and ideologically neutral" (1995, p. 163), Fennimore argued that "the hegemonic focus on parent participation in school support activities presumes ideologically neutral public schools that hold all parents in equal regard" (p. 161). Moreover, this scholar highlighted how the law requires "negotiation with institutional scripts," whereby "racism and related injustices are now deeply embedded in complex social and legal constructs such as court decisions that ignore apartheid schools and eliminate race from legal equations" (p. 166).

Following Fennimore's analysis, we find that the DisCrit lens (Connor et al., 2016) provides a deeply troubling view of the nature of nondominant parents' participation within the confines of special education law and within the context of the society's endemic racism. While it is certainly true that the "institutional scripts" of the law are daunting for most parents regardless of ethnicity or language, research shows that in special education, there is a chasm of difference between expected or required practices and the normative participation of parents who are not schooled in the knowledge base or communication styles of mainstream U.S. culture.

Thus, at the inception of the EHA it was evident that two intimidating trends would provide the main obstacles to implementation of the parent-participation mandate: first, the nationwide endemic racism that had only just begun to be challenged and, second, the law itself, with its procedural and technocratic framing of parent participation. The literature on parent participation has continued to highlight these two trends ever since the establishment of the EHA/IDEA. Overall, the legalistic framing of parent involvement in special education has proven challenging for all parents, and particularly for those least familiar with the discourse style that has come to dominate the IEP process. We begin our review with literature focusing on parents from nondominant cultural, socioeconomic, and linguistic backgrounds.

CHALLENGES OF RACISM, ETHNOCENTRISM, AND CONTEXT

With parent participation specified as a requirement under the EHA, the convergence of disability and race in the special education system catapulted parents of color directly into the advocacy conversation. Within 2 years of the enactment of the EHA, researchers were already documenting the difficulties that parents of color were having in participating in the IEP process. The first research reports noted that professionals were providing such parents with minimal information regarding their rights (Sullivan, 1980; Tomlinson, Acker, Canter, & Lindborg, 1977). Marion (1979) furthered this point, arguing that the traditional stigma of race and social class could be seen in school personnel's disrespectful and exclusionary treatment of African American parents attempting to participate in the IEP process. On the parents' side, Marion noted that the process was also undermined by Black parents' historical mistrust of school authorities under the desegregation orders. This report was quickly followed by similar analyses by Patton and Braithwaite (1984) and Cassidy (1988). Within the same decade, studies documenting similar patterns among other culturally/linguistically diverse (CLD) families included Hispanic, Native American, and Asian families (Bennett, 1988; Chan, 1986; Connery, 1987; Lynch & Stein, 1987; Sharp, 1983).

In over four decades since the passage of the law, studies of CLD parents and professionals' interactions around the IEP have continued to reveal numerous challenges related to racial, cultural, and linguistic differences. Reviews by Harry (2008) and Harry and Fenton (2017) identified four main themes in this literature: (a) cross-cultural misunderstandings regarding the meanings of disability, (b) professionals' deficit views of these families, (c) differences in parents' versus professionals' goals for children and young adults, (d) and differences in parents' versus professionals' interpretations of parental roles. While these four themes continue to be present in studies of CLD families, there are new trends that reveal the continuing hegemony of racism.

The Hegemony of Race Over Class

Several studies point to a movement toward greater attention to the intersections of family identity. Specifically, there has been an increasing trend toward grappling with the relative influence of race and socioeconomic status or perceived social class. It is apparent that, while minority groups have increased their economic and social capital, the residue of historical racism continues to provide the main lens through which school personnel view families of color.

The category of ASD presents a case in point. As noted by Ong-Dean (2009), the category of ASD has traditionally included a disproportionate number of high-income, predominantly White families. However, as the category has become more institutionalized and has grown to include a wider range of children, the hegemony of race at the intersection of race and disability has become evident. In spite of the high prevalence of ASD in the population and the extensive research on the benefits of early intervention services, studies have reported significant delays in the diagnosis and identification of ASD for African American children, leading to delays in interventions and needed services (Gourdine, Baffour, & Teasley, 2011; Pearson & Meadan, 2018). Some researchers have attributed this gap to practitioners' lack of understanding of African American families as well as a historical mistrust of health care providers by the African American community. However, studies have also highlighted the hegemony of negative social perceptions that have a tremendous impact upon African American parents of children with ASD.

A case study by Gourdine and associates (2011) of 11 African American mothers reported that the mothers had intuitive concerns about their children very early on, noticing a lack of speech development by 18 months of age. Even when they suspected that something was wrong, the parents were quite devastated by the autism diagnosis and were further disturbed by the assumptions on the part of the clinicians, who, using insensitive, deficit-laden language, presumed the parents to be uneducated and perhaps unable to care for their children. Highlighting the biases and assumptions about race and class, parents in this study, who were middle-class, African American, college-educated parents, expressed how surprised the staff was to discover that the mother of a child was a health care professional herself. In response to their sense that the clinicians at this site did not want their child to continue, these parents decided to pay privately for services that would benefit their son. The findings of this study are similar to the work of Gillborn, Rollock, Vincent, and Ball (2016), who found that middle-class African American parents in the U.K. found difficulty getting their children diagnosed with ASD and LD.

These and other studies suggest that parents who may have bypassed many of the financial and social-status barriers are unable to escape the social perceptions at the intersection of race and disability. In a qualitative study by Pearson and Meadan (2018), Black mothers interviewed described how practitioners ignored their initial and subsequent concerns about their child's development and emergent behaviors that suggested a diagnosis of ASD. In response, these mothers would seek alternative means of obtaining an appropriate diagnosis and a professional who would address their concerns, centralizing a role for parent advocacy. The researchers noted, "one of the most fundamental ways that mothers were able to gain access to services for their children was through advocacy. During the interviews, nine out of eleven mothers explained how they have often advocated for the rights and services of their children" (Pearson & Meadan, 2018, p. 26).

In our study, the intersections of parents' racial, socioeconomic, and sexual orientations illustrated the complexity of identity, pointing to the impossibility of simple hierarchies or typologies. Nevertheless, it was evident that race was still perceived as the master status, alongside the other dimensions of parents' identities. This hegemonic position of race was made clear by two African American mothers, Rhonda and Zoe, but in very different scenarios. For Rhonda, both she and her daughter, Amira, felt the sting of racism but in opposite directions. For Zoe, the issue hit home when she made decisions about how to adjust her advocacy style as compared to that of her spouse, Sonia.

Rhonda: "I felt that."

Rhonda's story includes her range of experiences with schools, health care settings, family members, and community members that involve both her and her daughter, Amira. Rhonda describes her experiences when seeking placement in a private school that catered to students with the ASD diagnosis and seemed to be a good fit for her daughter. She felt discriminated against by the school staff, who seemed to question whether she would be a good fit at the school or would make empty promises to get back to her. Even though her daughter may have met some of the criteria for admission to the school, Rhonda describes not being a part of the socially accepted group:

> I started going to some of the private schools that I'd heard catered to kids with autism or on the spectrum. And even they . . . I was discriminated against. I felt that . . . the color of my skin. And the fact that maybe I wasn't a part of "the group" or whatever "the group" was. 'Cause, I could see that Amira probably *was* a fit for some of the programs.

Ultimately, Rhonda ended up enrolling Amira in her neighborhood's public school, which was her last choice. At the school and within the classroom of students with varying exceptionalities, however, her daughter experienced discrimination based on some of her features, specifically, being "othered" by members of her own ethnic background. Rhonda found this particularly unsettling:

> Mine is ostracized because she has long hair, she has curly hair. "Oh you're not Black. You're not this." You'd be surprised!

Zoe: "The Angry Black Woman"

Zoe describes her identity as a Black woman in understanding the power dynamics of the world when it comes to race and her child's disability. Her experiences have led her to hold back on her advocacy at times, allowing her spouse, Sonia, who is White Hispanic, to speak on their child's behalf. Because of this identity, in the geographic region in which this family resides, Sonia's ethnicity holds greater status, particularly when engaging with professionals, many of whom share the same cultural identity. She describes Sonia as being savvier, being able to use the "lingo" that is appropriate and recognized. Zoe also describes others' implicit biases about her features "not looking all delicate," which she suggests may magnify their negative perceptions of her. Although they are both in a nontraditional union, the power of race is still highly influential, as Zoe perceives Sonia as having a look that is more socially acceptable to others. Yet Zoe also recognizes that there are times that call for her to implement the "angry Black woman" role. However, generally, they feel that this affects whether or not their daughter Giselle receives services as well as the quality of services received:

It's something that I felt was necessary for [Giselle] to get the kind of attention she needs and deserves. I've been in this skin my whole entire life. And so, you know, I know the difference between the way I'm readily perceived by others as opposed to Sonia, who is a Hispanic, but if you look at her, you don't see Hispanic. You see you know, a perfectly good White woman. And here I am, you know, Angry Black Woman, you know. Lookin' a certain way. You know, I'm not looking all delicate and not perceived to be that way by anybody. So yeah . . . she takes the lead now. If a situation arises where she needs Angry Black Woman to come out, and you know, be angry—then I jump on course!

While being strategic and knowing when to speak out, Zoe also admits that this is a painful experience for her, having to hold back her voice because of the social perceptions of her identities. Though she may recognize this as unjust, she also recognizes the need to participate in unjust processes as means of supporting her child. This highlights the power differences that are evident at the intersections of race and disability:

Not that . . . it doesn't make me feel a certain way, that you know, people are that way. Because it does. But in that moment, I know that I need to do what's best for her.

Our study showed that the racism some parents experienced was likely to be experienced by their children also. In mixed-race families these issues could further complicate the decisions parents had to make in their child-rearing practices. In Patty's case, she was surprised to find her grandson faced with the double marginalization of race and disability within the family itself.

Patty: "How do you teach that?"

Patty's son Richard is medium brown-skinned in complexion with dark, curly hair. His racial and ethnic identity is Black Hispanic. However, Patty describes her frustration with experiencing unexpected discrimination within her own family. While her family is an ethnic blend, Richard is the only child who is identified as Black Hispanic, while the rest of his family members, including his sister and nephews, are identified as White Hispanic. While this isn't of any particular significance to Patty, she was disappointed to discover how this came to play in the family dynamics. In addition, because Richard has a disability, he may not recognize many of the cultural and social nuances, good or bad, that are a part of everyday social experiences for children.

Patty describes her feelings of conflict. While she wants to intercede immediately, a part of her approach to supporting Richard's growth and self-advocacy is to allow him to have natural social experiences, to see how he responds to these encounters, and to teach him how to respond. However, because she was unprepared for one particular conversation between Richard and his nephew of the same age, she was not sure how to intervene. She describes having to "fight" even within her own family:

> Or you're fighting for them. Because . . . like yesterday, um, the little one—and I was listening, but I didn't interfere. But I'm in the kitchen and the little one goes, "Come on, nigga."
>
> So he has never heard that expression so he goes, "Um, you called me a negro?"
>
> "Yeah, nigga."
>
> "You're calling me a nig—abuela!"
>
> I go, "Yes?" I had heard the whole thing.
>
> "[Name of nephew] called me a nigger."
>
> I said, "Well, that's not nice, to call people a name." I said, "You may be Black, you may be White, but you know, that's not a name that you call each other." And so he kept on, "N—, but it's like the expression that they use."

At first, Patty's concern about how to handle this situation was how to reconcile the word in its original origin and intent as compared with its commonplace usage in today's society. Is there a difference? she wondered. She began to chalk this up to the latter conceptualization, as her grandson using it as a term of endearment. However, she learned that a few moments later, when Richard went to report the incident to his sister, expecting her to reprimand him, his sister replied, "Well, you *are*." Patty was even more disappointed by how her granddaughter managed this encounter, saying, "We are trying to teach here!" Perhaps this is something that is understated: Beyond the understanding of race and disability are the power of colorism and other divisive forces.

Cultural Values, Context, and Goals for Adulthood

Parent input during the transition period has become a key focus of research on family participation. Beyond explicit expressions of racist attitudes, this literature highlights cultural dissonance in goals for children with disabilities as well as poor professional communication with parents. Studies by Rueda, Monzo, Shapiro, Gomez, and Blacher (2005); Wilder, Jackson, and Smith (2001); and Kalyanpur (1998) described the contrast between Hispanic and Native American families' more collectivist expectations for their adult children and the individualistic goals identified by service providers. Smith and Routel (2010) emphasized that how transition and its key component, self-determination, are defined and operationalized is based on the mainstream ideals of individualism and independence, which often contradict the values of diverse families. Acknowledging this discord, Smith and Routel state that these ideals are still the standard markers for success under the legislation of IDEA, and they add that

> the transition success of students with involved parents and enhanced self-determination abilities, as defined by the dominant culture, can be viewed as reflective of the level of assimilation of families and professionals into the hegemony of Anglo-European cultural geographies. (2010)

The following vignette, from one of the caregivers in our study, Jenny, describes the type of customization and individualized approach that advocacy could take. Jenny is White Hispanic and is a teacher where her foster daughter, Nora, attends school. Although Jenny is quite familiar with the intricacies of the dual systems of school and foster care, her goals for transition and independence for the child under her care do not fall under the preset domains of transition under IDEA.

Jenny: "Sometimes you can't control that to the fullest."

Jenny self-describes as White Hispanic and is the teacher and the foster caregiver to an 18-year-old adolescent named Nora. Nora is Hispanic from Central America, with long dark hair, brown skin, dark eyes, and a radiant smile. She has the label of ID. However, Nora also has multiple, concurrent diagnostic labels under the DSM-V that are related to her background of trauma and loss. Nora is described by her teachers as a hardworking student who held a summer job in the local parks, and is currently doing some community-based employment through the transition services offered by the district.

Although Nora's foster-care status may have presented some challenges, Jenny is in a unique position by working at the school Nora attends. Jenny does not perceive there to be any educational challenges for Nora, and Nora's and her own interactions with school personnel have been smooth. Noting the benefits of working at the school, Jenny adds, "Let me tell you, working at the school has its advantages." Jenny also has access to advocacy support through the legal clinic whose attorneys represent Nora. However, she may not perceive the need to utilize this advocacy support as other foster parents would, or even to be present herself at the IEP and transition meetings. Sending her husband, Nora's foster father, in her place, Jenny perceives these meetings and establishing the IEP goals to be very "customary," a formality rather than a platform for advocacy, stating, "To be honest, I haven't really thought about those kind of goals. The hosting teacher does."

Regarding transition goals, however, Jenny takes a less deferential stance. Her concerns are related to internal factors rather than to things that are external to Nora. While Jenny reports the benefits of Nora's therapy medications and positive concerted efforts of her mental health care providers, her long-term concerns for Nora's transition have little to do with the established domains that are typically emphasized for transitioning students with disabilities; her focus is on Nora's mental health:

> My main concern, goals for her in general, is how to be as independent as possible. How to control her emotions and stabilize more. But I do know that has to do with her mental health. Sometimes, you can't control that to the fullest.

Jenny's testimony illustrates how some families' goals and perceptions may not be in alignment with the established protocols under special education law. Nora's intersecting identities of being a foster care youth, having mental illness, and carrying the ID label affect her ability to navigate her own spaces, and they affect the decisions made on her behalf, which must consider her caregiver's goals for her. What speaks to our case for how caregivers value the personhood of the children they care for is that although she reports the benefits of therapies and medications, Jenny emphasizes that many of Nora's challenges are a part of her and cannot be "controlled" or managed. Jenny's own cultural and familial values guide her priorities for Nora above the established recommendations for transition. While Jenny is situated in the dual role of school personnel and caregiver, she gives less weight to legalized protocols for transition, such as independent living, focusing her energies instead on providing a safe and nurturing home environment for Nora. Her hopes are that Nora will be able to overcome some of her emotional obstacles. Jenny's next plan is to accept another foster adolescent at their home so that Nora can have an even richer family experience.

   The inattentiveness to home, family, and contextual considerations is one way in which schools may constrain or ignore the advocacy of parents and caregivers like Jenny. In spite of the number of studies and guidelines supporting the family's essential role in successful transitional planning and postschool success, several studies of parents of transitioning students have expressed the minimalization of their role by school personnel. A study by Francis, Stride, Reed, and Chiu (2017) highlighted parents' desires for school personnel to recognize the interdependence and involvement of the family members for transitioning students. Similarly, a study by Hirano and colleagues (2016) carved out several roles for parents of transitioning students. These researchers adapted the earlier work of Walker, Wilkins, Dallaire, Sandler, and Hoover-Dempsey (2005), exploring the role of parent involvement for transitioning students. A clear distinction between home- and school-based activities supporting transition was reported in this study.

   The dichotomy between home and school was noted in the earlier work of Epstein (1995) on families of children with special needs. As a result, they proposed a multidimensional model for parent involvement at the transition level, emphasizing the importance of expanding the role of families in the transition process outside of school-based contexts. This approach, researchers note, "expands traditional involvement activities beyond attending meetings and helping with homework to parents who act as decision-makers and evaluators, collaborators, instructors, coaches, and advocates" (Hirano et al., 2016, p. 3546). These studies are also in alignment with the seminal work of Leake and Boone (2007), whose study also highlighted the family's role in the transition.

While one aspect of parents' concerns may be focused on being a part of the collaborative process, they are also concerned about how well the schools actually meet the goals of transition for their children. Parents in the study by Rabren and Evans (2016) emphasized how transition goals and services at the secondary level should incorporate the integration of their children with disabilities with peers and community members without disabilities. Parents expressed how such opportunities should occur within school and community contexts, noting the profound lack of disability awareness in the community, which serves as a primary barrier to their children's integration. In a similar vein, a study by Francis and colleagues (2017) explored perspectives among parents of young adults with intellectual and developmental disabilities who have graduated from postsecondary educational programs. Parents described how they would have wanted more opportunities for inclusion at the secondary level in order to better prepare their emerging adults for community inclusion. These parents also recommended that transition planning and services begin sooner rather than later, in order for their child to have more time to develop critical skills.

In our study, the parents highlighted the importance of having both career-based and recreational activities that support the children developmentally as well as some culturally rooted goals that are valued by some families. Rhonda's description of the services at her school as "the transition thing" and Patty's wishes for Richard to be able to engage in family traditions are described in the vignettes below.

Rhonda: "Every kid doesn't want to do home health or cooking!"

Rhonda, a former athlete, describes how she appreciated the efforts of Amira's coach in middle school in exposing students to a variety of sports. Through a school–community partnership, he was responsible for introducing Special Olympics as an extracurricular activity. The Special Olympics allowed students with disabilities, who may or may not have been engaged in academics or given the opportunity to participate in other school-level extracurricular activities, to, at the very least, try a different sport.

Imagine Rhonda's disappointment when it was time for Amira to enter high school and she discovered that there was no availability for this type of program. Rhonda tried to show *how* it could be implemented, and that it in fact had been implemented at the school, offering to call the program coordinator to help the school establish it. The school refused her requests, which she felt would have been so important for Amira's well-rounded development, forcing her to find community-based opportunities:

Because she did sports outside, now mind you, they don't provide sports. They had nothing. We came in in 9th grade and it was nothing. . . . Nothing, nothing. So I'm like, *Oh my gosh!* Then, I have to tap into outside.

In addition to the lack of recreational activities, Rhonda was disappointed by the transition services offered by the school. She describes how limited the opportunities for career exploration were and how they were restricted to the hospitality and culinary arts, yet another example of failing to meet students' interests and preferences,

Their transition. So they tell me—I don't know if it's every school. . . . I'm thinking, every school has a, um, partnership per se. . . . So they'll tap into those careers. Now I'm finding that a lot of times with our kids, they want to push them into home health or cooking. Every kid doesn't want to do home health or cooking! There you are wanting to do a one-fit-all!

Patty: "You're hoping that that too, will happen."

In describing some of the goals she had for Richard, Patty describes how his sensitivity and pickiness regarding food was frustrating to her. Patty added a nutritionist to his team of providers, who has given her recommendations for his dietary needs. However, what she was hoping for was for Richard to be able to try different foods. She brought this up to a developmental pediatrician, who didn't see this as a priority for Richard:

I know that [the developmental pediatrician] told me that it wasn't important, but I wanted him to learn how to eat different foods. I think because of the Latin part and the socializing, I think it will help him to be able to sit at a table with friends and enjoy a meal . . . later on in life if he meets, like a young lady, you know 'cause you're hoping that that too, will happen.

One issue that has surfaced in these parent testimonials relates to the contradictory role of the developmental pediatrician and the neurologist. While neurologists are generally handing down a label or prescribing a medication, the developmental pediatrician may typically use a nondeficit approach in addressing the needs of the child. The developmental pediatrician, while concerned about acute and/or chronic health problems, may respond differently to developmental concerns, expecting that some issues may take longer to resolve or, in some cases, not at all, as they are part of that child's unique profile. We believe this represents a paradox—an approach that may be comforting to some parents who are continually exposed to deficit-framed language and recommendations for treatments, while others may perceive this as dismissive and lacking in responsiveness to their goals for their children.

Patty's exchange with the developmental pediatrician also underscores the need for valuing parents' goals through a cultural lens. She talks about the "Latin part" of cuisine, which is strongly tied to family and social gatherings and which has high value in Hispanic culture. For Patty, the ability to share meals within and outside of the family, therefore, is a marker of successful transition, a goal that she has for Richard. Family and culturally centered transition goals may contradict the values of the practitioners from whom parents seek advice. Compare this to a culturally reciprocal approach (Kalyanpur & Harry, 2012), by which the professional would have asked the mother to explain why the food was so important to her, rather than assuming that it was not.

Parent Advocacy Styles

As some of the foregoing vignettes show, the complex identities of parents cannot be captured by a one-size-fits-all philosophy of advocacy. Within the traditional framework, White middle-class parents have historically been the parents with the type of cultural capital valued by professionals. This type of capital emphasizes formalized advocacy training, knowledge of the law, and ability to navigate and use the technical jargon embedded throughout the special education process (Balcazar, Keys, Bertram,& Rizzo, 1996; Burke & Goldman, 2017; Ong-Dean, 2009; Trainor, 2010). This is often to the exclusion of families whose forms of advocating may be diverse, overlooked, or even contradictory to the schools (Auerbach, 2007; Groce, 1999; Khalifa, Arnold, & Newcomb, 2015; Quiñones & Kiyama, 2014; Sauer & Lalvani, 2017; Stanley, 2015; Wilson, 2015).

Differences in cultural styles present important differences in modes of advocacy across disability, race, and socioeconomic status. A study by Trainor (2010) showed that while parents of lower socioeconomic status implemented more intuitive knowledge about their children to advocate for them, parents with greater access to resources utilized this knowledge as well as an array of strategies to advocate, therefore being more successful in their efforts. Parents of color were less inclined to advocate for their children, although they described both ambiguity and disagreement with the labels assigned to their children. African American, Latino, and Native American parents in this study, while agreeing with their children's within-school difficulties, doubted the fitness of the assigned disability categories to their children and raised questions about whether their "academic difficulties were a result of disabilities rather than problems within the classroom and/or instructional method" (p. 45). An interesting finding from Trainor's (2010) study was that across socioeconomic and racial/ethnic classifications, advocates of children with ASD were more likely to have successful outcomes in their advocacy by working with professionals. This points to an additional inequity—the privileging of certain disabilities over others, which we referred to in the previous chapter as the shifting and drifting phenomenon among disability categories. Our vignettes in the previous chapter included statements from mothers in our study indicating that a diagnosis of ASD was seen by parents as an "elite diagnosis" because of its power to bring additional services. We cannot be sure whether this preferential treatment may have developed because of the specialized behavioral and communication needs of this population or because of the high status of the parents who have lobbied for this disability and the increased resources that have come to many school districts as a result. However, we tend to favor the latter explanation and note that parents with much less status, such as those in our study, may now be benefiting from the widespread application of this label, whether or not it is appropriately applied.

A study by Rehm and colleagues (2013) of parent advocacy during the transition period brings additional dimensions to the work of Auerbach (2007) and Trainor (2010), who described the power differences among parents advocating for their children. Rehm and colleagues sought to illuminate the experiences of parents of adolescents who had both a chronic health condition and a developmental disability. The rationale for the study was based on prior research that reported the increased spending on health care services among children with chronic health care needs enrolled in special education as compared to families of children without a chronic health condition or without special education services. The researchers detailed the breakdown of educational attainment among the parents in their study, the highest level of education occurring among Whites, followed by African American and Asian parents with some college education, and finally Latino families, who had the lowest educational attainment in the sample. Highlighted in the study was the advocating power among these parents, to whom the researchers assigned the terms *high-profile* parents, *strategic* parents, *grateful-gratifier* parents, and parents with unsuccessful negotiations. The researchers noted that the high-profile parents were mostly White with education beyond a postsecondary degree. These parents were well-known in the school district and could be characterized as intimidating, as researchers noted:

A pervasive culture of advocacy arose from parents' interpretations of broad and complex laws, regulations, court judgments, and entitlements, and this information motivated parents to pursue what they perceived they were due. (p. 1381)

An interesting finding in this study was that the majority of the African American, Latino, and Asian parents fell into the categories of grateful-gratifier and parents with unsuccessful negotiations. The former described parents whose advocacy efforts were in alignment with school personnel preferences because professionals felt the parents had realistic expectations of their children, while the latter described parents whose requests for services were unmet. Although the researchers note that this category of parents—those with unsuccessful negotiations—was represented by every racial/ethnic group, these parents generally identified the following three reasons for their lack of success in advocacy efforts: a lack of knowledge of the law, limited awareness of the available services, and insufficient skills to negotiate for their concerns. The researchers described these parents as "seen by teachers as poorly focused and unable to prioritize their child's education above more pressing personal concerns such as emotional or physical health challenges, financial pressures, and legal difficulties" (p. 1384). Similar logistical issues, including work schedules and transportation, were also reported by Cavendish and Connor (2018) regarding the ability of parents of urban high school students with LD to attend school meetings. Although parents in all categories described having multiple stressors, the researchers noted that these parents often had other resources and social supports to offset them.

Building upon the literature that reveals African American parents' reluctance to speak up during IEP meetings with professionals, Wilson (2015) described the question-asking among African American parents as a form of their advocacy. Consistent with previous literature, she describes how collaborating with professionals prior to the IEP meeting in order to formulate questions could enhance the implementation and success in the meetings. Wilson described the importance for culturally and linguistically diverse parents to acquire the forms of social and cultural capital that were deemed successful among parent advocates in the study by Trainor (2010). While we fully endorse Wilson's recommendation, we note that the deficit-laden views that many service providers hold of African American families living in poverty can be particularly hard to overcome (Harry, Klingner, & Hart, 2005; Knotek, 2003; Rao, 2000). Indeed, researchers in the first cited study described these families as being "under fire" from school personnel.

The Limitations of Typologies

Several educational researchers have introduced typologies in their studies to describe parent advocacy styles and to distinguish one type from another. Though scholars such as Alper, Schloss, and Schloss (1995) and Groce (1999) have effectively described how parent advocates employed a range of strategies, research continues to suggest a hierarchy among these classifications.

Across studies that offer typologies of advocacy, the intuitive knowledge that parents have may be considered less powerful. Trainor's (2010) classification of parent advocates viewed their advocacy through the lens of social and cultural capital. This placed the parents whose advocacy efforts were based on their intuitive knowledge on the opposite end of the continuum from parents whose expert style of advocacy had an impact at the systems level. Similarly, Rehm and colleague's (2013) study of parent advocates distinguished high-profile parents, described as being most successful in their advocacy efforts, from the other categories of parent advocates and, even more alarming, from the parents who were deemed unsuccessful in their advocacy efforts, who therefore had no advocacy classification at all.

By assigning categories to the ways in which families advocate, based on certain criteria such as their knowledge of special education legislation, for example, are we subtly reproducing the classification systems that often divide our children? Is the question of whether they are successful—or, for example, whether they are even considered to be advocates—attached to the outcomes of their advocacy efforts? While it may be evident that the results of some families' advocacy styles may achieve their goals and preferences more than others, it is worth examining how we as researchers may unintentionally reproduce these distinctions.

In our study, we found a range of advocacy styles among the parents. Of the nine parents, only Myra, described in a previous vignette as fighting for services under the ASD label, would be readily described as having the resources and style of advocacy that are typically acknowledged by practitioners. Ana and Jenny, who both managed to leverage the same power through their employment and networking advantages, might also have had their concerns dismissed were they in a different geographical region that did not match their cultural identity. For the most part, however, the rest of the parents displayed a range of adaptive processes by which they learned to negotiate the system, maneuvering in whichever ways best fitted their personalities and resources.

We begin this series of vignettes with Rhonda's approach to advocacy and the response by professionals when they encounter her.

Rhonda: "I'm not dead yet!"

Rhonda describes how she recognizes personnel's initial assumptions about her, judging her based on race and presumed socioeconomic status, though she is a working middle-class parent. She could sense their attempts to place her in a category along with other parents whom they would likely dismiss as uneducated or uninvolved. Yet she adds that her strategy of maintaining cordiality while standing her ground may cause them to question their own assumptions. She steps forward with a growing confidence in her own advocacy:

> they try to tread lightly 'cause they've probably gotten checked about it and they probably look at me like . . . I don't know. This one here, it looks like she might be more educated than—or whatever. But I try to kill them with kindness. And I just say you—you get what you get. You bring it, now you better be prepared for how I'm gonna respond. That's what I say. 'Cause I'm getting better . . . at learning. Yeah. I'm not dead yet!

Similar to Rhonda's experiences, Patty also describes the personnel's negative assumptions about her, as demonstrated through the constant ignoring of her requests. Though she felt that increasing her presence at the school was an effective approach, she also found that utilizing her network of formal advocates would help her gain traction.

Patty: "They help him . . . and me . . . get the response."

Patty was in a unique legal situation, as she was in the final stages of review by the agencies and courts in order to adopt her grandson. Like the many other *abuelas* that she describes who have stepped forward to become the primary providers for their grandchildren, Patty had to learn to quickly navigate the delicacies of the legal process. However, when discovering that her grandson has come home from the first day of school with bruises on his body, her demands for an incident report from the school were ignored. Patty felt there was not only a lack of understanding of complex situations but also a lack of accountability, as the teacher referred to her grandson as "no saint" when she asked how this could have happened on her watch. Fueled by her own sense of powerlessness and the imminent fear of losing custody, Patty increased her presence at the school by serving as a volunteer. What was instrumental in gathering much-needed documents, however, was the assistance of the legal interns working on her case to advocate on her behalf at no cost to her. While school personnel had been repeatedly unresponsive to Patty, they complied with the legal team's request for documentation. Subsequently, the teacher expressed her disapproval of Patty's combined advocacy efforts:

> And she always felt I was, you know, watching her or whatnot. And so, she said, "Why did you have to get attorneys out here?" I said, "Because

I've been asking you and I'm not getting a response." I said, "And they are attorneys for him. They help him . . . and me . . . get the response."

Although Ana shared the social identities of school personnel and was therefore not subjected to any of the negative culturally based assumptions, she also experienced ongoing tensions with the school and a dismissal of her own concerns. Although, like Rhonda and Patty, she was aware of the power differentials between herself and school personnel, she was also well-versed in the procedural and implicit rules for advocacy.

Ana: "If you don't put that in writing . . . "

Because her son has high cognitive ability, Ana sometimes experiences tensions with the school when they do not address the socioemotional and behavioral aspects of his autism. In spite of her numerous requests for more specialized support, the school has persisted in placing her son in a general education kindergarten setting, ignoring her verbal requests and discussions with school personnel. Ana explains her frustrations with the school as they continue to presume to know what is best for her child, prioritizing his academic abilities over his social needs. Drawing on her personal experience with school dynamics and the input of her sister, who is an exceptional special education teacher, Ana explains the importance of being explicit with the school about her concerns and goals for her son, while documenting these on the IEP. Although she describes this as more procedural than collaborative, she recognizes these established protocols as the only means of getting her requests honored:

> And I had to explain all this, and I had to go over every detail as far as even, like I said, drop-off and pick-up. You know, if you don't put that in writing on this legal document then they won't abide by it, and frankly . . . I've been a teacher, my sister's a teacher, I really have my . . . hesitation with IEPs you know.

PARENT ADVOCACY: THE LAW AS THE OBSTACLE

While the legalistic framing of the law may present more intense challenges for parents who do not normally participate in mainstream discourse styles, this framing has been noted as an obstacle to most parents ever since the early days of the EHA. For example, in less than 2 decades after the law's enactment, a review of literature by Lindle (1992) presented "a dismal picture" (p. 9) of professional approaches that tended to address the "letter" rather than the "spirit" of the law. In addition, while studies indicated that IEPs were being written "to fulfill the law rather than plan instructional activities" (p. 9), numerous articles and pamphlets for parents included condescending attitudes toward parents, such as advice on how to dress for meetings and how to use professional-sounding language (such as words like "generalization").

Unfortunately, literature since that time indicates that a procedural approach has become the norm. Ong-Dean's (2009) study of parent involvement is very instructive in understanding how this works. Describing the parents' role as "individualized in form and technical in content" (p. 39), he argues that this type of interaction intimidates and limits the participation of parents with low incomes and limited formal education. Thus, he says, "parents who are more privileged are better able to advocate successfully for their children" (p. 39). Citing Lareau's (2003) well-known argument that social and cultural capital account for most of the difference in parents' participation in their children's education, Ong-Dean concludes:

> What distinguishes privileged parents, then, is not their desire to see their children succeed, but their belief that they can and should help them succeed in school, and their possessing the economic and cultural resources to do so. In short, parents' social class does affect their ability to advocate for their children. (p. 41)

Ong-Dean takes this argument further, describing a combination of economic capital with what he calls "elite cultural capital." This form of capital, he argues, provides some parents with knowledge and skills by which they are able present their case not only with technical evidence but also in a carefully reasoned manner that signifies that they are "sensitive to the institutional requirements for objectivity" (p. 119). By this means, such parents can "persuade the presiding hearing officer that their claims conform to demanding legal and technical standards" (p. 116). In other words, the most successful parent advocates are able to present themselves like professionals on the subject of their child's condition and needs. While most parents are indeed the experts on their children, this style of interaction around the intensely personal matter of parenthood is a tall order for most parents!

A qualitative study by Zeitlen and Curcic (2013) with 20 parents offered powerful examples of the debilitating effects of the IEP's procedural focus. The interviews highlighted parents' sense of depersonalization and their feeling of being unrecognized in a process that caused them "emotional angst surrounding feelings of being judged and not being able to live up to the expectations of the school" (p. 6). One parent captured the deficit focus of the process, stating that "the hardest thing about the meeting is getting your nose rubbed in your child's shortcomings" (p. 6). The process of these meetings was perceived by parents as "ritualistic" and "mechanical" (p. 9) and the IEP document itself as a meaningless legalistic document meant for lawyers rather than parents.

While the foregoing research reveals the angst felt by typical parents, Ong-Dean's (2009) discussion of parents at the elite end of the spectrum demonstrated how the possession of cultural capital has the potential for creating or furthering schisms within the field of parent advocacy. Borrowing a term from Bourdieu (1986), Ong-Dean (2009) argued that both professionals and parents are likely to "misrecognize" the skills of those with "elite cultural capital" as indicators of "superior parental values as parents" (p. 118) and to "misrecognize" the relatively ineffective advocacy of less privileged parents as lack of involvement or commitment. This attitude was seen in the fact that privileged parents in Ong-Dean's survey interpreted their own advocacy as a sign of their superior commitment to their children rather than as a reflection of the cultural and possibly economic capital that provided them with the opportunity to exercise such advocacy.

The observation of social-class schisms within the broad field of parent advocacy appears as a continuing theme in the history of parent advocacy. While the technical approach of regular IEP meetings can be intimidating to many parents, the process of formally challenging school personnel's decisions takes this form of advocacy to another level. Indeed, parents with "elite capital" are the ones most likely to be able to pursue a claim for services beyond the regular IEP process to the level of requesting a hearing. Ong-Dean points out that such parents educate themselves not only on their and their children's rights under the law but also on the technicalities of potential diagnoses for their children's conditions. Ong-Dean's survey in California of special education hearing requests, a level of parental challenge to a school district that requires considerable know-how, revealed that wealthy White districts had the largest percentage and the highest rate of requests for hearings, while poor minority districts made such requests at roughly one-fourth of that rate.

Perhaps the most chilling example of the social-class divide comes in Ong-Dean's presentation of figures on the rate of special education hearings in the Los Angeles Unified School District (LAUSD) in the years following the initiation of remedies for the Chandra Smith lawsuit (1993). This class-action suit, brought against the district by the mother of an African American student, represented all 65,000 students receiving special education services in the district, which Ong-Dean described as being "on the cusp of being a poor minority district" (p. 124). Initial concerns identified by the court included limited translations of IEPs for non-English-speaking students, delayed and inappropriate evaluations and placement, unduly segregated special education placements, and unacceptably high rates of suspension and African American disproportionality. Despite the district's overall low income level, the rate of special education hearing requests was surprisingly high. Ong-Dean explains that this pattern reflected affluent families' objections to the court's efforts to mandate greater inclusion and to reduce the rate of private placements being accessed mainly by privileged families.

In the previous examples, we see the continuing influence of historical racial and social class divisions. We argue that, on a more subtle level, the very epistemology underlying special education is, in itself, an obstacle to equitable parent participation in advocacy under special education law.

Epistemology and the Law: A Hegemonic Alliance

In describing the concept of "elite cultural capital" outlined by Ong-Dean (2009), we commented that the objectified, seemingly neutral style acquired by the most effective advocates would be a tall order for most parents. We ask why the very personal process of parent advocacy should be represented in such a depersonalized manner. To answer this question, we note that the thinking underlying this framing of parent participation in special education derives directly from two key principles of current Western societies—individual rights and a belief in the scientific method as the superior mode of acquiring knowledge.

Individualism and individual rights. The principle of individual rights is a cornerstone of special education law. On this principle is built the requirement for individualized planning and treatment of children with disabilities. Elaborating this point, Kalyanpur and Harry (2012), in an analysis of the cultural underpinnings of special education, linked the procedural approach of the law to underlying legal values of individualism, choice, and equity, and to the epistemological values embodied in science. Based on these perspectives, two paradoxes emerge. In terms of legal principles, parent participation is cast as an individual endeavor to be enacted by individual choice by which the parent can seek what they perceive as the most equitable services for their child. This does not mean that all parents will get what they ask for, since the pursuit of equity must include consideration of what is available to all children through the school's resources. Moreover, as policy analyst Diane Ravitch (2010) observed, there is a tension between equity and choice, by which increased options for choice result in a decrease in equity, as in the case of charter schools, for example. However, the individualized nature of the parent participation process also means that no public comparisons are made of the granting of resources, setting the stage for private negotiations whose outcomes depend both on parental personal and financial resources and school district's resources and policies. The creation of due process procedures, in itself, also sets the stage for potentially adversarial positioning of parents and school personnel.

A positivistic epistemology. The second paradox emerges from the epistemology underlying the construction of special education. By espousing science as the basis for its knowledge, the field relies on two main models— the medical model of pathology and the statistical model derived from psychology's model of the bell curve. In his analysis of the paradigms of modern social scientific thought, Skrtic (1991, 1995) envisioned the range of thinking as falling into four quadrants based on contrasting perspectives of objective versus subjective and microscopic versus macroscopic. Placing special education epistemology in the micro-objective corner of the quadrant, where the dominant mode of analysis is based on functionalism, Skrtic (1991) described the field as falling in "the most extreme objectivist region of the functionalist paradigm" (p. 106). This perspective, he argued, "takes a more or less microscopic view of social reality and studies its subject matter from an objectivist point of view" (Skrtic, 1995, p. 31).

Kalyanpur and Harry (2012) argued that, with disability viewed as a physical phenomenon reflecting pathology and falling outside the bounds of normalcy, proof of "disability" relies on presumably objective measurement of differences. Intelligence, however, is an abstract concept whose measurement is only approximated by scores on culturally derived tests of skills and knowledge. Even more important is the fact that decisions about how far from the norm one should fall in order to be designated "disabled" varies not only from culture to culture but also within cultures. One only has to recall the American Association on Mental Deficiency's change in IQ cut-off scores for mental retardation in 1969, from a score of 85 to 70, to understand that this disability can be "cured" simply by a stroke of the pen! The belief in "objective" measurement of human functioning, however, negates the obvious social construction aspect of disability definitions and, instead, promotes a reified view of disability as a "thing" possessed by an individual.

Seeking to establish its credibility through an alliance with science, traditional special education assessments largely exclude holistic, interpretive understandings of children's abilities, which are exactly the kind of everyday knowledge typically held by parents. A far cry from the heartfelt testimonies of distress and confusion in the parent narratives of the post–World War II period, parents' advocacy must now reflect a level of technical comprehension, even expertise, to navigate the legal pathways of the system within which their children receive services.

Technical language. The skills needed for this type of advocacy include the use of technical language that seeks to mirror the idea of objectivity. Kalyanpur and Harry (2012) analyzed this objectifying process as reflecting a belief in expert knowledge as categorical and objective. The language of objectivity, they argued, includes a "value-neutral or euphemizing" process (p. 61), which works by presenting an abstract version of a thing or activity or a medicalized version of a daily process, for example, abstracting the essence of toys—things children play with—and referring to them as "manipulatives"; making the action of serving a family sound more systematic, even mechanistic, by saying "service" rather than "serve"; medicalizing everyday concepts by saying "auditory or visual processing" rather than "interpreting/understanding what you heard or saw." Thus, as we observed earlier, effective parent advocates will need to present themselves as almost as neutral as this language (Ong-Dean, 2009). Indeed, Harry and colleagues (1995) reported the paternalistic approach to a mother who, upon becoming emotional in her request for a change of services, was quickly escorted out of the room by a team member, in order to give her time to recover her composure.

The meaningless IEP paperwork. It is disheartening to note in many of the studies cited previously that Harry's (1992) findings with Puerto Rican mothers are still dominant, showing how the use of technical language limits parent–professional relationships because of "written materials and technical language being substituted for meaningful communication with parents" (p. 490). Indeed, parents' frustration on this issue has continued to be a common theme in this research (Fitzgerald & Watkins, 2006; Lian & Fontánez-Phelan, 2001), leaving parents to advocate only if they can navigate the educational process through "individualized, technical disputes" with professionals (Ong-Dean, 2009, p. 10). This exclusivity continues to be doubly excluding with families whose cultural belief systems require deference rather than equity with professionals (Kalyanpur & Harry, 2012; Ong-Dean, 2009; Stanley, 2015).

In our study, parents expressed much frustration with the reliance on paperwork in place of genuine participation and compliance, as the following vignette of Rhonda's experience illustrates.

Rhonda's Journey/Amira's Journey: From Diagnosis to Transition

---

Diagnosis: "People didn't act like they cared."

From Amira's birth, Rhonda noticed that something was different about her daughter's development. Referencing her eldest daughters' growth, she noted Amira's delays in walking and speaking. She brought this to the attention of the providers. Yet they dismissed her concerns, telling her to wait to see what would happen, which she interpreted as a lack of concern:

And then, I started to ask questions, but nobody seemed to—people didn't act like they cared, for lack of a better word.

Amira's school experiences with personnel also mirrored the same dismissiveness as in the early years. Rhonda describes how the administrators implied that she did not accept her own child's level of functioning, because Rhonda had questioned the appropriateness of a full-day self-contained placement for Amira:

> Look, mom, now. She's 8th grade, she's going into high school, nothing's gonna change. You have to start accepting that this is what's going on with your child. And know that some of these services are not gonna be in place.

IEP process: "Noncompliant compliance"

Rhonda describes the nuanced ways in which the personnel excluded her from the IEP process by not providing her with the documentation of her goals. Rhonda was especially interested in seeing whether they had documented her requests for vision support through large-print material or whether this was simply face talk. She notes how the documentation would arrive well after the school year had ended:

> Sometimes the people wouldn't even be in the meetings so they wouldn't have their signatures, so they would tell me, "Oh, you'll get your copy by the end of the day, we'll send it home with your daughter." There were times we'd get it—school was in—the IEP was in March, April, May—we would get it . . . in the mail, maybe June, July.

Fidelity: "I want to see what's on there."

Even when receiving the copy of the IEP in the mail, Rhonda noticed that the forms were not signed. Recognizing the importance of this document and its legal status, she immediately went to the school's office at the very beginning of the school year to ask the special education coordinator for the official copy.

> And she gave me my, what they call, I guess my IEP, without the signatures. I left several messages, 'cause I have a card like this [holding up a business card] for her, asking, "Where's the signed copy?" 'Cause I want to see—did they actually put—'Cause that's like a rough draft. I want to see what's on there.

"Invisible but Tangible Norms" and the Torturing of Compliance

Beyond epistemology, the legal construction of parents' advocacy under the IDEA has had worrying implications for school policies as well as for parents' practices. The heart of the problem lies in the heavy focus on structured procedures with which school personnel feel they must comply in order to demonstrate that they are functioning within the law. However, as evidenced in several studies of parent participation under the law, the reliance on procedures does not in any way ensure equity. Rather, as Connor and Cavendish (2018) explain, the pressure for compliance and the "invisible but nevertheless tangible norms that are invoked by professionals within IEP meetings" result in a "production-line quality" that alienates rather than engages parents (p. 82). As stated by Skrtic and Knackstedt (2018), equity is further undermined by the fact that, "although IDEA's procedural safeguard provisions atomize advocacy, the degree to which parents are reduced to passive cases in the special education process depends on their economic and cultural capital" (p. 161). This pattern is undergirded by the "colorblind" framing of the regulations for parent participation, which do not acknowledge the power differentials between professionals and parents.

Certainly, research indicates that the power imbalance is normally in the direction of the school. However, a fascinating study by Voulgarides (2018), published in full book form, presents a stark portrait of the way the law can be distorted to tip the balance in either direction. First, the study reveals extremes of variable implementation of the requirements for parent participation in three school districts within the same state and the role of parents' cultural and economic capital in these processes. Second, the study shows how this differential implementation was accomplished in all three districts through a mechanistic framing of procedural compliance in order to avoid being cited for inappropriate disproportionality.

The three school districts in this year-long study were noticeably different in racial and socioeconomic demographics, the latter indicated by free and reduced lunch (FRL): White students comprised 7%, 65%, and 85% of the student populations in the three districts, with Black and Hispanic students making up the balance in varying percentages across the three districts. As expected, in the district that was predominantly White, only 15% of students received FRL, as compared with 33% in the more mixed district and 65% in the predominantly minority district. Another important feature was the rates of citation for disproportionality, with the White district having been cited for disproportionality in special education placements between 2004 and 2011 but not in the year of the research, and the other two schools having been cited for disproportionality in suspensions in both time periods.

The districts' practices regarding parent participation were shockingly different, ranging from total accountability to parents in the wealthy White district, to a rigid compliance-based approach in the midrange district, to a disorganized process in the low-income predominantly minority district, where "educators had little to no accountability to families and to the broader community" (p. 77). Specifically, in the high-income district, parents' high rate of demand for special education and other resources and services were fully supported by school personnel, who, in "time-consuming and labor-intensive" meetings, "would accommodate almost anything imaginable" (p. 71). The low-income predominantly minority district illustrated the opposite extreme, where parents were seen "through a deficit lens." Here, the researcher documented an IEP meeting to which the student came alone and asked if his mother should be present. The boy's mother was then easily reached by phone and expressed surprise that the meeting was being held because she had not received notice of it.

In the midrange district, the approach was to preplan meetings as tightly as possible in order to control the delivery of educational resources. This approach served to severely limit parent input and placed "technical language and bureaucratic compliance with IDEA at the forefront of district interactions with families" (p. 74). The researcher's description of a meeting for a manifestation determination regarding repeated suspensions of a 17-year-old Black girl illuminated the preset plan of the telephone conference with the parent, which was explained in the following way: "It's good for our budget to predetermine the outcome before a meeting starts," and "I always tell chairs hold the line, strip services, shave down IEPs, and don't send kids to alternative settings" (pp. 75–76). The researcher's concluding comments on this case pointed to the way this focus on stripped-down compliance undermined the intent of a law that was designed to serve students in an individualized manner:

> No one asked why Cindy's infractions were so predictable. And no one questioned what her relationships were like with adults in the district. . . . Lastly, in controlling a meeting's outcome, the administrative team inadvertently ensured that colorblind and context-neutral norms shaped the tone and tenor of special education meetings. . . . This approach does not sufficiently account for the shifting demographic context of [these] schools and the growing racial and class tensions that were present in the district. The technical approach also erased the humanity behind the regulations. (p. 77)

All three patterns presented distortions of the law. While parents in the wealthy White district were able to "hoard resources" in ways that ensured attainment of their goals, their advocacy was successful for their own children but was not equitable in the larger picture of available resources. In the low-income district the absence of a coherent policy left the door open to gross neglect of the law. In the midrange district, the microscopic focus on procedural compliance with the letter of the law made a mockery of its intent.

Another way in which the law became a two-edged sword in these school districts was evident in the midrange district where the administration's advice to keep students out of alternative settings reflected an effort to avoid being cited for exclusionary practices. In fact, the need to avoid being cited for disproportionality drove much of the practice in this district. Sadly, and ironically, both the district administrator and school personnel were aware of the inadequacy of their practices. The administrator acknowledged that he believed that "the root of the problems in [the district] and a contributor to disproportionality, were the 'deep-seated tensions' in the community surrounding issues of race and class," yet the bulk of his workflow "was focused on ensuring that compliance was met at any cost" (p. 90). Similarly, school personnel involved in the case of Cindy indicated that they were concerned about the student's difficulties and faulted the district's limited provision of more staff to provide supportive services. In the face of "budget issues," school personnel felt "stuck in a cycle" (p. 76) that constrained them to rely on ineffective functional behavioral assessments (FBAs) and behavior implementation plans (BIPs). This concern further illustrates the mechanistic implementation of the letter of the law: FBAs, which are mandated by the law, and BIPs should actually be effective tools when used in a manner that includes responsiveness to the full contexts of students' motivations and needs (Skiba, Ormiston, Martinez, & Cummings, 2016).

Parents in our study described perspectives very similar to that of Voulgarides's regarding professionals' limited attempts to understand the motivations and underlying needs experienced by students such as Cindy. For example, Patty expressed her concern with the mechanistic approach to assessment of her child and the need for a more holistic model of evaluation.

Patty: "Other people are able to speak about them."

Patty describes her concerns about how professionals focus on other aspects of children with special needs, such as their intelligence or behavioral functioning, yet may dismiss their psychological or emotional needs and feelings. She interprets this as the attitude of some professionals who may assume that these children do not have feelings:

> Psychologically they don't get evaluated, um, for their emotions. They think, "Okay, that's nonsense" or they're—you know—they don't feel or who knows what they think. And there is a component that I've noticed, to the special needs emotions that are not being—nobody's aware of them.

Patty adds that this should be a part of assessing children because of their possible experiences with trauma. She furthers the point that any child may have been exposed to trauma. Yet the situation is even more profound for children with special needs, who are unable to express themselves:

I don't know. Like the emotional part of you thinking—what could it have done? You know, um, and they test for autism and they test for this, but they don't do like an emotional IQ or whatever it's called. 'Cause there's triggers . . . traumas that every child—you know—other people are able to speak about them.

Voulgarides's study shouts the questions, How do these distortions of the law affect parent advocacy? Does the splintering of advocacy by social class and cultural/economic capital matter? What needs to be done to create equitable and meaningful implementation of the law's intent to include parents in decisionmaking? How could this be done differently?

So, What Is Parent Advocacy Under the Law, and Who Qualify as "Advocates"?

Parents' identities, communities, first language, formal knowledge, and participation in systems and goals for their children with disabilities may not stand out against the backdrop of preset expectations and the bureaucratic process through which one is expected to advocate. Often, these parents, though highly aware of how the system works, are disqualified as advocates. Our participant, Marie, is one such example of a working Black mother who is aware of what assigning labels can provide and what removing them can take away. She fought for her son to maintain his speech-language support. She described invoking the support of a teacher at the school, who knows her, knows her son, and provides her with advice in order to appropriately meet the needs of her son.

Marie: "You can still have your own specialty."

Marie is a Haitian mother of a child who has the LD/SLI label. She is a hardworking single mother of two children. This mother recognized that something was perhaps "not right" with her son very early on. While pregnant with her eldest son, she was working security in a building where she would greet a Jewish mother who was pregnant at the same time. After their children were born and reached the toddler phase, she noticed how different this child's interaction with her family was from her own. She describes how the child would ask questions, expressing a natural curiosity about the things around her. She recognized how this woman's daughter would identify and name things, like "Look Mom, a baby!" Yet from her own son, only a few sounds.

She expressed these concerns to the pediatrician, but it took several attempts for them to respond. Finally she received the phone call from a family disability support agency. By this time, her child was about 33 months in age, with only 3 months before the eligibility for early intervention services would end. Though they were able to set up home visits, where they would come in to provide services and give the mother some support, they advised her to let him rest and wait until the school year began before enrolling him. They provided her with some strategies at home and told her to "spend as much time with him as possible" in order to provide lots of language input.

Following this advice, she did everything she could at home with what she felt would prepare him for school. This child had been doing very well academically. She said she has kept up the high language input, having conversations about things that interest him. He knows his multiplication tables and has a strong interest in mathematics. When the IEP goals were being written, the only area that the school would provide him with was reading support. However, he has been reading, at the advice of his mother, for several years. She described recently giving him books from the Harry Potter series to read, which she says stimulates his imagination and interest.

Her son has been recently identified as gifted, as the result of a psychoeducational evaluation. During the IEP meeting, the team decided to remove the IEP, which provided supports for his speech and other learning challenges. His former teacher, supporting the concerns expressed by the parent over the removal of his IEP, advised her to go back into the school and request a new IEP meeting. She did just this and the plan to reconvene for an IEP meeting is on the agenda. Marie acknowledges and values her child's difference:

> Me and the teacher have been working with him for 2 years already. So she knows . . . and I was gonna be like, "We still want this for him. And you can still continue with your gifted." Because someone could be . . . look at Einstein. So you could be . . . have your own specialty. But you still have your [needs].

One point to mention here is the hands-on nurturing of her child's learning, communication, and gifts. This sits in contradiction to the number of assumptions that educators make about working-class parents and about Black parents. Though she implemented some of the strategies provided by the support agencies, Marie noted that it was home learning and the support she received from her son's former teacher that helped him to achieve his goals.

We close our review with a brief consideration of an overarching question facing researchers and professionals: What constitutes parent advocacy, and how can it be facilitated? The literature includes contrasting views of the specific actions that constitute parent advocacy. One body of research reveals a greater focus on formalized advocacy, marked by structural and systemic frameworks (Balcazar, Keys, Bertram, & Rizzo, 1996; Burke et al., 2018; Burke, Goldman, Hart, & Hodapp, 2016; Trainor, 2010). Other studies have reported a broader range of advocacy activities, including both intuitive and prescribed knowledge, formal and informal strategies, and efforts that may or may not be recognized by professionals (Alper, Schloss, & Schloss, 1995; Auerbach, 2007; Groce, 1999; Trainor, 2010). For example, for Wilson (2015) the question-asking among African American mothers of children with autism during IEP meetings is an expression of their advocacy. Similarly, Stanley (2015), in a study of 12 mothers residing in one of the most economically distressed counties in a Southern state, identified a range of advocacy activities, including individual efforts, that parents felt they did intuitively on the basis of their knowledge of their child's skills and needs. These activities included the following: collective efforts, in which mothers got together to attend and address school board meetings; locating and accessing community resources such as private tutoring and recreation programs; and communicating with school administrators by asking questions, making specific requests, disagreeing with the teachers' recommendations, "standing up for the child," "being present" by attending meetings, stopping by at lunchtime, and doing "impromptu visits" to the school (p. 7). Despite all these efforts, the research also revealed barriers to their efficacy, including deference to professionals' perceived expertise, feeling that their concerns were not heard or validated by school personnel, and work and time constraints. Overall, the researcher concluded that the fact of living in a rural area constrained the amount of services available to children and contributed to mothers' fear of retribution to their children if they complained too much.

In summary, we cite Alper, Schloss, and Schloss (1995), who, in addition to describing a wide range of parent advocate typologies, stated the following:

> We have emphasized the range of advocates and advocacy goals to correct the often-mistaken notion that advocacy is synonymous with professional support during a formal hearing. Based on our conceptualization, advocacy occurs any time people speak or act on behalf of themselves or others. (1995, p. 264)

What can be concluded from this range of typologies is that how advocates and advocacy are described may depend greatly upon how their actions and methods are perceived and valued, which may influence the recognition of parent advocacy across populations by practitioners, institutions, and other stakeholders.

We close this chapter with Rhonda's heartfelt answer to the question of how she would describe her advocacy. Rhonda speaks for all the parents in the study, indeed, for all the parents we have known, including ourselves, as we ponder the question of what it means to be an advocate.

"I owe it to my daughter."

Kids are first. And to have a kid with special needs . . . I . . . I don't feel like I've missed out. 'Cause I chose to have her. We all have choices. You know, so. Those people that don't raise their children, I don't know what to tell them. I guess, you know, somebody'll have to step in and do what they do, the system or whatever. But I just feel like I owe it to my daughter to make sure that she's best—whatever her best is.

"I'm her voice, I'm her ears."

If I had known that word—advocacy—I would answer it truthfully if I say yes, because that's a popular word. But if I had to choose my word, I would say a voice. I'm her eyes, her ears, her voice. And I'm getting emotional because. It's just been . . . an uphill battle. And . . . it's not over. And sometimes I say . . . if not me, then who? You know . . . so . . . advocacy. Long-term, yes. But I'm her voice, I'm her ears."

CHAPTER 8

Reframing Advocacy, Repositioning the Advocate

In this chapter we return to our initial questions in studying parent advocacy for children with special needs. First is the question of the valuing of personhood as understood through a long history of disenfranchisement reinforced by deficit-framed language and attitudes in professional, educational, and community contexts. Second is the process by which parents seek services and supports for their children, a process that, it would appear, was not intended for all to navigate, privileging access and power to those who may already have it. We have peered through the lens of several disciplines, including sociology, education, bioethics, health care, psychology, philosophy, and law, as well as through several subdisciplines such as special education, multicultural education, critical studies, and disability studies. We call for particular attention to identity and community contextual intersections, for it is evident that we undermine the good intent of advocacy when we unintentionally assign privileges to the already privileged and further marginalize the already marginalized. We present the words of our participant Rhonda, a Black mother of a teenager with special needs, who eloquently describes her experiences of community exclusion even among other parents of teenagers with special needs:

> 'Cause people tend to . . . you know, judge a book by its cover. If you don't look a certain way or talk a certain way, then, you know, you don't fit into our *scheme* of things, or whatever. . . . People like to form cliques. But I like to welcome everybody; we're all the same, we're all parents. We all have in common; we want something for our children. So, I don't really see color, gender, none of that. We are who we are, let's advocate for our kids and have a good time. But even that now, with some new people coming in, they want to form—based on status, you know what I'm saying? Don't look down on her! Just because—so, so what? And it's a shame because it does exist.

ADVOCACY THROUGH A DISCRIT LENS

Only three generations ago, initiatives and programs began to emerge across the United States that would redefine the status of parents of children with disabilities. These were reflected in policy, the delivery of services, and efforts to increase communication. The shift in paradigm, driven by parents and other stakeholders with a personal interest in improving the lives of those with disabilities, initiated the gradual process of recasting parents as partners with professionals across systems. Responsive to the needs and concerns of families, national and state policymakers began to look toward developing leadership among parents, realizing that they are knowledgeable, experienced, and the best means of support and education for other parents. Through such programs, parents were perceived as the best advocates for the needs of their children with disabilities, for their own needs, for the needs of other parents of children with disabilities, and as representatives of the disability groups and communities they represented.

More recent programs have looked at increasing capacity and social capital of parents through the parent-training model, which seems to demonstrate success. These are federally or regionally funded programs that aim to address the needs of family and individual constituents, preparing them for individual, systemic, and policy-level advocacy. Several local initiatives, inspired by the success of these strategies, have developed programs that seek to increase the empowerment and leadership among parents and self-advocates in order to address the needs of the local communities. While these have been successful in their own right, they are often responding to identified needs at a macro level rather than responding to the local-level concerns of communities with complex situations and identities.

However, there are clusters of national and local family disability-support organizations that have incorporated into their mission the specific needs and concerns of families and communities at the intersections, such as the aforementioned National Black Deaf Association (NBDA) and Sinergia in New York City. Organizations such as these are dedicated to providing support for families who are facing those aspects of identity that coexist with the disability and make them more vulnerable, for example through racial discrimination, language barriers, and the challenges of living in urban centers. Furthermore, such organizations develop leadership among representatives from these communities and identities, by purposely including on their boards a wide representation of racial, ethnic, cultural, linguistic, socioeconomic, and gender identities.

With the exception of these pockets of diversity, the trouble with well-intended programs that seek to empower and support families of children with disabilities is that they are still operating under the assumption that universality means equity. Therefore, we will now explore the challenges of parent advocacy models through the seven tenets of DisCrit.

The Interdependence of Racism and Ableism

Challenging the traditional view that racism and ableism are discrete forces, DisCrit explores the ways in which these social constructs operate together, interdependently. Unlike the past, where discrimination was explicit and legalized, the more subtle, implicit forms of racism that have replaced it are perhaps more insidious, though sometimes unintentional (Bonilla-Silva, 2006; Delgado & Stefancic, 2017). Scholarship has described the exposure of minority families to microaggressions, as described by Davis (1989), the "stunning, automatic acts of disregard that stem from unconscious attitudes of White superiority and constitute a verification of Black inferiority" (p. 1576, as cited in Fenton, Ocasio-Stoutenburg, & Harry, 2017). In addition, literature has revealed a historical construction of "elite" and powerful disability categories that operate in the same discriminatory ways, to overtly exclude or unintentionally mute the voices and concerns of other families (Ong-Dean, 2009). Furthermore, although the intent is not malicious, continuing to look at the disability experience through colorblind and color-, disability-, and context-neutral lenses, as if racism, ableism, colorism, sexism, and elitism are not operational throughout society, limits the kind of self-reflection that is needed to transform thinking (Bonilla-Silva, 2006; Fenton, Ocasio-Stoutenburg, & Harry, 2017).

The Multidimensionality of Identities

Identity can be both perceived and constructed in various ways. We look at constructed racial identities, for example, Black, Hispanic, or White, as if they are discrete categories and the definition is applicable across contexts. However, the urban, geographical region in which our study takes place and how our participants self-identify exemplifies how wide the variation of cultures is across and within these constructed categories. While Ana, for example, self-identifies as White Hispanic (a common identity marker in this region), she notes how she has certain advantages that other families may not:

> There are a million parents out there, I'm sure like that, and my heart breaks because you know, where we live, there's a lot of cultures here. There's people who English is not their main language and I, I just don't know how they navigate the system. It's confusing for me, and I'd like to think that I'm, you know, pretty sharp and I ask questions, and I, I, I know how to do research, and I know how to find phone numbers and make calls, and there's people who don't know how to do that and it's still confusing for me. So, I know that there's so many kids out there not getting the help that they need because it's hard to navigate.

Recognizing the Real-Life Implications of Socially Constructed Identities

Beyond the "identity" is the implication of such an identity. As noted by Bonilla-Silva (2006), despite the socially constructed nature of the categories of race and disability, these carry true social implications that manifest in the experiences of families, especially at the intersections. This was especially evident for our mixed-race family, Sonia and Zoe, the "perfectly good White woman" and the "angry Black woman," whose identities translate into how they are perceived by others and affect the services their daughter would receive. Here is testimony from Zoe about her experience in the waiting room for her daughter's therapy:

> I think that they looked at me—and it wasn't any different from the way that they looked at anyone else because they were all minorities there in the waiting room. That the expectations, my expectations would be low. That I would just accept whatever they were giving . . . and not that the personnel there weren't minorities either because they were! But you expect me to just give my child over like, "I need a break from her, girl, take her!" No. Honey, I'm sorry. I need to be in there with her to see, to make sure I know what you're doing. She's here to get certain services but I want to know what the services are.

Privileging the Voices of the Marginalized

Harry and Ocasio-Stoutenburg (2018) described the collection of research studies on parent and professional relationships that envision "a collaboration between parents and professionals that has gone beyond a professional-superior/parent-inferior dichotomy to one that involves a customized and holistic approach" (pp. 246–247). However, this model can be challenging to realize. For example, in our small study, we have so far succeeded in recruiting a group of parents who vary widely in race, culture, language, sexual orientation, and marriage status, but socioeconomic status remains more challenging. Of our nine parents, we would identify only one as being of working-class status, which we attribute both to the more extreme time and family demands experienced by families with more limited resources and to the historical lack of trust occasioned by families' knowledge of evident power differentials. After all, we are not only "university types" but also strangers to the families. Despite our intention to meet the parents in their homes or wherever they prefer, we found that the distribution of an attractive flyer had less success with these families. The approach that facilitated our access to Marie's family was seeking an introduction to the family from a Haitian American service provider with whom she had a good relationship. In completing our study we believe that following this lesson will yield a more equitable range of participants.

The Legal and Historical Aspects of Race and Disability Constructions

In addition to acknowledging the elitist ideologies that constrain understanding the complex nature of families' needs, any attempt to provide a cultural framework for parent advocacy requires knowledge of the historical trajectory of parents' roles within the context of a racially and economically stratified society. Based on the tenets of DisCrit, which provide a framework for exploring this phenomenon, a complete history would include (a) the historical removal of power and rights from the parents of children with disabilities and (b) the historical removal of power and rights from the parents of children who belong to racial and ethnic minorities and who are poor, and (c) because of the power of race over class, the historical removal of power and rights from parents of children with disabilities who belong to racial and ethnic minority groups, regardless of their socioeconomic status. Sauer and Lalvani (2017) described the intentionality in addressing the needs of culturally and linguistically diverse families in their reconstruction of advocacy to empower families of children with disabilities. The authors proposed a model that begins with sharing disability history through a disability studies perspective that specifically incorporates the injustices experienced by families of other marginalized identities.

The Role of Whiteness and Ability as a Property Right

What is often left out of the dialogue on parent advocacy is that the issues of the minority matter just as much as the issues of the majority. The literature supports how failure to explicitly reach out to the former may further constrain many families' advocacy efforts in fighting against disparities in services and outcomes. While it is tempting to feel relief that many of the battles for equity have been won with the passage of key legislation such as the Americans with Disabilities Act (ADA) or the Individuals with Disabilities Education Act (IDEA), the fact is that the fruits of success are not equitably distributed, particularly for groups that have historically experienced discrimination, stigma, and marginalization. Artiles (2011) illuminates this issue by adding that, in spite of the "shared histories of struggle for equity" (p. 431) between racial and ethnic minority families of children with disabilities and their White, middle-class counterparts, the very gains experienced by the disability community may have had the unintended consequence of contributing to the disparities experienced by racial and ethnic minority families. Many African American parents, for example, found that the educational outcomes were still inequitable after so much hope and promise had gone into the passage of IDEA (Blanchett, Mumford, & Beachum, 2005). In addition, literature has supported a historical construction of "elite" and powerful disability categories that operate in the same discriminatory ways, to the overt exclusion or unintentional muting of the voices and concerns of other families. Following this tenet of DisCrit, we contend that parent advocacy, therefore, has been demonstrated to be a *property right*; the coded wording of "social and cultural capital" in this context means an exclusive right for White, middle-class families with more socially acceptable, less stigmatized disabilities. This appeared to be the case in the experience of Rhonda, whose daughter was excluded from this diagnosis, even though, as she said, "the big name was always autism."

Activism and Resistance in Co-Constructed Efforts Among Stakeholders

Throughout the contexts in which families and children are situated, teachers, other school personnel, health care providers, community members, therapists, family members, and even other parents of children with disabilities may serve as agents of both equity and inequity in co-constructive efforts. They are agents of inequity when they fail to do the following: (a) consider each individual and family in a socioecological context; (b) emphasize the many identity intersections that challenge the "one-size-fits-all" philosophy; (c) explore the circumstances that contribute to the fluidity, complexity, and dynamic nature of each family system; and (d) engage with families from diverse cultural, contextual, social, and linguistic backgrounds in a way that is beyond courteous, but meaningful and respectful.

These stakeholders become agents of equity when they do the following: (a) implement a culturally reciprocal method of addressing the needs and concerns of families through their perspective (Kalyanpur & Harry, 2012), (b) consider the experiences among multiply marginalized groups, (c) help to alleviate the additional burdens that proposed universal and prescriptive remedies placed upon them, and (d) design and rethink new ways of co-constructing advocacy though a grassroots, child- , family- , and community-centered perspective.

In a review of studies utilizing DisCrit, the originators of the concept (Annamma, Ferri, & Connor, 2018) called for the development of more "expansive" interpretations of activism. Specifically, they highlighted the notion of "intellectual activism," by which scholars "situated multiply marginalized students of color, their families and their communities as knowledge generators" and "reexamined normative discourse, policies and practices" (p. 62). An effort in co-construction, therefore, is to support parents in their understanding of and resistance to decisions, processes, placements, and interactions that disempower them and their children. Consistent with the "speaking out" and "standing up for a cause" definitions of advocacy, the resistance and activism are implied. However, considering the forces that empower some parents as agents of change for their own lives while restraining and dismissing others, particular attention needs to be given to supporting the resistance among families whose voices are so often muted in society.

REVISITING "DIFFERENCE"

As we present some of our findings, we re-present the framework of Minow (1990), who outlined the three main assumptions about the norms: (a) that having a disability means that a person is intrinsically different from the norm, (b) that the norm is often unstated yet is consistently seen as desirable, and (c) that objective observers' determinations of the meaning of "difference" represent truth, to the exclusion of the perspectives of others. The following summary of findings illustrates the meanings of these concepts, which may have critical implications for teachers, school personnel, medical practitioners, therapists, community members, and even for other families of children with and without disabilities. This collective list of stakeholders has been identified by our caregivers as having an impact, both positive and negative, on their advocacy efforts.

"Differing from the Norm"

One common theme that has been found throughout our review of the literature and within the voices of our study participants is that advocacy that addresses the issue of their child differing from a "norm" begins very early on, within the self and within the family. For our parents receiving an early diagnosis for their child, differing may have begun even while the child was still within the womb, with expectant and new-parent joys truncated by professionals' suspicions of disability and negative judgment of the value of our as-yet-unborn children.

Two of our families of children with Down syndrome demonstrated advocacy during the prenatal period by ignoring these statements and electing to "enjoy the rest of the pregnancy" despite anticipated problems. These caregivers describe how they wrestled with all of the information they had stored in their memories about experiences of children with disabilities in their families, communities, and trainings, which seemed to have been inundated with struggle. After the birth, these families were presented with grappling with their child's difference from "the norm," as compared to typically developing children as well as children with the same diagnosis. For the three families of young children with Down syndrome, for example, these were entirely different experiences. For Carlos and Betty, though an initial step involved recognizing the chasm between their own expectations for their child and his diagnosis, their newborn son's medical crisis helped them to put into perspective what really mattered to them, which was his life. Although their connections with supportive services, nurturing school placements, and caring professionals seemed to alleviate many of their concerns, they still expressed concern about their son's delays in speech. Betty describes how, although she hoped that the therapies would help, she would accept whatever outcome may be and not allow this to define his capabilities:

I know he's very advanced. But he's still not talking. Is he gonna be a nonverbal adult with Down syndrome? I don't know. He could be. But I don't think that whether he talks or not has anything to do with his potential or what he's capable of, you know?

For Zoe and Sonia, whose toddler Giselle has a rare type of Down syndrome that attenuated her eye development, there were multiple identity intersections that did and could prove challenging. First, although Sonia recognized in the hospital that Giselle had Down syndrome, this was rejected by the doctors, whose focus was on her vision. Sonia had fallen into depression, without support or advice on how to care for her visually impaired child, when she received the diagnosis of Down syndrome 2 weeks later. Connecting with a specialized school for children who are blind and visually impaired, witnessing other families, and receiving the nurturing support of the administrators and staff was comforting to Sonia and helped her family to accept her child's blindness. There came a recognition that Giselle was in fact different from the "norms" of typical children, from the "norms" of children with visual impairments, and from the "norms" of children with Down syndrome. Although her parents did not mention this, we also note that Giselle is a biracial child of a biracial same-sex couple, identity markers that could elicit further stigmatizing, depending on the contexts in which the family lives. In addition, her parents describe how their daughter's experience is also different from the rest of her sighted family. However, Zoe describes this as "Giselle's norm," explaining that, in spite of these differences, this is what Giselle knows:

It's what she has—it's her normal. It took us some adjusting, you know, to get used to, you know, how do we deal with it? How do we prepare her? But it's her normal. Darkness is all she knows. She doesn't know we see. She still doesn't. You know, but she goes about her days and nights and likes and dislikes just like anybody else.

Linda, whose 12-year-old son has a dual diagnosis of Down syndrome and autism, describes her relief that many of his former struggles with health and school placement issues have been resolved. However, she expresses ongoing concerns and tensions with providers who lack the perspective in recognizing behaviors that are part of his unique profile. She is disappointed to learn that the clinicians' final "offering" to support her concerns about his new vocalizations is to medicalize him, and she interprets this as an attempt to keep her son within the exclusive "norms" of what they recognize to be "part of Down syndrome" and "part of autism"—but not both. She expresses her worries that there isn't greater support for her child's "norm":

What's going to happen to him when he graduates from school? I'm not being negative about his behaviors. I'm just being realistic about what he's capable of. And if at this age, he's still not talking and, at this age, he's still dependent, and at this age, you know, showing all of these sensory behaviors, like I don't know if in 6 years when he's an adult, he's not gonna be one of these people with Down syndrome who works in a supermarket or goes to a rec center on a bus. I don't know. I worry about what is that transition gonna look like for him.

For all of the parents in our study, however, acknowledging and accepting their child's differences also meant understanding what kind of supports would help them, especially for children with intersecting identities. Jenny, the foster mother of an adolescent with ID, ADHD, and other concurrent mental illnesses, expresses how one of her goals would be for her daughter to be able to manage her emotions. She realizes that even with the benefits of therapies and medications, only some of that is within her control. In fact, like all of our caregivers, she is resigned to the belief that although they would seek interventions and supports, it is important to value the individuality and uniqueness of the children under their care.

The Hegemony of the Norm

Many of the parents in our study described the constant pressure placed upon them to be a part of the "norm" in ways that were both visible and invisible. Visible ways in which this ideology was reinforced were the behaviors and actions of health care professionals, other parents, and members of the community at large. Speaking of their prenatal experience, Carlos and Betty described having to defend their right to have and care for their child, against the explicit pressure by the providers to consider either termination or adoption. Their resistance was demonstrated by advocating for their child's life. Linda described how in her postnatal experiences the practitioner's constant questioning as to why she did not have prenatal screening was inappropriate and insulting, considering that her child was already born. She explained that the shock of how she was treated outweighed the shock of the diagnosis, stating, "If anything needs to be done, it should start at the delivery. It wasn't just the surprise; it was the *questions.*"

Parents described ways in which these experiences continued over time, in different ways, with different actors and settings. Perhaps among the most disturbing were the accounts given by Rhonda of the deficit-focused, degrading, and offensive statements made by medical professionals in the clinical facility where her daughter was receiving vision services. This experience had a profound impact on Rhonda, given the value that people place on medical professionals as experts:

I overhead them speaking about my child . . . prior to the doctor getting in there. . . . What they didn't know was that I heard them . . . I guess you could say making light of a situation that wasn't true. So, when the doctor saw my child, he already had this preconception. But he cleared it up later to say to them, "Well, I didn't see the same child that y'all said"—'cause what they told the doctor was that my child was out of control. First of all, she's a child. She does have a learning disability. So . . . was she not sitting? Yes. But . . . what you said was like she was an animal. . . . And they don't know me from earth. So, to make that—and you're a medical professional? It ripped my soul.

Other ways in which the norm was reinforced as something desirable were invisible, occurring in the silent ostracism of the community. Several of the parents, including Rhonda, Patty, Ana, Linda, and Marie, describe the negative reactions of others to their children's behaviors in everyday settings. Ana, however, drew a contrast between the reactions of her son's teachers and providers, whom she felt actually did understand her son's invisible disability of autism, and reactions in the community, which she felt was less understanding of her son's behaviors that didn't fit into the normative expectations:

Just in the community, just out and about you know. If the kid is throwing a tantrum, it's not because he's a spoiled brat, it's cause he's got sensory overload here in the supermarket you know. . . . He doesn't understand that "No, you can't open this gallon of milk," where I can't have a discussion, I can't have a negotiation with him, it doesn't work. I've had to leave places you know, because . . . one because it's too much for my kid and because of the stares and you know. So, it's more, I feel like you know the people who understand the disorder, the teachers and the therapist and the physicians, I've had good experiences 'cause they get it. My worry is the rest of the community sometimes. And my son doesn't have a disorder that is visible. That's also the thing, he looks like a normal kid you know. But he's got a neural, neurological disorder so you can't see it. I don't know if you know, if it makes a difference to other adults if it looks like you could physically see something on the child but . . . I think that they, . . . the connection doesn't happen for them.

Still, some families, though recognizing the differences in their child, had accepted their child's reality as situated against a general lack of understanding in the world. What they desired most was that the world could value their child while acknowledging their differences. Rhonda describes her family members' perception of disability:

'Cause when you see somebody else—and sometimes my daughter tells me too, she says, "Mom, what if that was our story?" When you see kids that are on ventilators. Some kids that are not walking—you know, she's a late walker. You know, your story could always be different. And I say, we have a lot to be thankful for.

The valuing of difference was echoed in Patty's statement about her grandson, diagnosed with Williams syndrome:

Because if somebody loves too much or somebody . . . you know, doesn't communicate a certain way, why is it that they're wrong? Why is it that we're right and not—you know, make *them* labeled, like *they're* disabled?

Objective Observers' Determinations of "Difference" as Truth

One major challenge experienced by our parents was recognizing that the power of others' assessment of their children as being "different" could make critical and permanent decisions for them, at the exclusion of their input. Marie, the Haitian-American mother of a Black boy with the dual label of SLI/LD and gifted/exceptional, described how professionals determined that he may be too large for his age and growing too fast. They determined that her son, outside of the parameters of what they determined to be appropriate size and stature, should receive hormone treatment to retard his growth. Although Marie felt this was wrong, the doctors filled her mind with concerns about how she would be able to manage him as he grew older, generating a fear of her own child. Ultimately, Marie was thankful that they did not proceed with the hormone treatment. As we sat in her neighborhood, she pointed out other Black children who were considered large for their age. She commented that from now on, she would feel compelled to warn other parents so that they don't experience the same thing.

A similar account, though with the opposite objective, was given by Linda, whose son was assessed by his endocrinologist as being too small in stature because they felt he was outside of the parameters of the growth curves for typical children as well as the adjusted "Down syndrome" charts. Their recommendation was for her to get a second opinion, which she details below:

And then that doctor, which I had never met before, wanted him to be put on growth hormones before he did any kind of bloodwork or anything. To prove like the medical necessity. I just had like a very bad vibe. So, I went on my own. And I went to a third endocrinologist. And he agreed with me. He did the test over and didn't see anything wrong with his growth hormones. That he didn't need them medically, that we would be injecting him every day. That if we were okay with his height, that he was probably going to be 4' 8", if we were fine with that. If he's not complaining about his height, which he's not, then probably could just leave him alone because there's no reason to do it. I told the doctor I just didn't understand why he kept insisting on the growth hormone when there was no need. . . . I guess in my own way I was advocating for him. I just didn't go back.

In the school system, parents also experienced how the perceptions of others about their child was assumed to be truth. Rhonda describes her challenges in seeking an appropriate school placement for Amira, who was automatically assigned a class rather than assessed for the most appropriate classroom placement:

So, I just kept running into all these little things. By this time, my mom . . . is gone. So, I don't have my mom in my ear trying to help me navigate being back here, and a child with special needs. So [the school] was like okay—and I guess why one of my sisters went with me, 'cause they were demanding to do the psychological. They were demanding because at 3rd grade is when the [state testing] and all this stuff. She wasn't in normal classes, but they kept putting her in, what they called . . . EBD . . . and . . . recommended ABA therapy . . . but I feel like at that time, that's not where she belonged. Because nobody tested her, so how did you come—how did you come to this?

Another issue highlighted by our participants is how professionals fail to make their decisions through the family-level disability perspective. Not all problems are the same across family systems, contexts, and at any point in time. In a family life cycle and life course perspective, described by Turnbull and colleagues (2015), the family is ever in a state of flux. Its key players, their interactions with one another, and their interactions with their environments change. Rhonda's account is an example of the impact of changing family dynamics on her own advocacy because her mother was a valued member of her support team. While a few of the parents in our study were confident in their own skills for advocating, many described their reliance on family members or teachers they have a rapport with as supporters of their advocacy.

While the observer may be considered to be the determinant of the objective truth, it often falls short of understanding the child and his or her potential. The ultimate determination by such observers across settings, however, can limit the experience and opportunities offered to children. As Rhonda expresses, "That's why I say notes can be . . . I don't know, detrimental, I guess. 'Cause you don't really give a person a chance. You kind of just write 'em off, they can't do that."

CO-CONSTRUCTING ADVOCACY: DEVELOPING A NEW MODEL

We emphasize that we do not intend to be unduly critical in our discussion of current advocacy models and training programs. While we note the numerous attempts at increasing diversity in some models, we highlight the need to develop multiple, intersectional rather than singular cultural lenses. Regarding how educators can tap into parents' own knowledge about their children, for example, Fenton, Ocasio-Stoutenburg, and Harry (2017) note, "many of the current models are not necessarily broken; they may simply need a more deeply entrenched, culturally responsive stance" (p. 221). We envision the same for parent advocacy, to cast a wider, yet deeper net.

Fennimore (2017) recommends designing and orienting studies that position the researcher in the co-constructive position with his or her participants, in order to create solutions rather than propose solutions for them. She adds,

> I pose that activist-participant-observer paradigms offer resolution to issues of discrimination and conflict of interest in research on nondominant family involvement. Through such paradigms, researchers share the experience of school-based resistance and dismissal faced by parents who are struggling for their educational rights. (p. 175)

This is the spirit of community-driven, grassroots advocacy that is also endorsed by scholars such as Khalifa, Arnold, and Newcomb (2015) and Sauer and Lalvani (2017). The latter propose that such approaches move advocacy from the "ivory tower" and even past individualistic aims to more collectivistic aims that align with communities and address the needs of culturally and linguistically diverse families. There is an emergence, a resistance from being put down and shut out. The instinctive and experiential knowledge that families and caregivers possess is valuable and essential to defining needs and has a great deal to offer in providing the depth and breadth of perspective needed to address such layered issues. We have engaged our parents in defining advocacy for us, identifying their concerns and ways that make the process of developing advocacy co-constructive rather than power-down. Their recommendations are summarized below in the sections "What Doesn't Work?," "What Works?," and "Paying It Forward."

What Doesn't Work?

Judgment, biases, and assumptions. Our participating families described barriers to co-constructing advocacy. They include judgment on the part of others based on their child's disability. Tying back to our theme about the value of personhood, these parents describe how their child's appearance or behavior may have an impact on how others perceive them.

Judgments based on parents' and caregivers' appearance and implicit bias toward their race and ethnicity have also been uncovered, as consistent with the literature and our DisCrit lens. Families describe situations in which they are presumed to be uneducated, not invested in their children's education beyond what is given to them, or wanting some respite rather than being present and active in their children's appointments. Based on their appearance, parents are presumed also to be on Medicaid, coded in the words "receiving services," which corresponds to the quality of care they should expect.

Lack of disability knowledge and ambiguity. Other barriers to a co-constructive process identified by parents is a general lack of knowledge or information about the disability. Caregivers have been disheartened by the lack of awareness in the community but are especially disappointed to see this among practitioners in clinical and educational settings. The lack of clarity and the ambiguity of labels affect how and when supports and services are received, as well as the quality of care delivered. Rhonda describes her early awareness of her child's disability that was met with ambivalence by professionals who didn't seem to care, saying, "We don't know, we'll just have to wait with time."

Elitism. Several parents felt as if they were on the outskirts of the higher priority disability labels. Parents felt their concerns were dismissed by medical professionals and by educators when their child could not receive a diagnosis or their child's unique profile did not fit in with the parameters that typically characterize the label. This elitism carried over into the community.

Many of the families faced other societal barriers that they felt prevented them from full engagement and participation as part of groups, education, and training programs and advocacy initiatives. Ana describes how the financial and time expectations of being involved in an advocacy organization prevented her from continuing on as a board member. Linda describes how her child's dual diagnosis prevents her from feeling as if she truly belongs to either the Down syndrome or the autism groups, a feeling of isolation because Tony's behaviors are not descriptive of the typical children in either group. Like Rhonda, she remains as a peripheral listener to conversations in the community because of the community members' very elitist behavior.

Parents reported the formation of social "cliques" based on various identities, such as race and social class. In addition, while the parents of the toddlers felt they still "got a pass" or experienced "communities of caring," several parents of older children felt excluded when their children behaved differently at playgrounds or activities in their own neighborhood. These experiences of exclusion were enacted by families of typically developing children as well as children with the same diagnosis (Linda).

Being powerful yet feeling disempowered. Although parents sometimes felt as if advocating for their children's needs required them to take on an assertive role during school meetings and health care appointments, they also recognized how this disrupted the synergy of working collaboratively with practitioners. Nearly all the parents felt that a significant barrier was not having their concerns and ideas acknowledged. Such incidences, as consistent with the literature, have led to delays in services in the critical years, as Linda explained. Parents felt disappointed that they were not included as a partner in developing and sharing strategies that they could use at home to support their children. While the parents of younger children felt it was important to be knowledgeable about strategies in therapeutic settings, the parents of older children felt that it was a barrier to not be able to share resources and strategies *with* the teachers. They considered themselves to be just as knowledgeable and resourceful as the teachers about their children and felt frustrated in not being able to discuss ideas for their children.

Systemic barriers to advocacy. Our study also uncovered some systemic barriers to advocacy. We presumed a relief from economic stressors among parents who were in the middle-income range. However, what we found was the contrary. Some of the caregivers (e.g., Ana, Rhonda, Zoe) reported being ineligible for services because they were above the poverty level and having to manage the expenses of co-pays for therapies and doctor visits. Some mothers are feeling the economic impact of this reality, especially being a single- or sole-family provider. Linda and Ana describe having to "pick and choose" which therapies are a priority because they cannot do all. Ana, for example, recalls the systemic and legal barriers that had an impact on her son's ability to receive services:

> There was some loophole in the law . . . where based on this number of size of your employees, if you have 50 or less or 100 or less, I forget the number, you have to offer it. If you don't, there's some loophole where you don't have to. So, I spent years not being able to access ABA in those critical beginning months when he was 18 months, up until about when he was 4 years old.

Though there were families that were eligible for health care and therapeutic services to be covered through their insurance, there were other expenses that were required to support their children's needs and well-rounded development. Working mothers, such as Marie, for example, describe the challenges of working multiple jobs so that they can provide for activities, outings, and other recreational needs of their children. Similarly, though Rhonda manages her daughter's medical expenses through her private insurance, she describes the pinch of out-of-pocket expenses to keep her daughter in community activities such as cheerleading and gymnastics.

What Works?

Caregiver-initiated supports. Pockets of co-construction were demonstrated in the study as well as parents' suggestions for what would make their advocacy work ideally. On their part, they felt that their compliance with school requests, such as purchasing supplies for the classroom, attending meetings, and volunteering at the school, was a way in which they supported and modeled co-construction of their own advocacy. They perceived this as their contribution to the synergistic relationship they wanted.

Intangible ways in which they supported these relationships in order to contribute to a climate for co-advocacy included acknowledging the competence of the teacher, creating a rapport with staff members at hospitals and clinical offices, and participating in community events. Caregivers emphasized a two-way relationship characterized by using the words "working as a team" and "partnerships" in describing their ideal relationships with teachers and practitioners.

Some of these co-constructive efforts included printing information and materials for the teachers and therapists about their child's disability as well as providing suggestions for helping their child comply with activities. Doing so, parents felt, reassured the professionals that they are "on their team" while ultimately helping them to better support their children. For example, Patty describes her efforts in providing brochures to practitioners in schools and medical offices to help them understand Williams syndrome:

> And I'd give it to the teachers. I said, "I don't know if you're interested in reading up. You know, I printed this out for you." And so, I did it for the therapist. I said, "You know, he may not need everything you're doing. Or maybe he needs something else that might be more interesting to you. But here, look at this and see what you think."

Practitioner-initiated supports. Our participants appreciated both the tangible and intangible supports they receive from teachers, health care professionals, and therapeutic practitioners. They described how helpful it was for teachers to take the time to provide classroom newsletters and communications, removing the veil of what happens at school. In addition, the verbal support, encouragement, guidance, and praise from practitioners were also perceived as co-constructive to their advocacy efforts, as these stakeholders knew their child and the parent, providing customized support. Moreover, caregivers could see the effects of co-advocacy when they saw their recommendations, efforts, and strategies being implemented by the practitioners.

Family and community-initiated supports. Family members, community members, and former school personnel offered their suggestions as well as physical presence at IEP and other school meetings when parents sometimes felt alone or "attacked" by school personnel. There were advantages to some parents being within the same school, having family members in the field of special education, or encountering strangers in the community who were willing to support them. In addition, the fact that some of their former supporters (e.g., guardians ad litem, former teachers) kept in contact with them provided them with the reassurance that they had some additional layers of support when they encountered barriers or the processes became too confusing.

Other resources and supports. Some of the sources of supports for advocacy that our participants identified were through reading books as well as social media posts that helped them to connect with the experiences of others, understanding and unpacking their mix of emotions. Spirituality and religion played an important role for many of the parents, as they referenced their own prayer life, and, though sometimes difficult, feeling the connectedness within their church community. Journaling and writing were also referenced by our parents as a way to organize their thoughts and plan for the future.

"No right or wrong way." Our parents emphasized that advocacy isn't prescriptive and that they often did what came naturally to them. Although it is sometimes helpful to know the regulations, they emphasized their feelings of competence when they knew it was right to go with their intuitions against a professional's recommendation that was inappropriate or ended up being poor advice.

Parents spoke about letting go of some of their own perceptions about disability, their own perceptions about parenting, and the judgment of others to be open to their own family experiences and seeking new opportunities for their children. They celebrated instances in which people worked with them to provide natural experiences that were age-appropriate and valuing of their children. Most importantly the parents talked about the importance of speaking up over formal knowledge, emphasizing how parents "know something about [their] child."

Paying It Forward

Maslow's hierarchy of needs model (1960) has often been used to provide insight on why the focus of some families of children with disabilities may be more on practical and physiological needs while those of others may be toward the higher needs of self-fulfillment. However, this was not the case in our study. In spite of the economic impact of disability on several of the families, *all* of the families, despite their income level, their children's physiological needs, their family circumstances, or their children's disability label, found it important to support other families like them. Several of them saw our recruitment flyer and expressed that they "wanted to help" us by giving their input. One reason for their outreach was the acknowledgment of others who had helped them. Although they emphasized how these experiences do not happen every day, these co-advocates have had a significant impact on their advocacy, as Rhonda comments, her voice trembling toward the end of the statement:

> And I've had two or three people that have made the way . . . I guess, the hill a little lighter. "You doing okay, Mom? You're doing it, you're doing it." There are times when you feel like, I'm—I'm not doing enough. But those people have said to me, "You're doing it." And they have no connection to me or my child, per se. In any shape, form, or fashion.

They encouraged other budding advocates to keep an open mind about their children, simply acknowledging and appreciating being their parent. What was truly compelling was our parents' humility in talking about being appreciated and acknowledged for what they do to advocate for their children and for others. They felt that this was part of their due diligence. They spoke of their "gratitude" by acknowledging how their situation could perhaps be worse. Our caregivers spoke of their desire to be "a voice for others," recalling what it felt like to experience the shock and loneliness for the first time. What was incredibly touching was their willingness to give back, cherishing those people who have made a difference in their lives, as Patty's powerful words resonate:

> You know? I've always been for that, "Okay, I'll help." "I'll give the 10 dollars." You know, because I want, like I tell these people, "Go forward, come on." You know, the thing is resolve. The main message here is let's resolve. Let's resolve, let's resolve. Don't stay wallowing in that same thing. Because you feel sorry for yourself, which, listen, it's true. But don't stay there. You know, resolve. Resolve the problem. So, if I can help you resolve it, I can't just sit there and say, "Hmm. Let them—" No. "Okay, what is your need? Let's go, right now."

FORGING AHEAD

The goal of this book is to propose a culturally and contextually responsive approach to parent advocacy by foregrounding the issues of context and family complexity. To do so, we have tried to practice what we preach—we co-construct the ways with our caregivers. The voices of our parents and caregivers, who represent a range of cultural, linguistic, family, and socio-economic descriptions, challenge the approach of universalizing the family disability experience as much as they challenge the approach of universalizing the advocate and his or her child. Even under the restrictions of special education legislation, however, these parents have learned to become border crossers, maintaining their position as advocates without yielding to the identity-subtractive process by which parents are forced to advocate.

We share a reflective memo (Charmaz, 2014) from Lydia, the second author of this book, which describes the very complexities and experiences that make advocacy a constructive, iterative, and reflective process.

Lydia: Reflective Memo

This research has caused me not only to continually think about the experiences of the caregivers but also to reflect upon my own role as an advocate. The question about what matters to me has changed so much over the years and will continue to change as time and circumstance progress. I realize that like the parents of the young children in my study, I fought past those same tensions within myself, with practitioners, against the judgment of my own family members, friends, and the community around us. Like many of these parents, I was comforted by the blissful atmosphere of the school where he first received early intervention that "normalized" his disability. I am thankful for those, in fact, because it helped me to know that there are pockets of hope in this world, of people who care about children and their families. I didn't think it got worse; in fact, I thought I could put my boxing gloves down.

Transitioning out of the early years was when my battle began. Placements that were awful, people trying to force him into the box that they felt Down syndrome was. His inability to use words to communicate magnified the issue. But then there were his health concerns, the chronic ear infections, croup, the valve in his heart that remained open. There were multiple surgeries and praying by his hospital bedside, realizing like many of the caregivers in this study that there are greater worries than his IQ level.

I also had to wake up and recognize the implicit biases about me, about my race and ethnicity, about the large size of my family. Presumptions about my sexuality as a Black woman, my educational level—that this should come as some surprise that I may know *something* about my child. I experienced the same kind of shock and othering as these participants when I thought I had the right to be on some of these disability organization boards. I thought these groups would truly be immune to elitism because they stood for something just, when I realized how quietly and subtly they boxed me out. I didn't have wealthy friends who could donate funds, nor did I have it in my own bank account to donate. I was running, trying to make those meetings after cooking dinner, trying to blow-dry my thick curly hair and doing what I thought was adding some real perspective to the good intent of the group. However, I remember one board member, my friend, sharing a hurtful reality with me:

> "I didn't want to tell you this. But Jose was talking about you when we were voting for you to be on the board. I tried to explain to him, but I don't know. He's ignorant, please ignore him."
> "Well, what did he say?" I asked.
> "He said, 'You know, I don't understand how these Black people have such a hard time and complain and don't do anything with their life, when I came here from Cuba with 7 cents in my pocket. And look at me.' So maybe you could explain to him—"
> "I don't owe him an explanation for who I am," I said. "And I don't need to qualify myself for him."

Though my friend apologized on his colleague's behalf, I learned, the hard way, I was not, nor was I ever going to be, a celebrated advocate. Shortly after I joined the board, he left.

My real development as an advocate, I believe, came when I stopped thinking that I had to be one, by all of the definitions I had learned in these advocacy training classes and community. I was free when I ceased trying to fit into spaces that weren't made for me and for my family. I shine as an advocate when I take it beyond myself and what I want for my own child to other people's children. I am thankful for the teachers at my son's first B-2 program who see me in passing and say, "Just look at you. I am so proud of you. Isaiah is so lucky." But I know in my heart I am the lucky one to have him.

THE NEXT CHAPTER

So, what's next? As we continue to follow up with our parents on the many different projects, groups, transition plans, social media platforms, and other initiatives they are undertaking, we will include these stories in our case study companion book. We are accompanying parents to therapy, attending their IEP meetings, getting to know their families and neighbors. As we learn about their lives and their work toward the goals they set for themselves and for their children, we view them as experts, not regardless of their cultural and linguistic background, race, class, and child's disability type, but precisely because of their multiple identities, which offer a collective advantage to our culture. We learn from one another the meanings of charged words like *freedom*, *privilege*, *equity*, *choice*, and *dignity*. By recasting our parents, who are raising our future, we can choose to unhinge our national and global culture from the confines and bounds of false ideologies and oppressive forces that were instituted when we *did not* know better and that continue to exist while we *do* know better. We also choose to celebrate the diversity of people, not as exceptionality on the ends of an erroneously applied and constructed curve, but as part of the natural variation of what it is to be human. Although being human has been socially, biologically, medically, politically, economically, and judicially constructed in various ways throughout history, we dare to say that individuals, with multiply traversing yet vulnerable and marginalized identities, with all comforts, statuses, power and privileges removed, not only know well what it means to be human but are at the level of mastery. We are indebted to upholding their dignity.

References

Abraham, W. (1958). *Barbara: A prologue.* New York, NY: Rhinehart.

Abraham, W. (1980). *You always lag one child behind (Barbara revisited).* Scottsdale, AZ: Sunshine Press

Albrecht, G. L., Seelman, K. D., & Bury, M. (2003). *Handbook of disability studies.* Thousand Oaks, CA: Sage.

Aldrich, C. A. (1947). Preventive medicine and mongolism. *American Journal of Mental Deficiency, 52,* 127–129.

Alper, S., Schloss, P. J., & Schloss, C. N. (1995). Families of children with disabilities in elementary and middle school: Advocacy models and strategies. *Exceptional Children, 62*(3), 261–270.

Andrews, L. B., & Hibbert, M. (2000). Courts and wrongful birth: Can disability itself be viewed as a legal wrong? In L. P. Francis & A. Silvers (Eds.), *Americans with disabilities: Exploring implications of the law for individuals and institutions* (pp. 318–330). New York, NY: Routledge.

Annamma, S. A., Ferri, B. A., & Connor, D. J. (2018). Disability critical race theory: Exploring the intersectional lineage, emergence, and potential futures of DisCrit. *Research in Education, 42,* 46–71.

Artiles, A. J. (1998). The dilemma of difference: Enriching the disproportionality discourse with theory and context. *The Journal of Special Education, 32*(1), 32–36.

Artiles, A. J. (2011). Toward an interdisciplinary understanding of educational equity and difference. *Educational Researcher, 40*(9), 431–445.

Artiles, A. J. (2013). Untangling the racialization of disabilities: An intersectionality critique across disability models. *Du Bois Review: Social Science Research on Race, 10*(2), 329–347

Auerbach, S. (2007). From moral supporters to struggling advocates: Reconceptualizing parent roles in education through the experience of working-class families of color. *Urban Education, 42*(3), 250–283.

Avis, D. (1985). Deinstitutionalization jet lag. In H. R. Turnbull & A. P. Turnbull (Eds.), *Parents speak out: Then and now* (pp. 185–199). Columbus, OH: Merrill.

Balcazar, F. E., Keys, C. B., Bertram, J. F., & Rizzo, T. (1996). Advocate development in the field of developmental disabilities: A data-based conceptual model. *Mental Retardation, 34*(6), 341–351.

Bell, D. (1980). *Brown v. Board of Education* and the interest convergence dilemma. *Harvard Law Review, 93,* 518–533.

Bennett, A. T. (1988). Gateways to powerlessness: Incorporating Hispanic deaf children and families into formal schooling. *Disability, Handicap & Society, 3*(2), 119–151.

Berry, J. O. (1995). Families and deinstitutionalization: An application of Bronfen-brenner's social ecology model. *Journal of Counseling and Development, 73*, 379–383.

Bérubé, M. (1998). *Life as we know it: A father, a family, and an exceptional child.* New York, NY: Pantheon Books

Bettelheim, B. (1967). *The empty fortress: Infantile autism and the birth of the self.* New York, NY: The Free Press.

Bhambra, G. K. (2014). A sociological dilemma: Race, segregation and U.S. sociology. *Current Sociology, 62*(4), 472–492.

Blanchett, W. J. (2010). Telling it like it is: The role of race, class, and culture in the perpetuation of learning disability as a privileged category for the white middle class. *Disability Studies Quarterly, 30*(2).

Blanchett, W. J., Mumford, V., & Beachum, F. (2005). Urban school failure and dis-proportionality in a post-*Brown* era: Benign neglect of the constitutional rights of students of color. *Remedial and Special Education, 26*(2), 70–81. Retrieved from doi.org/10.1177/07419325050260020201

Blatt, B. (1966). *Christmas in purgatory: A photographic essay on mental retardation.* Syracuse, NY: Human Policy Press.

Blatt, B. (1969). Purgatory. In R. B. Kugel & W. Wolfensberger (Eds.), *Changing patterns in residential services for the mentally retarded* (pp. 35–50). Washington, DC: President's Committee on Mental Retardation, U.S. Department of Health, Education and Welfare, Office of Education.

Block, P., Kasnitz, D., Nishida, A., & Pollard, N. (2016). Occupying disability: An introduction. In P. Block, D. Kasnitz, A. Nishida, & N. Pollard (Eds.), *Occupying disability: Critical approaches to community, justice, and decolonizing disability* (pp. 3–14). New York, NY: Springer.

Bogdan, R., & Biklen, D. (1977). Handicapism. *Social Policy, 7*(5), 14–19.

Bogdan, R., & Taylor, S. (1989). Relationships with severely disabled people: The social construction of humanness. *Social Problems, 36*(2), 35–148.

Boggs, E. M. (1978). Who is putting whose head in the sand? (Or in the clouds, as the case may be). In A. P. Turnbull & H. R. Turnbull (Eds.), *Parents speak out: Views from the other side of the two-way mirror* (pp. 50–68). New York, NY: Macmillan.

Boggs, E. M. (1985). Whose head is in the clouds? In H. R. Turnbull & A. P. Turnbull (Eds.), *Parents speak out: Then and now* (2nd ed, pp. 55–63). Columbus, OH: Merrill.

Bonilla-Silva, E. (2006). *Racism without racists: Color-blind racism and the persistence of racism in the United States.* Lanham, MD: Rowman & Littlefield.

Bourdieu, P. (1986). The forms of capital. In J. Richardson (Ed.), *Handbook of theory and research for the sociology of education* (pp. 241–258). Westport, CT: Greenwood.

Boyd, D. (1951). The three stages in the growth of a parent of a mentally retarded child. *American Journal of Mental Deficiency, 55*, 608–611.

Brosco, J., & Feudtner, C. (2006). Growth attenuation: A diminutive solution to a daunting problem. *Archives of Pediatric & Adolescent Medicine, 160*(10), 1077–1078.

Brown et al. v. Board of Education of Topeka, Shawnee County, Kan., et al., 74 S.Ct. 686, 692 (1955).

Buck, P. S. (1992). *The child who never grew.* Bethesda, MD: Woodbine House. (Original work published 1950)

Buck v. Bell, 143 Va. 310 (Va. Ct. App. 1927).

Bullard, W. (1908). The high-grade mental defectives. *The Boston Medical and Surgical Journal, 159*(8), 240–242.

Burke, M. M., & Goldman, S. E. (2017). Documenting the experiences of special education advocates. *The Journal of Special Education, 51*(1), 3–13.

Burke, M. M., Goldman, S. E., Hart, M. S., & Hodapp, R. M. (2016). Evaluating the efficacy of a special education advocacy training program. *Journal of Policy and Practice in Intellectual Disabilities, 13*(4), 269–276.

Burke, M. M., Meadan-Kaplansky, H., Patton, K., Pearson, J., Cummings, K., & Lee, C. (2018). Advocacy for children with social-communication needs: Perspectives from parents and school professionals. *The Journal of Special Education, 51*(4), 191–200.

Cameron, C. C. (1973). *A different drum.* Englewood Cliffs, NJ: Prentice-Hall.

Carey, A. C. (2009). *On the margins of citizenship.* Philadelphia, PA: Temple University Press.

Carlson, L., & Kittay, E. F. (2010). Introduction: Rethinking philosophical presumptions in light of cognitive disability. In E. F. Kittay & L. Carlson (Eds.), *Cognitive disability and its challenge to moral philosophy* (pp. 1–26). Malden, MA: Wiley-Blackwell.

Caruso, G. (2015, October). History of disability. Lecture presented at Partners in Policymaking, Orlando, FL.

Carver, J. N., & Carver, N. E. (1972). *The family of the retarded child.* Syracuse, NY: Syracuse University Press.

Cassidy, E. (1988). Reaching and involving Black parents of handicapped children in their child's education program. Lansing, MI: CAUSE Inc. (ERIC Document Reproduction Service No. Ed 302 982).

Castles, K. (2004). "Nice, average Americans": Postwar parents' groups and the defense of the normal family. In S. Noll & J. W. Trent Jr. (Eds.), *Mental retardation in America: A historical reader* (pp. 351–370). New York, NY: New York University Press.

Cavendish, W., & Connor, D. (2018). Toward authentic IEPs and transition plans: Student, parent, and teacher perspectives. *Learning Disability Quarterly, 41*(1), 32–43.

Cayea, W. (2006). *Feral child: The legacy of the wild boy of Aveyron in the domains of language acquisition and deaf education.* Rochester, NY: Rochester Institute of Technology.

Chan, K. S. (1986). Parents of exceptional Asian children. In M. K. Kitano & P. C. Chinn (Eds.), *Exceptional Asian children and youth* (pp. 36–59). Reston, VA: Council for Exceptional Children.

Charmaz, K. (2014). *Constructing grounded theory* (2nd ed.). Los Angeles, CA: Sage.

Clinkenbeard, W. W. (1989). On the trail of the holy humanhood. *Journal of Medical Ethics, 15,* 90–91.

Collins, P. H., & Bilge, S. (2016). *Intersectionality.* Hoboken, NJ: John Wiley & Sons.

Collins, R., & Camblin, L. D. (1983). The politics and science of learning disability classification: Implications for Black children. *Contemporary Education, 64*(2), 113–118.

Connery, A. R. (1987). A description and comparison of Native American and Anglo parents' knowledge of their handicapped children's rights (Unpublished doctoral dissertation). Northern Arizona University, Flagstaff.

Connor, D. J., & Cavendish, W. (2018). Sharing power with parents: Improving educational decision making for students with learning disabilities. *Learning Disability Quarterly, 41*(2), 79–84.

Connor, D. J., Ferri, B. A., & Annamma, S. A. (Eds.). (2016). *DisCrit: Disability studies and critical race theory in education.* New York, NY: Teachers College Press.

Corrigan, P. W., & Bink, A. B. (2016). The stigma of mental illness. In H. S. Friedman (Ed.), *Encyclopedia of mental health* (2nd ed., pp. 230–234). Oxford, England: Elsevier.

Crenshaw, K. (1989). Demarginalizing the intersection of race and sex: A Black feminist critique of antidiscrimination doctrine, feminist theory and antiracist politics. *The University of Chicago Legal Forum, 140,* 139–167.

Davis, P. (1989). Law as microaggression. *Yale Law Journal, 98,* 1559–1577.

Delgado, R., & Stefancic, J. (2017). *Critical race theory: An introduction.* New York, NY: New York University Press.

Disability Justice. (2017). The closing of Willowbrook: *New York State Association for Retarded Children v. Carey.* Retrieved from disabilityjustice.org/the-closing-of-willowbrook/

Disability Justice. (2019a). *Wyatt v. Stickney.* Retrieved from disabilityjustice.org/wyatt-v-stickney/

Disability Justice. (2019b). Dehumanization, discrimination, and segregation. Retrieved from disabilityjustice.org/justice-denied/dehumanization-discrimination-and-segregation/

Disability Justice. (2019c). The right to education. Retrieved from disabilityjustice.org/right-to-education

Donovan, M. S., & Cross, C. T. (2002). *Minority students in special and gifted education.* Washington, DC: National Research Council.

Du Bois, W. E. B. (1994). *The souls of Black folk.* New York, NY: Dover. (Original work published 1903).

Dudley-Marling, C., & Gurn, A. (2010). *The myth of the normal curve.* New York, NY: Peter Lang.

Dunn, L. M. (1968). Special education for the mildly retarded—Is much of it justifiable? *Exceptional Children, 35*(1), 5–22.

Epstein, J. L. (1995). School, family, and community partnerships: Caring for the children we share. *Phi Delta Kappan, 76*(9), 701–712.

Epstein, J., & Rosenbaum, S. A. (2019). Revisiting Ashley X: An essay on disabled bodily integrity, sexuality, dignity, and family caregiving. *Touro Law Review, 35*(1) 197–234.

Epstein, R., Blake, J., & Gonzalez, T. (2017). *Girlhood interrupted: The erasure of Black girls' childhood.* Washington, DC: The Georgetown Law Center on Poverty and Inequality.

Erevelles, N. (2011). *Disability and difference in global contexts: Enabling a transformative body politic.* New York, NY: Palgrave MacMillan.

Erevelles, N. (2017). The right to exclude: Locating Section 504 in the disproportionality debate. In J. Allan & A. Artiles (Eds.), *Assessment inequalities: World yearbook of education, 2017* (pp. 120–136). London, England: Routledge.

Evans, D. (1953). *Angel unaware*. Grand Rapids, MI: Revell/Baker Publishing Group.

Fadiman, A. (1997). *The spirit catches you and you fall down: A Hmong child, her American doctors, and the collision of two cultures*. New York, NY: Macmillan.

Featherstone, H. (1981). *A difference in the family: Living with a disabled child*. New York, NY: Penguin.

Fennimore, B. S. (2017). Permission not required: The power of parents to disrupt educational hypocrisy. *Review of Research in Education, 41*(1), 159–181.

Fenton, P., Ocasio-Stoutenburg, L., & Harry, B. (2017). The power of parent engagement: Sociocultural considerations in the quest for equity. *Theory into Practice, 56*(3), 214–225.

Fenton, Z. (2016). Disability does not discriminate: Toward a theory of multiple identity through coalition. In D. J. Connor, B. A. Ferri, & S. A. Annamma (Eds.), *DisCrit: Disability studies and critical race theory in education* (pp. 203–222). New York, NY: Teachers College Press.

Fernald, W. E. (1912). The burden of feeble-mindedness. *The Boston Medical and Surgical Journal, 166*(25), 911–915.

Fitzgerald, J. L., & Watkins, M. W. (2006). Parents' rights in special education: The readability of procedural safeguards. *Exceptional Children, 72*(4), 497–510.

Fletcher, J. (1972). Indicators of humanhood: A tentative profile of man. *The Hastings Center Report, 2*(5), 1–4.

Fletcher, J. (1974). Four indicators of humanhood: The enquiry matures. *Hastings Center Report, 4*(6), 4-7.

Francis, G. L., Stride, A., Reed, S., & Chiu, C. Y. (2017). Family-professional partnerships in postsecondary education programs: Perceptions of professionals. *Inclusion, 5*(4), 263–278.

Frohock, F. M. (1986). *Special care*. Chicago, IL: University of Chicago Press.

Fuller, N. (2013, October 13). "Baby Jane Doe" at 30: Happy, joking, learning. *Newsday*. Retrieved from newsday.com/news/health/baby-jane-doe-at-30-happy-joking-learning-1.6249597

Gelb, S. A. (2010). Evolutionary anxiety, monstrosity, and the birth of normality. In C. Dudley-Marling & A. Gurn (Eds.), *The myth of the normal curve* (pp. 71–86). New York, NY: Peter Lang.

Gillborn, D., Rollock, N., Vincent, C., & Ball, S. (2016). The black middle classes, education, racism, and dis/ability: An intersectional analysis. In D. Connor, B. Ferri, & S. Annamma (Eds.), *DisCrit: Disability studies and critical race theory in education* (pp. 35–54). New York, NY: Teachers College Press.

Glaser, B. G., & Strauss, A. L. (1967). *The discovery of grounded theory: Strategies for qualitative research*. New York, NY: Aldine de Gruyter.

Goddard, H. H. (1913). The improvability of feeble-minded children. *Journal of Psychoasthenics, 17*, 121–131.

Goddard, H. H., & Green, C. D. (1913). *The Kallikak family: A study in the heredity of feeble-mindedness*. New York, NY: Macmillan.

Goff, P. A., Jackson, M. C., Di Leone, B. A. L., Culotta, C. M., & DiTomaso, N. A. (2014). The essence of innocence: Consequences of dehumanizing Black children. *Journal of Personality and Social Psychology, 106*, 526–545. dx.doi.org/10.1037/a0035663

Goffman, E. (1963). *Stigma: Notes on the management of spoiled identity*. Englewood Cliffs, NJ: Prentice-Hall.

Goode, D. A. (1983). "Who is Bobby?" Ideology and method in the discovery of a Down's syndrome person's competence. In G. Kielhofner (Ed.), *Health through occupation* (pp. 237–248). Philadelphia, PA: Davis.

Gould, S. J. (1996). *The mismeasure of man* (2nd ed.). New York, NY: W. W. Norton & Co.

Gourdine, R. M., Baffour, T. D., & Teasley, M. (2011). Autism and the African American community. *Social Work in Public Health, 26*(4), 454–470.

Gramm, E. (1951). Peter the beautiful: The story of an enchanted child. *American Journal of Mental Deficiency, 56,* 271–274.

Greenfield, J. (1972). *A child called Noah.* San Diego, CA: Harcourt.

Groce, N. E., & Zola, I. K. (1993). Multiculturalism, chronic illness, and disability. *Pediatrics, 91*(5), 1048–1055.

Groce, N. (1999). Disability in cross-cultural perspective: Rethinking disability. *The Lancet, 354*(9180), 756–757.

Gunther, D. F., & Diekema, D. S. (2006). Attenuating growth in children with profound developmental disability: A new approach to an old dilemma. *Archives of Pediatrics & Adolescent Medicine, 160*(10), 1013–1017.

Gutierrez, J., & Sameroff, A. (1990). Determinants of complexity in Mexican-American and Anglo-American mothers' conceptions of child development. *Child Development, 61,* 384–394.

Hanline, M. F., & Daley, S. E. (1992). Family coping strategies and strengths in Hispanic, African-American, and Caucasian families of young children. *Topics in Early Childhood Special Education, 12*(3), 351–366.

Harris, C. I. (1993). Whiteness as property. *Harvard Law Review, 106*(8), 1707–1791.

Harry, B. (1992). An ethnographic study of cross-cultural communication with Puerto Rican-American families in the special education system. *American Educational Research Journal, 29*(3), 471–494.

Harry, B. (2008). Collaboration with culturally and linguistically diverse families: Ideal versus reality. *Exceptional Children, 74*(3), 372–388.

Harry, B. (2020). *Childhood disability, advocacy, and inclusion in the Caribbean: A Trinidad and Tobago case study.* London, England: Palgrave-Macmillan.

Harry, B., Allen, N., & McLaughlin, M. (1995). Communication versus compliance: African-American parents' involvement in special education. *Exceptional Children, 61*(4), 364–377.

Harry, B., & Fenton, P. (2017). Family diversity. In M. T. Hughes & E. Talbott (Eds.), *The Wiley handbook of diversity in special education* (pp. 149–166). Hoboken, NJ: John Wiley & Sons.

Harry, B., & Klingner, J. (2014). *Why are so many minority students in special education?* (2nd ed.). New York, NY: Teachers College Press.

Harry, B., Klingner, J. K., & Hart, J. (2005). African American families under fire: Ethnographic views of family strengths. *Remedial and Special Education, 26*(2), 101–112.

Harry, B., & Ocasio-Stoutenburg, L. (2018). Leadership and collaboration in home–school partnerships. In J. B. Crockett, B. Billingsley, & M. L. Boscardin (Eds.), *Handbook of leadership and administration for special education* (pp. 243–264). New York, NY: Routledge.

Hart, J. E., Cheatham, G., & Jimenez-Silva, M. (2012). Facilitating quality language interpretation for families of diverse students with special needs.

Preventing School Failure: Alternative Education for Children and Youth,
56(4), 207–213.

Heller, K. A., Holtzman, W. H., & Messick, S. (1982). *Placing children in special education: A strategy for equity.* Washington, DC: National Academy Press.

Herr, S. S. (1986). The agony of Phillip Becker: Parental autonomy versus the best interests of the child. In A. Carmi, S. Schneider, & A. Hefez (Eds.), *Psychiatry law and ethics, Medicolegal Library* (Vol. 5, pp. 236–240). Berlin, Germany: Springer.

Hess, R., Molina, A., & Kozleski, E. (2006). Until somebody hears me: Parent voice and advocacy in special educational decision making. *British Journal of Special Education, 33*(3), 148–157.

Hirano, K. A., Garbacz, S. A., Shanley, L., & Rowe, D. A. (2016). Parent involvement in secondary special education and transition: An exploratory psychometric study. *Journal of Child and Family Studies, 25*(12), 3537–3553.

Hmong family prevents forced surgery on son. (1991, January). *Omaha World Herald,* p. 16.

Hughes, E. C. (1945). Dilemmas and contradictions of status. *American Journal of Sociology, 50,* 353–359.

Hughes, J. S. (1992). Labeling and treating Black mental illness in Alabama, 1861–1910. *The Journal of Southern History, 58*(3), 435–460.

Hunt, P. (1966a). A critical condition. In P. Hunt (Ed.), *Stigma: The experience of disability* (pp. 145–159). London, England: Geoffrey Chapman.

Hunt, P. (1966b). *Stigma: The experience of disability.* London, England: Geoffrey Chapman.

Immigration Act of 1907, 11 § 59 U.S.C. §1134 (1907).

Individuals with Disabilities Education Improvement Act, Pub. L. No. 108–446 (2004).

Institute of Clinical Bioethics. (2013, May). Is the "Ashley treatment" ethical? Retrieved from sites.sju.edu/icb/is-the-ashley-treatment-ethical

Jackson, V. (2001). In our own voice: African-American stories of oppression, survival, and recovery in mental health systems. Retrieved from power2u.org/in-our-own-voice-african-american-stories-of-oppression-survival-and-recovery-in-mental-health-systems-by-vanessa-jackson

Jones, K. W. (2004). Education for children with mental retardation: Parent activism, public policy, and family ideology in the1950s. In S. Noll & J. W. Trent Jr. (Eds.), *Mental retardation in America: A historical reader* (pp. 322–350). New York, NY: New York University Press.

Kalyanpur, M. (1998). The challenge of cultural blindness: Implications for family-focused service delivery. *Journal of Child and Family Studies, 7*(3), 317–332.

Kalyanpur, M., & Harry, B. (2012). *Culture in special education: Building reciprocal family-professional relationships.* Baltimore, MD: Brookes.

Khalifa, M., Arnold, N. W., & Newcomb, W. (2015). Understand and advocate for communities first. *Phi Delta Kappan, 96*(7), 20–25.

Killilea, M. (1952). *Karen.* New York, NY: Buccaneer Books.

Kirk, S. A., & Becker, W. C. (Eds.). (1963, January 13–15). *Conference on children with minimal brain impairment.* National Society for Crippled Children and Adults.

Kittay, E. F. (2011). Forever small: The strange case of Ashley X. *Hypatia, 26*(3), 610–631.

Kittay, E. F. (2019). *Learning from my daughter: The value and care of disabled minds*. Oxford, England: Oxford University Press.

Knighton, E., & Knighton, W. (1985). The colors of the rainbow. In H. R. Turnbull & A. P. Turnbull (Eds.), *Parents speak out: Then and now* (pp. 270–278). Columbus, OH: Merrill

Knotek, S. (2003). Bias in problem-solving and the social process of student study teams: A qualitative investigation. *The Journal of Special Education, 37*(1), 2–14.

Kübler-Ross, E. (1969). *On death and dying*. New York, NY: Routledge.

Lareau, A. (2003). *Unequal childhoods: Class, race, and family life*. Berkeley, CA: University of California Press.

Larry P. v. Riles, NO. C-71–2270 RFP (N.D. Cal. 1971).

Lau v. Nichols, 414 U.S. 563 (1974).

Lea, D. (2006). "You don't know me like that": Patterns of disconnect between adolescent mothers of children with disabilities and their early interventionists. *Journal of Early Intervention, 28*(4), 264–282.

Leake, D., & Boone, R. (2007). Multicultural perspectives on self-determination from youth, parent, and teacher focus groups. *Career Development for Exceptional Individuals, 20*, 104–115.

Lee, C. (1961). *Tender tyrant*. Minneapolis, MN: Augsburg.

Lian, M. G. J., & Fontánez-Phelan, S. M. (2001). Perceptions of Latino parents regarding cultural and linguistic issues and advocacy for children with disabilities. *Journal of the Association for Persons with Severe Handicaps, 26*(3), 189–194.

Lindle, J. C. (1992). School leadership and educational reform: Parent involvement, the Education for Handicapped Children Act, and the principal. *Occasional Papers: School Leadership and Education Reform* (OP #4). Retrieved from tigerprints .clemson.edu/cgi/viewcontent.cgi?article=1002&context=eugene_pubs

Linton, S. (2007). *My body politic: A memoir*. Ann Arbor, MI: University of Michigan Press.

Liptak, G. S., Benzoni, L. B., Mruzek, D. W., Nolan, K. W., Thingvoll, M. A., Wade, C. M., & Fryer, G. E. (2008). Disparities in diagnosis and access to health services for children with autism: Data from the National Survey of Children's Health. *Journal of Developmental & Behavioral Pediatrics, 29*(3), 152–160.

Losen, D. J., & Orfield, G. (2002). *Racial inequity in special education*. Cambridge, MA: Harvard Education Publishing Group.

Lynch, E. W., & Stein, R. (1987). Parent participation by ethnicity: A comparison of Hispanic, Black, and Anglo families. *Exceptional Children, 54*, 105–111.

Marion, R. (1979). Minority parent involvement in the IEP process: A systematic model approach. *Focus on Exceptional Children, 10*(8), 1–16.

Mary, N. (1990). Reactions of Black, Hispanic and White mothers to having a child with handicaps. *Mental Retardation, 28*(1), 1–5.

McIntosh, P. (1989, July/August). White privilege: Unpacking the invisible knapsack. *Peace & Freedom Magazine*, 10–12.

McLaren, P. (2015). *Life in schools: An introduction to critical pedagogy in the foundations of education*. New York, NY: Routledge.

Mehan, H., Hartwick, A., & Meihls, J. L. (1986). *Handicapping the handicapped: Decision-making in students' educational careers*. Stanford, CA: Stanford University Press.

Mendoza, E., Paguyo, C., & Gutierrez, K. (2016). Understanding the intersection of race and dis/ability: Common sense notions of learning and culture. In D. J.

Connor, B. Ferri, & S. A. Annamma (Eds.), *DisCrit: Disability studies and critical race theory in education* (pp. 71–86). New York, NY: Teachers College Press.

Mercer, J. R. (1973). *Labeling the mentally retarded*. Berkeley, CA: University of California Press.

Meyers, C. E., Borthwick, S. A., & Eymen, R. K. (1985). Place of residence by age, ethnicity, and level of retardation of the mentally retarded/developmentally disabled population of California. *American Journal on Mental Deficiency, 90*(3), 266–270.

Mills v. Board of Education of District of Columbia, 348 F. Supp. 866, 871 (DC Dist. of Columbia 1972). Retrieved from law.justia.com/cases/federal/district-courts/FSupp/348/866/2010674/

Minow, M. (1990). *Making all the difference: Inclusion, exclusion, and American law*. Ithaca, NY: Cornell University Press.

Moore, L. (n.d.). Krip-Hop Nation is Moore than music [Blog post]. Retrieved from wordgathering.com/past_issues/issue22/essays/moore2.html

Morrier, M. J., & Hess, K. L. (2012). Ethnic differences in autism eligibility in the United States public schools. *The Journal of Special Education, 46*(1), 49–63.

National African American Autism Community Network (NAAACN). (n.d.) About us. Retrieved from naaacn.com/about-us/

Nowicki, J. M. (2018). *K–12 education: Discipline disparities for Black students, boys, and students with disabilities*. Report to Congressional Requesters. GAO-18-258. Washington, DC: U.S. Government Accountability Office.

Nussbaum, M. C. (2002). Capabilities and disabilities: Justice for mentally disabled citizens. *Philosophical Topics, 30*(2), 133–165.

Nussbaum, M. C. (2009). *Frontiers of justice: Disability, nationality, species membership*. Cambridge, MA: Harvard University Press.

Ogunyipe, B. (2016). Black Deaf culture through the lens of Black Deaf history. *Described and Captioned Media Program*. Retrieved from dcmp.org/ai/366/#books

Oliver, M. (1990). *The politics of disablement*. London, England: Macmillan.

Oliver, M. (2013). The social model of disability: Thirty years on. *Disability and Society, 28*(7), 1024–1026.

Oliver, M., & Barnes, C. (1998). *Social policy and disabled people: From exclusion to inclusion*. London, England: Longman.

Olshansky, S. (1962). Chronic sorrow: A response to having mentally defective children. *Social Work, 43*, 190–193.

Ong-Dean, C. (2009). *Distinguishing disability: Parents, privilege, and special education*. Chicago, IL: University of Chicago Press.

Outterson, K. (2005). Tragedy and remedy: Reparations for disparities in Black health. *DePaul Journal of Health Care Law, 9*(1), 735–792.

Park, C. C. (1982). *The siege: A family's journey into the world of an autistic child*. New York, NY: Back Bay Books.

Patton, J., & Braithwaite, R. (1984, August). Obstacles to the participation of black parents in the education programs of their handicapped children. *Centering Teacher Education, 34*–37.

Pearson, J. N., & Meadan, H. (2018). African American parents' perceptions of diagnosis and services for children with autism. *Education and Training in Autism and Developmental Disabilities, 53*(1), 17–32.

Pennsylvania Association for Retarded Children v. Commonwealth of Pennsylvania, 334 F. Supp. 1257, 1259 (E.D. Pa 1971).

Pennsylvania Association for Retarded Children v. Commonwealth of Pennsylvania, 343 F. Supp. 279, 307 (E.D. Pa 1972).

Pickett, B. (2018, Spring). Homosexuality. In E. N. Zalta (Ed.), *The Stanford Encyclopedia of Philosophy*. Retrieved from plato.stanford.edu/archives/spr2018/entries/homosexuality/>

Quiñones, S., & Kiyama, J. M. (2014). *"Contra la corriente"* [Against the current]: The role of Latino fathers in family-school engagement. *School Community Journal, 24*(1), 149–176.

Rabren, K. M., & Evans, A. M. (2016). A consensual qualitative analysis of parental concerns and strategies for transition. *Journal of Vocational Rehabilitation, 44*, 307–321.

Rao, S. (2000). Perspectives of an African American mother on parent-professional relationships in special education. *Mental Retardation, 38*, 475–488.

Ravitch, D. (2010). *The death and life of the great American school system: How testing and choice are undermining education*. New York, NY: Basic Books.

Rehm, R., Fisher, L., Fuentes-Afflick, E., & Chesla, C. (2013). Parental advocacy styles for special education students during the transition to adulthood. *Qualitative Health Research, 23*(10), 1377–1387.

Rembis, M. A. (2011). *Defining deviance: Sex, science, and delinquent girls, 1890–1960*. Chicago, IL: University of Illinois Press.

Resnik, J. (2011). The Baby Doe rules. *Embryo project encyclopedia*. Retrieved from embryo.asu.edu/handle/10776/2103

Richards, P. L. (2004). Beside her sat her idiot child: Families and developmental disability in mid-nineteenth century America. In S. Noll & J. W. Trent (Eds.), *Mental retardation in America: A historical reader* (pp. 65–84). New York, NY: New York University Press.

Richardson, J. G., & Powell, J. W. (2011). *Comparing special education: Origins to contemporary paradoxes*. Stanford, CA: Stanford University Press.

Rogers-Dulan, J., & Blacher, J. (1995). African American families, religion, and disability: A conceptual framework. *Mental Retardation, 33*(4). 226–238.

Ronald, A. T. J. (1993). *(Dis)forming the American canon: African-Arabic slave narratives and the vernacular*. Minneapolis, MN: University of Minnesota Press.

Rothstein, R. (2017). *The color of law: A forgotten history of how our government segregated America*. New York, NY: Liveright.

Rueda, R., Monzo, L., Shapiro, J., Gomez, J., & Blacher, J. (2005). Cultural models of transition: Latina mothers of young adults with developmental disabilities. *Exceptional Children, 71*(4), 401–414.

Saatcioglu, A., & Skrtic, T. (2019). Categorization by organizations: Manipulation of disability categories in a racially desegregated school district. *American Journal of Sociology, 125*(1), 184–260.

Sauer, J. S., & Lalvani, P. (2017). From advocacy to activism: Families, communities, and collective change. *Journal of Policy and Practice in Intellectual Disabilities, 14*(1), 51–58.

Sayad, A. (2006). *L'Immigration ou les paradoxes de l'altérité: L'illusion du provisoire* [Immigration or the paradoxes of otherness: The illusion of the provisional]. Paris, France: Raisons d'agir.

Schneps, M. (2014). *I see your face before me: A father's promise.* A Murray B. Schneps Publication.

Schuster, W. R. (2016). Rights gone wrong: A case against wrongful life. *William & Mary Law Review, 57*(6), 2329–2367.

Segal, R. (1970). *Mental retardation and social action: A study of the associations for retarded children as a force for social change.* Sprinfield, IL: Thomas.

Sharp, E. Y. (1983). *Analysis of determinants impacting on educational services of handicapped Papago students.* Tucson, AZ: University of Arizona, College of Education. (ERIC Document Reproduction Service No. ED 239 468)

Shaywitz, B. A., & Shaywitz, S. E. (2009). Brain imaging in studies of reading and dyslexia. *Encyclopedia of Language and Literacy Development* (pp. 1–6). London, ON: Canadian Language and Literacy Research Network.

Shaywitz, S. E., & Shaywitz, B. A. (2004). Reading disability and the brain. *Educational Leadership, 61*(6), 6–11.

Shoot, B. (2017). The 1977 disability rights protest that broke records and changed laws. *Atlas Obscura.* Retrieved from www.atlasobscura.com/articles/504-sit-in-san-francisco-1977-disability-rights-advocacy

Skiba, R. J., Knesting, K., & Bush, L. D. (2001). Culturally competent assessment: More than nonbiased tests. *Journal of Child and Family Studies, 11*(1), 61–78.

Skiba, R., Ormiston, H., Martinez, S., & Cummings, J. (2016). Teaching the social curriculum: Classroom management as behavioral instruction. *Theory into Practice, 55*(2), 120–128.

Skloot, R. (2010). *The immortal life of Henrietta Lacks.* New York, NY: Crown Publishers.

Skrtic, T. M. (1991). *Behind special education: A critical analysis of professional culture and school organization.* Denver, CO: Love Publishing.

Skrtic, T. M. (1995). Deconstructing/reconstructing the professions. In T. M. Skrtic (Ed.), *Disability and democracy: Reconstructing (special) education for postmodernity* (pp. 3–62). New York, NY: Teachers College Press.

Skrtic, T. M., & Knackstedt, K. M. (2018). Disability, difference and justice: Strong democratic leadership for undemocratic times. In J. B. Crockett, B. Billingsley, & M. L. Boscardin (Eds.), *Handbook of leadership and administration for special education* (2nd ed., pp. 148–174). New York, NY: Routledge.

Sleeter, C. (1986). Learning disabilities: The social construction of a special education category. *Exceptional Children, 53*, 46–54.

Smith, D. (1957). Public schools and the mentally retarded. *The Elementary School Journal, 57*(7), 375–378.

Smith, P., & Routel, C. (2010). Transition failure: The cultural bias of self-determination and the journey to adulthood for people with disabilities. *Disability Studies Quarterly, 30*(1). Retrieved from dsq-sds.org/article/view/1012/1224

Solnit A. J., & Stark M. H. (1961). Mourning and the birth of a defective child. *The Psychoanalytic Study of the Child, 16*, 523–537.

Spring, J. (2016). *Deculturalization and the struggle for equality: A brief history of the education of dominated cultures in the United States* (8th ed). New York, NY: Routledge.

Stafford, M. C., & Scott, R. R. (1986). Stigma, deviance, and social control: Some conceptual issues. In S. C Ainlay, G. Becker, & L. M. Coleman (Eds.), *The dilemma of difference: A multidisciplinary view of stigma* (pp. 77–90). New York, NY: Plenum Press.

Stanley, S. L. G. (2015). The advocacy efforts of African American mothers of children with disabilities in rural special education: Considerations for school professionals. *Rural Special Education Quarterly, 34*(4), 3–17.

Stern, A. M. (2010). Gender and sexuality: A global tour and compass. In A. Bashford & P. Levine (Eds.), *The Oxford handbook of the history of eugenics* (pp. 173–191). Oxford, UK: Oxford University Press.

Stinson, R., & Stinson, P. (1979). *The long dying of Baby Andrew.* New York, NY: Little Brown & Co.

Strauss, A. A., & Lehtinen, L. E. (1947). *Psychopathology and education of the brain-injured child: Fundamentals and treatment* (Vol. 1). New York, NY: Grune & Stratton.

Stuckey, Z. (2017). Race, apology, and public memory at Maryland's Hospital for the "Negro" Insane. *Disability Studies Quarterly, 37*(1), 1–22.

Sullivan, O. T. (1980). *Meeting the needs of low-income families with handicapped children.* Washington, DC: U.S. Department of Health and Welfare, National Institute of Education. (ERIC Document Reproduction Service No. ED 201 091)

Summers, M. (2010). "Suitable care of the African when afflicted with insanity": Race, madness, and social order in comparative perspective. *Bulletin of the History of Medicine, 84*(1), 58–91.

Takaki, R. (1993). *A different mirror: A history of multicultural America.* New York, NY: Little-Brown and Company.

Taylor, A. (2013). "Lives worth living": Theorizing moral status and expressions of human life. *Disability Studies Quarterly, 33*(4). Retrieved from dsq-sds.org/article/view/3875

Terman, L. (1916). *The measurement of intelligence.* Boston, MA: Houghton Mifflin.

Tomlinson, J. R., Acker, N., Canter, A., & Lindborg, S. (1977). Minority status, sex, and school psychological services. *Psychology in the Schools, 14*(4), 456–460.

Trainor, A. (2010). Diverse approaches to parent advocacy during special education home–school interactions. *Remedial and Special Education, 31*(1), 34–47.

Travers, J., & Krezmien, M. (2018). Racial disparities in autism identification in the United States during 2014. *Exceptional Children, 84*(4), 403–419.

Turnbull, A. P., & Turnbull, H. R. (Eds.). (1978). *Parents speak out: Views from the other side of the two-way mirror.* Columbus, OH: Merrill.

Turnbull, A. P., Turnbull, H. R., Erwin, E. J., Soodak, L. C., & Shogren, K. A. (2015). *Families, professionals, and exceptionality: Positive outcomes through partnerships and trust.* Upper Saddle River, NJ: Pearson.

Turnbull, H. R. (2011). *The exceptional life of Jay Turnbull: Disability and dignity in America, 1967–2009.* Amherst, MA: White Poppy Press.

Turnbull, H. R. (2014). Quality of life: Four under-considered intersections. *International Public Health Journal, 6*(4), 403–411.

Turnbull, H. R., & Turnbull, A. P. (Eds.). (1985). *Parents speak out: Then and now.* Columbus, OH: Merrill.

Turnbull, H. R., & Turnbull, A. P. (2015). Looking backward and framing the future for parents' aspirations for their children with disabilities. *Remedial and Special Education, 36*(1), 52–57.

Turnbull, H. R., Wehmeyer, M., Turnbull, A. P., & Stowe, J. J. (2006). Growth attenuation and due process: A response to Gunther and Diekema. *Research and Practice for Persons with Severe Disabilities 31*(4), 348–351.

Tyler, I. (2018). Resituating Erving Goffman: From stigma power to Black power. *The Sociological Review, 66*(4), 744–765.

United Nations. (2006). Convention on the rights of persons with disabilities. New York.

United States President's Committee on Mental Retardation. (1977). *MR: Report of the President's Committee on Mental Retardation.* Washington, DC: U.S. Government Printing Office. Retrieved from acf.hhs.gov/sites/default/files/add/gm_1976.pdf

Vasquez, A. M. (1973). Race and culture variables in the acceptance-rejection attitudes of parents of mentally retarded children in the lower socioeconomic class (Unpublished doctoral dissertation). California School of Professional Psychology, Los Angeles.

Voulgarides, C. K. (2018). *Does compliance matter in special education? IDEA and the hidden inequities of practice.* New York, NY: Teachers College Press.

Walker, J. M., Wilkins, A. S., Dallaire, J., Sandler, H. M., & Hoover-Dempsey, K. V. (2005). Parental involvement: Model revision through scale development. *Elementary School Journal, 106,* 85–104. doi:10.1086/499193.

Wang, M., & Singer, G. H. (2016). *Supporting families of children with developmental disabilities: Evidence-based and emerging practices.* New York, NY: Oxford University Press.

Wilder, L. K., Jackson, A. P., & Smith, T. (2001). Secondary transition of multicultural learners: Lessons from the Navajo Native American experience. *Preventing School Failure, 45*(3), 119–124.

Wilson, N. M. (2015). Question-asking and advocacy by African American parents at Individualized Education Program meetings: A social and cultural capital perspective. *Multiple Voices for Ethnically Diverse Exceptional Learners, 15*(2), 36–49.

Wolf-Branigin, M. (2007). Supporting persons with intellectual and developmental disability: Will our emerging political leaders build on President Kennedy's legacy? *Intellectual and Developmental Disabilities, 45*(6), 412–414.

Wolfensberger, W. (1983). Social role valorization: A proposed new term for the principle of normalization. *Mental Retardation, 21*(6), 234–239.

World Health Organization. (2011). *World report on disability.* Geneva, Switzerland: Author.

Wyatt v. Stickney, 325 F. Supp. 781, 783 (M.D. Ala. 1971).

Yackle, L. W. (1989). *Reform and regret: The story of federal judicial involvement in the Alabama prison system.* Oxford, England: Oxford University Press.

Zeitlen, V. M., & Curcic, S. (2013). Parental voices on Individualized Education Programs: "Oh, IEP meeting tomorrow? Rum tonight!" *Disability & Society 29*(3), 373–387. doi:10.1080/09687599.2013.776493

Zirkel, P. A., & Huang, T. (2018). State rates of 504-only students in K–12 public schools: An update. *West's Education Law Reporter*—354 Ed. Law Rep. 621. Retrieved from perryzirkel.files.wordpress.com/2018/07/zirkel-and-huang-state-by-state-504-only-rates-article-061118.pdf

Zirkel, P. A., & Weathers, J. M. (2015). Section 504-only students: National incidence data. *Journal of Disability Policy Studies, 26*(3), 184–193.

Ziskin, L. (1985). Transition—from home to residential care. In H. R. Turnbull & A. P. Turnbull (Eds.), *Parents speak out: Then and now* (2nd ed., pp. 75–78). Columbus, OH: Merrill.

Index

Normative position
  appeal of, 85–89, 147–149
  characteristics of personhood, 26, 73–75
  construction of difference (Minow), 1,
    22–23, 49, 76–77, 84, 145–151
  desire for, 84–85
  meaning of disability, 75–77, 145–147
  normalcy as God-given state, 49–50
  "normalizing" disability, 81
  objective observers in determining, 149–150
  perceptions of social value and, 84–85
  stigma of disability. See Stigma/
    stigmatization
  whole person and, 92
  wider parameters of normalcy within
    definitions of disability, 25, 89–91
Novelty shock (Wolfensberger), 18
Nowicki, J. M., 81–82
Nussbaum, Martha C., 74–75

Ocasio-Stoutenburg, Lydia, 141, 142, 151
  background information, 3
  Isaiah (son), 3–4, 5–6, 14–15, 46–47,
    71–72, 157–158
  journal entries, 46–47, 51, 71–72
  reflective memo, 157–158
Ogunyipe, Benro, 59
Oliver, Michael, 75–76
Olshansky, S., 44–45
Ong-Dean, C., 5–6, 17–18, 95, 97–101, 111,
  120, 126–128, 130, 141
On the Origin of Species (Darwin), 32
Orfield, G., 101
Ormiston, H., 134
Other
  African Americans viewed as, 68–69
  in Biblical references to disability, 25
Other Health Impaired (OHI), 91
Outterson, K., 31

Paguyo, C., 36
Parent advocacy
  advocacy organizations and, 56, 58,
    59–64, 140
  approaches to, 16–18, 120–125, 137
  assumptions in construction of difference
    (Minow), 1, 22–23, 49, 76–77, 84,
    145–151
  authors' lenses in, 3–4, 14–16, 23–24,
    46–47, 157–158
  challenges of, 71–72, 77–92
  challenging societal norms in, 49–50,
    52–53, 54–55, 74, 145–147
  co-constructing. See Co-constructing
    advocacy
  cultural and social capital in, 6–7, 16–18,
    57–59, 96–98, 111, 126–128, 140,
    143–144

  in cultural-historical lens, 6–7
  de-constructing, 140–144
  "denial" vs. "disagreement" and, 49–50
  developmental phases of, 6–8, 96. See also
    Liberatory phase of parent advocacy
  differences in social privilege and power,
    16–18
  DisCrit and. See DisCrit
  equity vs. deficit perspective in, 11
  goals of, 18
  identity in intersectionality, 1–2
  law as vehicle for. See Liberatory phase of
    parent advocacy
  in life-death decisions, 78–79
  marginalization within advocacy, 11
  moving toward empowerment, 69
  need for, 3–4, 18–23
  new model for, 151–156
  parents as experts and, 14–15
  in prenatal period, 71–73, 83–87,
    145–146, 147
  as process and force for change, 2
  published narratives of parents, 15, 51–59
  qualifying as "advocates," 135–138
  racism as obstacle to parent participation,
    110–125
  in special education context, 8
  vignettes. See Vignettes
Parent autonomy
  medical ethics and, 72, 79–81
  in quality of life decisions, 79–83
Parents and family
  advocacy and. See Parent advocacy
  disempowerment in 20th century, 42–46
  professional theories on, 44–46
  removal of disabled children from, 43–44
  stage theory of responses to disability, 45,
    52–53
Parent Training and Information Centers
  (PTIs), 64
Park, Clara Claiborne, 56
Parks, Rosa, 93
Partlow State School (Alabama), 66, 67–68
Patton, J., 110
Patton, K., 136–137
Patty/Richard, 75, 77, 102, 107, 114–115,
  119–120, 124–125, 134–135, 149, 154,
  156
Pearson, J., 136–137
Pearson, J. N., 111, 112
Pennhurst Institution (Pennsylvania), 66
Pennsylvania
  Pennhurst Institution, 66
  Pennsylvania Association for Retarded
    Citizens (PARC), 93–94
People-first language, 21
Peter the Beautiful (Gramm), 53–55
Pickett, B., 19

About the Authors

Beth Harry is a professor of special education at the University of Miami. A native of Jamaica, she received her bachelor's and master's degrees from the University of Toronto and her PhD from Syracuse University. Her work focuses on issues of disability, families, and diversity. Beth's research and teaching have been inspired by her experience as a parent of a child with cerebral palsy, as told in her memoir, *Melanie, Bird with a Broken Wing: A Mother's Story* (2010).

Lydia Ocasio-Stoutenburg is an advocate for families of children with special needs in Miami. Educated in the New York City public schools, she received her bachelor's and master's degrees in Biology at Stony Brook University and Adelphi University. The birth of her youngest son, Isaiah, who has Down syndrome, was her inspiration for furthering her education. She has since received a Master's degree in bioethics from St. Thomas University and is a PhD candidate in special education at the University of Miami.